# HOMAN INHOMANITY
The Oxymoron of Racism

# HOMAN INHOMANITY
## The Oxymoron of Racism

## Edward R W Makhene

Edward R W Makhene
2018

Copyright © Edward R W Makhene 2014.
Revised edition 2018.
All rights Reserved. This book or any portion thereof may not be reproduced or used in any manner whatsoever without the express written permission of the publisher except for the use of brief quotations in a book review or scholarly journal.

First Printing: 2014

ISBN 978-0-9876970-0-4

Edward R W Makhene
Mississauga, Ontario.
Canada.
edmakhene@icloud.com

For the peoples of this world who are oppressed and discriminated against, overtly and mostly covertly, solely on the basis of the colour of their skins.

# Contents

| | | |
|---|---|---|
| Acknowledgements | | ix |
| Chapter 1 | The "killer bees" | 1 |
| Chapter 2 | Twin world – a preview | 7 |
| Chapter 3 | The oxymoron | 13 |
| Chapter 4 | Representative scenarios | 28 |
| Chapter 5 | Religion to the rescue | 39 |
| Chapter 6 | Religion indicted | 50 |
| Chapter 7 | Religious inhomanity | 63 |
| Chapter 8 | Emergence of racism | 76 |
| Chapter 9 | Social inhomanity | 93 |
| Chapter 10 | More Social inhomanity | 109 |
| Chapter 11 | Governmental inhomanity | 122 |
| Chapter 12 | Governmental terror | 137 |
| Chapter 13 | Economic Inhomanity | 151 |
| Chapter 14 | Political inhomanity | 166 |
| Chapter 15 | Racism and Inhomanity burgeon | 182 |
| Chapter 16 | The varied meanings of life | 201 |
| Chapter 17 | The road ahead | 219 |
| Notes | | 239 |
| Index | | 245 |

## Acknowledgments

Thank you to my wife Eileen, as usual, for her steadfast support.

My thanks also go to the scores of unnamed authors whose works helped to enrich my understanding of many of the issues discussed in this book.

# Chapter 1
# The "killer bees"

Mention of the phrase "homan inhomanity" immediately brings to mind the word 'oxymoron'. Thereafter, many other words come to mind as competitors for primacy in depictions of situations where they beget oxymorons when combined with 'homan', a variation on 'human' that I will define later. For instance, caddishness, jingoism, and schadenfreude, the bedfellows of inhomanity, are incompatible with homanity. Accordingly, I have selected appropriate conceptual terms that begin with successive letters of the alphabet to portray some of the many ways in which this inconsistent concept (homan inhomanity) can be expressed: antinomianism, bigotry, caddishness, depravity, egregiousness, fiendishness, greed, hubris, immorality, jingoism, knavery, loathsomeness, maleficence, nefariousness, opprobriousness, prevarication, quarrelsomeness, repression, schadenfreude, travesty, usufruct, vilification, warmongering, xenophobia, yahooism, and zealotry. As we will see in discussions that follow, many words that refer to situations in the world that I shall describe qualify eminently, individually or in combination with 'homan', as living examples of one or more of the concepts embraced by these and similar descriptive terms, and by the concept "homan inhomanity".

Let us understand one clear fact from the beginning: anyone who consistently and maliciously interferes with a beehive should expect the bees to attack him in the process of protecting their home and their produce. He should not then bore his whole world with cries of being the victim of unfair and unprovoked attack by these creatures, and then devote the rest of his life viciously and futilely trying to eliminate them from the world where he found them, in the first place. Foolishly chasing them all over the world for decades, capturing, confining, and killing them and all other innocent insects to vent his anger at the bees that stung him for disdainfully messing with them and their store of sustenance only serves to expose his witlessness and suicidal hubris by eventually uniting the victims of his wrath against him. He sows the seed of his own destruction by unleashing his lethal power on creatures that are minding their own business; but he also cries hypocritically for sympathy from other people for his cavalierly self-inflicted predicament.

Instead of stopping and looking at what he has been doing to bring the wrath of the bees upon himself, he engages in more of his foolish and arrogant behaviour of dominion over property that does not belong to him by demolishing their habitat, devising more and more deadly means of exterminating them, and becoming obsessed with continually intensifying security around his house and environs against their dreaded and anticipated attacks. His sniffish behaviour, which is anchored in egotism and foolishness, condemns the otherwise peaceful lives of the people who live with him to uncertainty and tension. He is so cozy in his persistent self-assuredness and contempt for peaceful coexistence with the rest of his world that he hardly envisages a time when the tide will turn against him, as it surely will, with all the joy that it will bring to his many victims who have been wishing for such a catastrophic event. Then he will lose his life to a series of anaphylactic bee-sting reactions or to just one major sting—a just reward for his hubristic injustice to his world's inhabitants.

You fool, we can justifiably ask him, when are you going to look at yourself and see how daft you are, although you keep blaming the bees for escalating your conflict with them and exonerating yourself, because you think you alone are God's gift to your joint world, the paragon of his creation? Why don't you stay in your house and be content with your endless possessions, instead of trying to wrest the possessions of others from them and trying to make them live their lives according to your depraved, hypocritical consuetude. They are happy with their modest living, making honey for their livelihood, not for your covetous all-devouring appetite. Live your own life your way, and let the bees live their lives their way, and you, the bees, and the rest of the insect world that has become the object of your vile wrath and envy driven by greed, arrogance, and strategic preference of strife to peace will live together amicably in the same world. If you stay out of their business and stop assaulting them and treating them like dirt, they won't come after you. Then you won't need to endlessly multiply security measures and personnel for your safety and subject your fellow citizens to the needless inconvenience of continual, escalating harassment in their daily lives and travels "for their safety", while pretending that your reckless, domineering behaviour is not the source of everyone's misery. Stop assaulting the bees and treating them like dirt, and they will have no reason to seek revenge, for which you also seek revenge, for which they in turn seek revenge, prompting you to seek revenge for the revenge that they have exacted, *ad infinitum*. It makes no sense.

The essay that follows stems from many dismal settings that are akin to the one depicted above; but it is only a limited conceptual sketch of an even smaller part of the extensive problem of homan inhumanity. It is based on the actions of people who label themselves superior homan beings and dub others inferior subhomans by their own jaundiced criteria; who engage in bigoted, egoistic, hubristic, and dehumanizing actions to uphold and perpetuate their tribal "supremacy" through successive generations by any means available to them, but mostly by immoral means that include oppression, exploitation, and decimation of their unyielding victims; people who are ruled by unbridled and naked jealousy at the stellar achievements of those that they have subjugated, achievements over which they rant and rave uncontrollably in the most vitriolic racist language, as if that will ever undo those achievements; people whose racism is blatantly blind to the pain and suffering that it is causing their unfortunate victims; people whose inveterate hatred dominates their character and runs beneath and guides all their racist actions that should always—repeat always—be interpreted in that light. Their brutality and inhumanity is born of this hatred-based racism. Regrettably, however, it rarely begets the response in kind that it fully merits.

It is also a sorry account of the Krustan (equivalent of Christian in twin world[1]—a fictitious counterpart of our world that I will describe later) foundations of the despicable invention and reification of race for the perpetuation of tribal supremacy through homan inhumanity. It tells of intolerance born of the superiority complex of Krustans that makes them wreak savagery on their victims, churning out guck that they expect them to swallow blithely and gratefully (even while they are being dispossessed, degraded, and decimated), guck on which they choke violently and self-pityingly when they have to swallow it; of chickens coming home to roost in many fitting ways on relatively too few occasions; of oppressors (those who "crush or burden by abuse of power or authority", as defined in Webster's dictionary) who are inextricably welded to mendacities that they use to justify their heinous practices; of the insatiable greed that propels their selfish actions, which engulf and consume everyone in their path and far beyond; and finally, of religion that has descended from the high pedestal of command on which it had arbitrarily placed itself, into the gutter with every other sordid tool that is used to squelch, abuse, and dominate both Krustan homans and non-Krustan "subhomans".

These people have imposed their uninvited and odious

presence on the natural existence of all the other people of their world and subjected them to alien governance that is meant only to enslave them in the artificial and schizophrenic environment that they have created for them, however much they may deny their intent in words that belie their deeds. When they claim respect for homanity, they mean only their supercilious and belligerent homanity that inveighs churlishly against any person who talks peace to those that they have been intimidating or those on whom they are waging war to show off their might and to steal from them; when they profess justice as due or deserved treatment, grounded on basic need for survival and other relevant, universal, moral, and legal credentials that transcend societal limitations and prejudicial (mostly racist) pre-judgment, they refer only to their own just and fair treatment, which does not recognize fairness as consistent treatment of all who share the same moral homanity with them; when they proselytize rights to life and other values, they mean only their own that are "more equal" than those of others; and when they claim that Gudd, the god of twin world, is the father of all homankind, they mean that he is their father alone who listens only to them and will damn all other people who holler into his selectively deaf ears at their behest.

Within this background, those who are clearly earmarked for discrimination should regard all discriminatory acts with the gravity that they deserve, never condoning them, never dismissing them as of little or no consequence, and never accepting them as jokes, but always responding to them with the forceful and unwavering contempt that their vile perpetrators deserve. They shouldn't confuse the expected avoidance of others who are different in some ways from oneself with the vile, racially motivated imposition of vulgar, malicious, dehomanizing, discriminatory, oppressive, dominating, and enslaving restrictions that they are compelled to endure everywhere, including the workplace, the church, and the educational institutions. One is by choice; the other is by coercion. Examples of these sorts of insult abound in the daily lives of all brown peoples, the primary focus of this essay, and also in the lives of other less privileged groups that will receive only passing mention.

Fortunately for us, these abominable events and attitudes belong to another world, twin world. In our world we only speculate about them and we write factual and fictional volumes about them (e.g., fictional "Protocols"), not because we believe in them, but simply to give everyone a clearer understanding of the evil that prevails in twin world, as evidenced in the many references quoted in the text that follows. Our world does not harbour breeds of scurvy economists and their corrupt corporate bosses and political friends in government whose joint and sole nefarious intentions are to impose misery on the people by arbitrarily privatizing their hard-earned, highly-priced, steady-income-generating national assets, which they purchase for peanuts and then lease or rent to them at escalating prices, callously plunging them into deep oceans of debt with its absurd compound interests. We have the inimitable moral decency to know not to engage in such practices. Do we?.

Nowhere in our world do we find governments doling out enslaving loans for development or for rebuilding infrastructure that they damaged deliberately in wars of greed and hubris; ruthlessly cutting the budgets of their beneficiaries and taking off with 40% of their gross national product in partial repayment of those loans, but putting nothing back into the tottering economies that they continue to denude as they pilfer raw materials and minerals from them; inexorably siphoning off their means of subsistence by lifting price controls on everyone of their commodities, including food, and thus placing essentials beyond their reach; blatantly filching enormous sums of money that they invest outside the countries from which they are stealing it while they are in executive positions; cavalierly foisting on unwary citizens corporate dictatorship disguised in the garb of democracy and gleaned from the crises and confusing situations that they have engineered to diffuse the people's opposition to their plans for stealing power and control of their local assets from them; and engaging in other impoverishing and dehomanizing acts that will be highlighted in the pages that follow.

Nowhere in our world do we also find diabolical Krustans whose religion of hypocrisy tolerates and practices profane, depraved, and inhomane oppression of their non-Krustan brothers that they still regard as inferior beings; who prejudicially and glibly heap blame on non-Krustan churches for the evil deeds of anonymous non-members whose only sin is to belong to their tribe (they are all the same, bad), while Krustan churches are not settled with similar blame for equally heinous deeds of some of their tribe. Their deeds are condoned as the deeds of mere deviants, not representative of their illustrious tribe. ('tribe' is defined on page 18).

Nowhere in our world are there Krustans who rail against the right of non-Krustans to worship where and as they choose, or Non-Krustan churches that receive death threats from the Krustan rabble for daring to erect worship houses near hallowed ground that is close to Krustan houses of sin, or bigoted Krustan tribes who have bombed churches where brown Krustans worship with inevitable loss of life or else bombed to smithereens and incinerated millions of people of other lands without compunction or acknowledgment of violating the hallowed temples of the Gudd of all homanity as all persons should be. Are they not all made in his image, do their victims' lives not also count as sacred, and do they not also deserve the same respect and treatment as their killers? It appears that Krustanity is destined to follow the unrelenting course of personal and group moral bankruptcy, while it lacks the resources with which to redeem itself from the precipitous, dizzying, downward spiral in which it is ensnared, because its domain has been hijacked by people whose moral fibre has been digested away by inhomanity, greed, hatred, and lies. These people have not yet learned that respect for neighbours makes for better coexistence than perpetual attempts to steal from them, dragoon them into subservience, or continually try to decimate them.

The complex of scenarios outlined in this book happens against this background. But nothing goes on for ever. The day of reckoning has dawned for the oppressors who kill other persons with impunity but charge others with murder for responding in like manner. Their world of comfort flowing from self-service at the expense of other people has begun to crumble, and soon their good times will belong to the pages of history, like those of all the others of their kind who have preceded them. The existing turmoil in twin world bears ample witness to this fact, which is no longer the wishful thinking of fools. There is light further down the tunnel—before the end of brown existence that is being engineered by pink Krustans every minute of the day in every walk of life.

# Chapter 2
# Twin world – a preview

Throughout this essay, the reader should remember that any allegation that some persons from a particular tribe are guilty of doing something inhomane does not imply, entail, or justify the conclusion and interpretation that all persons from that group are guilty of doing the same thing; *some x are p* does not entail *all x are p*, even if 99.9% of all $x$ have been examined and found to be $p$. Some or all of the remaining 0.1% of $x$ may not be $p$, thereby refuting the general inductive conclusion that *all x are p*, simply because *some or most known x are p*. It should, therefore, be quite clear from the outset that some honourable persons with the best of intentions do not engage in the ignominious deeds of those whose agenda is to dehumanize others; also, that 18/1.82billion is not the whole tribe, except in the world of bigots. Furthermore, any resemblance between events in twin world and our real world or other possible worlds (any of the other ways that this world could have been) is entirely fortuitous and only goes to show that the principles and trends herein described can be universalized by virtue of the multifold particular occurrences that instantiate them all over twin world. So, nothing precludes the two worlds from being similar without being the same world. What obtains in twin world can also obtains in our world, even though they are different worlds. In other words, the two separate worlds can be qualitatively identical or replicas of each other without being quantitatively or numerically identical; i.e., one and the same world in place and time.

I have assumed an anthropocentric stance in discussing events in twin world and I am using one of the languages of this world to describe events that happen in a world other than our own, because our language is one of the means by which we can extend ourselves to other worlds to be able to understand what is happening there, in the same way that we use it to convey information about those parts and aspects of our world to which not every one of us has access. The languages of other worlds remain a mystery to us, even if we can speak and write about their worlds in our languages in parallel with how we think that they speak and write about our world. Therefore, the meanings and conceptual usages of the terms 'homan', 'inhoman', 'homane', 'inhomane', 'homaneness', 'homanity', and 'inhomanity in twin world correspond exactly to the meanings and conceptual usages of the terms 'human', 'inhuman', 'humane', 'inhumane', 'humaneness', 'humanity', and 'inhumanity' in our world.

It is noteworthy that the word 'homan' (human), which names the living person, is the source of all the attributes that have been enumerated above, and that without this homan being and her judgment on the worth of what exists or obtains in her world, there is no value in twin world, not even in money, which her male analogue seems to worship and value more than himself, other persons, and the deity that he has constructed in his own image. Furthermore, it is noteworthy that meaning doesn't end with the substitution of words or expressions that are equivalent to those that are being explicated; it spills over into the intended and unintended effects of the usage of the words or expressions employed; e.g., pink and brown, as used in this essay, suggest more than just appearance. They also convey selectively immoral practices prompted by deep-seated, plebeian attitudes of disrespect, inhomaneness, and hatred of some of the former toward most of the latter that often find expression in audacious acts of injury in its varied forms and murder that more often than not goes unpunished. I will assume the liberty to use these adjectival terms, i.e., 'pink' and 'brown' as nominals in some contexts.

Underlying this reprehensible behaviour of the pink tribe toward all other tribes, collectively known as browns, is the malevolent disposition to racism (defined in Merriam Webster's dictionary as "the belief that race is the primary determinant of human traits and capacities and that racial differences produce an inherent superiority of a particular race") that appears to be their imprimatur. Their immoral concept of racism is derived from their practice of distorting and prostituting the natural differences in skin colour that exist among the peoples of twin world by an illogical logic through which they arrive at the conclusion that they are the real homan beings and the rest of the people are subhomans, fit to be trampled upon by them and those that they select among their victims to act as their proxies and pawns in the execution of their selfish desires and dirty deeds.

In their cherished, hateful disposition toward the other, they display a two-pronged immoral and vicious attitude, which deters them from preventing harm from befalling her and also prompts them to strive to set up or abet injurious circumstances that will cause her harm. Furthermore, in their attempt to sidestep the vexing question of race, which originates from their tribe that is designedly exempt from the indignities to which browns are subjected as a people, some pinks have mistakenly (or designedly) subordinated the concept of racism to that of the wider exercise of political, socio-economic, and other kinds of power by one group over another, regardless of skin colour, since their pink laws and economy favour this self-assumed supremacy. They refuse to admit that while economic inequality of equals still leaves room for the underdog to catch up, inequality between arbitrary superiors and inferiors precludes that kind of catching up, but rather feeds and thrives on the vertical demarcation that has been willfully erected to perpetuate the resulting economic inequality and its concomitant enslavement of the other. They have also claimed that browns naturally prefer to gravitate toward their own kind, away from pinks, because they share common values, beliefs, traditions, and history, omitting to mention the common burdens of rejection and oppression that they carry. They even have the nerve to go so far as to assuage their guilty consciences by hiding behind the ineffective reactive racism of browns toward pinks, and by claiming that browns are the guilty ones for always brining up the question of race when it is far from their minds and not the motive behind many of their racist actions; in their world, racism that is not racist, if that oxymoron makes sense. By using this manoeuvre, bestowed on them by their age-old institutions of discrimination and oppression, they hope to obfuscate the roles of their modern institutions and them in the pernicious practice of racism and its devastating effects on its victims.

Their practice of turning the tables on their victims to avoid censure is just another one of their flagitious ploys, like their habit of accusing other people of being anti-them and of holding skewed views for criticizing their evil, racist practices, but claiming to be exercising their right to free speech when they vilify and concoct lies about their critics and those that they don't like, even edging them out of their jobs,. They claim victimization by brown malice in their feigned state of helplessness, so that they can earn the sympathy of their world and thereby smear their critics with guilt for chastising and persecuting them verbally. They plead self-pityingly for the right to inflict disproportionate, retributive collective harm on the victims of their racist ire, and their conniving pink brothers in crime gladly grant them that right, which is not theirs to grant, to the satisfaction of their ignorant constituencies who believe any lie that they are told. In their twisted minds, pinks can do no wrong, especially against browns.

For browns, however, it is the colour of their skins, and that alone, that makes them victims of all the imaginable categories of racism and shuts the exclusive doors of opportunity in their faces; and that is the real meaning of racism to them. The darker colour of one's skin is the criterion for refusing her admission to those avenues in life that will ensure that she prospers, while relegating her to the gutter where a great deal of pink effort will be expended to keep her, even at the expense of the progress of the whole of twin world. As expected, pinks use this same criterion to demean browns and inculcate in them a sense of worthlessness that will facilitate their own efforts to deprive them of civic and homan rights, as only cowards will do, denying them rights to which they are entitled by virtue of their personhood[1], because they think that they have the prerogative to decide who is a person and who is a $3/5$ person. First, they create and define rights as entitlements based on personhood, statehood, nationality, etc. Next, they define personhood to include only pinks, and then they brazenly define a class of "sub-persons" who are *ipso facto* precluded from holding those rights. They thus peremptorily withdraw recognition of browns as holders of rights and simultaneously exonerate themselves from their obligations to honour and respect their claims to those rights, which they have assigned to themselves as the only persons; and they think that their network of transparent ruses grounded in lies will hold for ever.

As will become apparent in the following pages, we are dealing with a world in which racist arrogance and malevolence have always been the order of the day; in which blatant theft from, incarceration, callous and cold-blooded murder of browns is the accepted pink practice; in which lies are the norm and truth the exception, especially in the highest circles of government; in which brown opinions are worth nothing, hence their systematic exclusion from appointed and other executive positions of consequence in the nation; in which all brown lives are always worth very much less than pink lives, even before the colour-blind, blindfolded, but still keenly colour-sensitive eyes of their justice system; in which brown dwellings can be bull-dozed with impunity by pink governments that care only about the welfare of their own kind; in which religious bigotry is used to control the thinking and actions of the citizenry and to inflict harm on browns; in which pinks resent the extension of health care benefits to browns under the pretext of infringement of their autonomy and their subjection to increased taxation but would rather comply with the use of their tax dullams (dollars of twin world) for engaging in and supporting evil wars that decimate the lives of millions of brown men, women, and children of small, weak, and defenceless nations all over twin world. Being plunged into that kind of astronomical debt from which no one benefits does not bother them, because such savage escapades add honour and glory to the petty egos of their rulers and them. They talk oxymoronically about the ethics of war (ethics of the unethical) as if an immoral undertaking can have ethics, like His Holiness The Devil. Holiness?

Miserable fools; they pay through their noses for the upkeep of vulturish corporations and their satellites who provide tools and services to keep wars going, so that they can bring huge fortunes to their owners who live off the citizens like the exsanguinating leeches that they are. Meanwhile, their health care, educational, social and other services are being slashed to the barest bones and surrendered to the plunder of the corporations to whom the funds that should be supporting these services are diverted. But they still don't get it, perhaps because the brunt of these vicious manoeuvres is borne largely by poor folk who are mainly browns. Instead, they prefer to separate their residences from those of poor citizens to avoid having to support them with their taxes and to enjoy exclusive amenities and services, while the poor languish for lack of basic services.

On the whole, these homans who live in better circumstances than the rest of the twin-worlders do not like to see their prerogative to wealth and comfort infringed upon by efforts to extend public assistance to those of their world who are just managing, and sometimes failing, to eke out a miserable existence on the barest minimum of essentials for survival in an economy created and derailed by the same persons who begrudge them the aid that they may be receiving from those who feel for them in their suffering. They prefer that those who do not have the means to pay for their health care should be left to die, while the filthy rich who are gouging them in premiums and other commodities refuse to admit that they are responsible for forcing them into that hopeless situation where they do not have a choice; their only painful choice is death. They will also not admit the plain truth that the sorry plight in which the rest of the people find themselves is a product of the trickle down, egocentric fiscal policies that did not do anything to cater to their welfare, but were geared solely to the prosperity of the fat cats. They enjoy benefits that have been bestowed on them and their corporations by governments that cater exclusively to their interests and which they control by intimidating them with strangulation of their economies by moving their industries to more pliant countries if they don't get their way; hence the obscene tax cuts for them at the expense of the social life, education, health, and survival of the poor. Governments have thus become corprocracies, i.e., government by corporations.

In this world of rot, self-destruction, hubris, pink inhomanity, and egotism that is already tottering toward its demise and is only held together, internally and externally, by armies and disrespectful, racist police forces, how does one match the morality of taking lives or wasting them for selfish, racist reasons against saving those lives? How does one justify the plight of thousands of soldiers who are suffering callous neglect of their mental and physical trauma after being used by politicians in their war games of self-glorification, politicians who wish that they had died in the wars than return to cost them money for tending to their health problems for many years to come, that they now commit suicide or become drug addicts and alienate everyone's sympathy for them to justify their neglect? These are people who revel in photo ops that depict them strutting the world stage and commiserating with bereaved military families, but also using transparent ploys to accuse the citizens of dishonouring these devoted patriots when they criticize them for waging self-serving, witless, immoral wars in which their own families do not participate. Such caddish attitudes can never be justified. The scurvy inhomanity and hypocrisy of these rascals deserve only severe reprobation, not the approbation that they seek and crave for. These rascals do not deserve any respect; they are a dishonour and disgrace to the offices that they hold, many of them by blatant theft of the electoral process.

# Chapter 3
# The oxymoron

In Webster's dictionary "oxymoron" is defined as "a combination of contradictory or incongruous words; something (as a concept) that is made up of contradictory or incongruous elements."[1] The point of combining such words is not to simply juxtapose them and still express separate and independent ideas, but to use them to express a unified idea in contradictory terms, which, as anyone will grant, is as manifest an absurdity as saying that a golf ball is white all over and black all over at the same time in the same locality. A being that is homan is expected to behave homanely. So, inhomanity in a homan being constitutes an inconsistency and absurdity that reduces the utterance to nonsense. Nevertheless, that is how absurdly many persons who wield power and authority over others behave toward them, in an absurd manner whose significance can be comprehended only if their ultimate aim is known. They do not only force them to act against their will and interests, but they also limit their choices of action to suit themselves and their heinous agendas.

In our world we call "human" any organism that satisfies certain biological criteria, like the possession of 46 chromosomes (with variations), a particular body shape and skin colour, and a certain array of behavioural patterns, all of which differ from those of any other living organisms. From the concept "human" are derived a) "humane", defined in Webster's dictionary as, "having or showing kindness, tenderness, compassion, etc.," b) its opposite, "inhumane", defined as, "having no compassion for others", which is a negative quality and misfit that should never define humanity. "Humanism", another derivative of "human", defines the behaviour of humans at their best, caring for one another and for other living organisms, caring for the earth and the clean atmosphere that sustain them, and promoting authentic human values without paying homage to religious dogma and myth; not the warped values that we will discover to be the norm in some worlds and should really be termed disvalues, as I have portrayed them in *Our World and its Values*. In some worlds e.g., twin world, some persons would like to interpret homanism — their equivalent of our humanism — as implying that each homan of a select tribe, and only that select tribe, is "the paragon of animals" (animals here refers only to the homan species), regardless of the survival costs that other people must bear to facilitate and sustain, however unwillingly, this hyperbolic characterization of him and his heedless self-imposition over them. His tribe and he think that they are indeed "the measure of all things", relegating every other person of every other tribe to second, third, and no class status, even though all of them are ultimately only "the quintessence of dust", however much they exalt themselves.

From these defining characteristics, it is easy to understand that homans are expected to perform homanistic or homanitarian acts of *ubuntu* (oo-boon-too) that are meant to promote only what is good and worthwhile in the lives of all people and their environment. (It is oxymoronic—the ultimate—that the oppressors of the brown people of South Africa called them "Bantu"; i.e., persons endowed with *ubuntu*, unlike themselves, after mulishly denying their personhood). The term *ubuntu* refers to the humaneness or personhood that is integral to the realization of one's being in the being of others with whom one has humane, caring, and respectful relationships, without losing one's individual moral and legal rights to the primacy and dominance of the group to which one belongs. *Ubuntu* denotes the cardinal role fulfilled by communalism in the realization of individual personhood, versus the "civilized" view of persons as profitable commodities for the marketplace, a view that extricates them from the communities to which they belong, so that they can be sold to the highest bidder for the greatest profit. Pink civilization dishonours them by regarding them as dispensable parts of a conglomerate that is less than its *ubuntu* whole, and not as integral constituents of a oneness that cannot be separated for humiliation without humiliating the whole with which they are intimately intertwined. One might as well completely detach a person's heart and lungs from his body and expect them to continue to serve their normal functions in the service of that body (in their separated state) as individual existents outside her body, while also expecting that body to survive as a person without its vital elements.

The thesis of *ubuntu*, as explicated by Mogobe Ramose in his book *African Philosophy Through Ubuntu*, that the molding of each person's character and her completeness as a person depend partly on the positive contributions of other persons to her personhood, so that it can be realized only in their joint personhood, is based on the priority of their joint existence over their individual existences, which are worthless without this preceding being. It is much like the philosophical concept of a person, which precedes its corporeal and psychic elements, rather than being derived from their conjunction.

For being the person that she is or ought to be in all aspects of her societal existence in this pre-established reciprocal relationship, each person depends on tacit, natal incorporation into her society, empowerment by it, and explicit support of others to live amicably, not in strife, with her neighbours within its tenets. At no time is any person's individuality denied, but at no time does it supersede the totality of personalities that constitutes the community to which she belongs and in which the being of every member is realized.

*Ubuntu* thus denotes coexistence of individuals within a social nexus at its best, since no single person can make all the items on which she would depend to live successfully in the milieu of the modern world apart from other people. Each person depends on others to supply and manage vaccines, medicines, sanitation, radios, food supplies, etc., while many of the conveniences and amenities that she enjoys in her world would have no meaning for her in her solitary life, since they are meant to be executed and enjoyed in the company of others; e.g. a game of soccer by a single, self-sufficient player who is also opposition and spectator is meaningless. From the circumscribed communality of her home region to a global sharing of her material goods with those who are deprived is as easy a step for the subscriber to *ubuntu* as it is difficult for the selfish hoarder who has much more than he needs to live in comfort (and luxury), but will not part with a minuscule fragment of it to feed the starving neighbours that he has created all over twin world.

When the architects of the hunger of twin world want to mock this noble concept so that they can highlight their self-serving capitalistic individualism, they speak disparagingly of "spreading the wealth around", as if it is a sin to extend a helping hand to those in need — a sure sign of a sick world. But *Ubuntu* entreats persons to aid, instead of exploiting other people: individuals and groups; save, instead of killing them; emancipate, instead of enslaving and oppressing them; be truthful, instead of lying to them; and be honest, ingenuous, and caring toward them, instead of being deceitful, manipulative, and callous to their interests and goals and to them. It also means that instead of polluting and stripping the environment of all its life-sustaining vegetation and animal population, which are at the root of life cycles and the balance of nature, people should preserve these elements of their world for the benefit of present and future generations and not appropriate them solely for their immediate, selfish, and extravagant use. For self-styled first world countries of twin world, which never cease to tout their supremacy in every one's face, it means taking the lead in cleaning up the environment, instead of hiding behind the silly and childish, but greed-inspired pout that "third world" countries should lead the way by first cleaning up their act, even as "first world" countries that are producing the bulk of the pollution are driving them into economic decline with their perverted money-lending institutions. (For arguments pro and con our duty in our world to uphold the "rights" of non-extant posterity, see chapter 4 of my *Our World and its Values*). Furthermore, it means facing up to the truth about their greed and inhomanity, which makes them kill others, instead of blaming it on their evolutionary animal origins and the persistence of the killer instinct in them. Animals don't kill for sport and greed of worldly possessions like homan beings; they kill only to feed and survive.

In the final chapter of *Our World and its values*, under the title "Whither Humanity?", I presented a bleak picture of where humanity is headed with its prevailing epidemic of greed and its warped concepts of values and their exercise in the words: "The weight of evidence points to alienation and the growth of increasingly inhumane relationships within and amongst the world's [human] communities."[2] Perhaps this view is unduly pessimistic; this world is not as bad and as doomed as I made it out to be, and optimism about the future of humanity would be a better attitude to assume. This world is studded with people who harbour only good intentions for others, altruistic heads of governments who live happily only if they can prevent the deaths of millions from disease, famine, cluster bombs, and purposely fomented sectarian violence for the express purpose of stealing the natural resources of the combatant third parties, and leaders whose every unselfish action can be rationally and logically accounted for only in humanitarian terms.

But there may be other worlds out there where these persons engage in irrational and logically contradictory actions like saying and trying to convince their audiences that rain could be falling and not falling in the same locality at the same time; e.g., my government believes in transparency, but we will not disclose any information to you to fulfill our accountability; also, my government doesn't believe in incurring deficits except when it borrows billions of dullams to buy the goodwill of its gullible electorate. These are persons who can also infuse money into one side of a contrived conflict to ensure the triumph of their protégés in that conflict and ensure their ongoing obsequious acquiescence to being used as pawns in executing the dirty work of their benefactor that is meant to exploit the unwary belligerent parties. Such a world is best described as an impossible, oxymoronic world, and that is what we will discover about twin world as the rest of this essay unfolds, although those who hold the trump card there want to confuse the rest of the people by claiming that what looks like an inconsistency is really a dialetheism or statement of the same kind as "all twin-worlders are liars" uttered by a twin-worlder. That means, if the statement is true, then the person uttering it is lying i.e., twin-worlders are not liars. If he is lying in his utterance (being a twin-worlder) then he is telling the truth i.e., they are liars. Confusing? Welcome to twin world where fame is rooted in infamy and popularity in foolishness of word and deed. Confuse them, dissuade them from thinking and opining, then exploit them.

In this age of interstellar travel, it is not outlandish to imagine travel to one of these oxymoron-studded worlds of our galaxy to learn their ways. That is why we will choose twin world, which is closer to our world than any other world out there, as we have already indicated. Twin world consists of five continents: Afibika, Asibia, Eubopa, Nomebika, and Somebika. Afibika is regarded by palaeontologists as one of the possible birth places of homanity (even with modern attempts to upset this belief with a solitary tooth of dubious early homan origin) and by sociologists to be the cradle of civilization of their world; only pink philosophers and racists have yet to reconcile themselves to the evidence being proffered that it is also the possible source of ancient Eubopan philosophy. The people of twin world run their affairs in the same way as we run ours, with some notable exceptions, and when an inhabitant of this world is in that world she feels more at home than she would if she were visiting one of the other possible worlds out there in our galaxy.

The only notable exception is that unlike the inhabitants of our world, the people of twin world shun our sloppy and ignorant use of language that is exemplified in the bandying about of words and expressions that do not make sense. They frown on expressions like neither $x$ or $y$ for neither $x$ nor $y$; neither one of you have... for neither one of you has...; do either one of you... for does either one of you...; with regards to for with regard to/as regards; continue on (carry on on) for continue (carry on); irregardless (regardlessless) for regardless; a phenomena for a phenomenon; a criteria for a criterion; is comprised of (no meaning) for is composed of, or comprises (includes)/(consists of); revert/return back (go back back) for revert/return (go back); he was laying there (laying eggs?) for he was lying there; utmost best (best best) for utmost (best); $\alpha$ is different than $\beta$ for $\alpha$ is different from $\beta$; between 7p.m. to 9p.m. (meaningless) for between 7p.m. and 9p.m.; 12 noon (tautology) or 12a.m. for noon (meaningless; noon is the boundary between a.m. and p.m., it can't be a.m. or p.m.); 12p.m. or 12 midnight for midnight; cold temperature for low temperature (-1 is lower on the temperature scale than +2); saying that the number -1 is colder than the number +2 is committing a category mistake like saying Monday is sleeping, days of the week don't sleep and numbers don't feel cold or warm to the touch); preventative for preventive (preventative is adjectival form of noun "preventation" and verb "preventate". Preventive is the corresponding form of prevention and prevent. Finally, the point of this exercise is is that... the juxtaposition of "is" and "is" in the construction of this sentence makes as little sense as the apostrophe in "he wear's two hat's" or "shoe's for boy's and girl's"; and many other absurdities.

Someone might argue that the meanings of words are determined by their use in language, and so people have the right to use words however they wish with the intent of conveying the meanings that they are entertaining. But that would constitute an unacceptable deviation from the conventional use of those words, and hence make nonsense of such use to persons whose usage of the words conforms with convention. We cannot attach our own meanings to words or deviate from their conventional use and expect other people to understand our meaning and intention. As Lewis Carroll stated,

> 'When I use a word,' Humpty Dumpty said, in rather a scornful tone, 'it means just what I choose it to mean — neither more nor less.'
> 'The question is,' said Alice, 'whether you *can* make words mean so many different things.[3]

Without entering into the fray about the utility or otherwise of the concept of possible worlds, like twin world, let us just assume that a possible world is another way that our world might have been, and let us imagine that we can take a trip to one of these possible worlds that are in competition with our actual world for the basic survival of its inhabitants and for supremacy in conquering and controlling, for good or for bad, adjacent parts of our common universe. We will note that in that world, the word 'tribe' is used in place of 'race' to refer to various members of their one, and only one, homan race in their different sizes, shapes, colours, languages, cultures, and mores; but the terms 'race', 'racial', 'racism', and 'racist' will be used in this essay as they are used in our world in reference to these tribes for convenience, necessity, and ease of comparison.

One of the oddities that we will discover on our arrival in twin world is that the Eubopans of that world have been trying their utmost over the years to discredit the facts surrounding the findings that situate Afibika at the centre of the history of their world and to attribute all these prestigious origins to their own continent. Their scholars, however, like those of our world, do not accord any credence to these claims. In our world, the Greek writer Herodotus, in 480BCE, is reported to have acknowledged the geometry of the Egyptians, their solar calendar, 12-part year etc., as evidence of their advanced (over Greek) learning. He also described them as having dark skins and curly hair, before they were invaded and diluted by light skinned tribes from the north. Lately, after his intensive, unbiased research, Richard Poe observed, "Nevertheless, twenty years after [Colin] Renfrew wrote his article [disclaiming the influence of Egyptian civilization on barbaric Europe], experts are no closer than they were in 1977 to moving the 'cradle of civilization' to Western Europe. And it seems a safe bet that they never will."[4]

At the same time, Martin Bernal, another intensive, unbiased researcher, has shown that 20 to 25% of Greek words were most probably derived from related Egyptian roots, because they have no connection with any of the European languages, lending credence to the claim that Egypt was the cradle of western civilization. George James, another student of Egyptology, states that "Egyptian temples carried inscriptions on the outside addressed to Neophytes, and among them was the inscription 'know thyself'. Socrates copied these words from the Egyptian temples."[5] With regard to the Pythagorean Theorem, he says, "the Egyptians taught Pythagoras and the Greeks what mathematics they knew."[6] About Greek Philosophy as a whole, he says, "Concerning the fact that Egypt was the greatest education centre of the ancient world which was also visited by the Greeks, reference must again be made to Plato in the Timaeus who tells us that Greek aspirants to wisdom visited Egypt for initiation."[7]

Realizing the weight of evidence against their shadowy claims of pink superiority in their world, Eubopans resorted to weaving chimerical theories based on cheap lies based on bogus scientific and anthropological studies into which Poe gives us an insight in his book *Black Spark, White Fire*. He quotes one master race exponent of phrenology who used the larger capacities of prejudicially selected larger skull sizes of white subjects (and therefore larger brains, but no mention of whether these were of hydrocephalic brains) versus their heights to prove his racist theory of the superior brain power of whites over that of blacks. Nevertheless, a notorious pink supremacist of twin world advised silence about their unhistoric and disreputable past, rather than reviving it and making a laughing stock of themselves as well known savages. He was, no doubt, aware of their oxymoronic claim to have civilized twin world while they "destroyed civilized life wherever they encountered it"[8].

Hagala, a twin world philosopher, admitted indirectly that the full identity of Eubopans can be appreciated when they are viewed against a background of Afibikans whose home continent, he claims, is the ahistorical primordium from which the history of their Eubopan continent and the world take off, leaving Afibika still groping in the dark. In constructing the type of Afibika that meets his biased tribal attitude, he pretends not to be aware, in writing the history of twin world, that everything has a history as long as it exists in time; it has a yesterday, today, and tomorrow, which, in retrospect, constitute its history. For him to suggest that Afibika is dormant in contrast with Eubopa where everything happens, that nothing happens in Afibika, is inexcusable bigotry bordering on foolish talk. Equally foolish sounding is any contention that debases Afibikans as strictly sensuous beings, because they live in a hot climate in a land that lacks abundant water, unlike the intellectually and socially superior Eubopans who live in temperate climates where water abounds. On these premises, he constructs his own Afibika by conjuring up a tectonic shift that will separate off its northern coastal areas and make it possible for him and like-minded racists to call them Eubopan-Afibika, while he condemns the rest of the continent to oblivion as unknowable, ahistorical, and without movement or change. The latter claim is, of course, a result of the preposterous manoeuvre of deriving an epistemological fiction from a phantasmal ontological fancy to feed his bigotry and lay the ground for further bigotry that defies philosophical wisdom and existing reality with figments of a perverted imagination.

Unfortunately for Hagala, the history of his tribe, known to all of twin world, bears witness to the disgusting barbarism, immorality, and reckless inhomanity of which he accuses Afibikans. Indeed, there is nothing harmonious with homanity to be found in the practice of suffocating people or vivisecting them alive. Instead, there is only praise to be heaped on the practice of *ubuntu* by which Afibikans live in their well organized communities where respect for other persons is their governing philosophy, not the I, me, myself philosophy of his tribe's lineage of thieves that motivated them to steal lands from the indigenous peoples by cunning and duplicity, making them sign treaties which only they understood (the fine print that they are still using today to bamboozle enlightened investors and purchasers of commodities in twin world), and now balking when they have to make good on long outstanding payments to honour those treaties. Their word has proved to be as good as the garbage from their homes that is left on their sidewalks to be carted to the dumps; it does not engender any respect for the source.

Pinks of twin world have assumed many painful contortions to try to discredit browns, carrying Hagala's antics further and also arbitrarily and audaciously dividing the continent of Afibika into a sliver in the north, in close proximity to Eubopa, which they claim as part of Eubopa. They have ignored the geographical barrier posed by the intervening sea that has been called "the axis of world history [and] the navel of the earth"[9], and they have expended tremendous energy and time trying to prove that the inhabitants of this northern region are not Afibikans, contrary to all the evidence that is starring them in the face, but which they are doing their best to distort. The rest of Afibika, which they acknowledge that they do not know, is their real Afibika. In our world, Egypt, with its rich educational, cultural, and philosophical history is one such area. As Bernal has observed,

> For eighteenth and nineteenth century Romanticists and racists it was simply intolerable for Greece, which was seen not merely as the epitome of Europe but also as its pure childhood, to have been the result of the mixture of native Europeans and colonizing Africans and Semites. Therefore, the Ancient Model had to be overthrown and replaced by something more acceptable[10]

to uphold the impression that "whatever the Greeks acquire from foreigners is finally turned by them into something finer."[11] The purpose of the exercise was always to advance the theory of European superiority; as one of them is reported to have said: "If the Egyptians were the inventors, this proves them to be [merely] ingenious, the Greeks showed themselves to possess superior genius."[12] But because Eubopans cannot convincingly deny these origins or sell the lie successfully, they have drawn an imaginary line in the sands of the northern Afibikan desert to justify their farcical fancies of Eubopan superiority, and they have incorporated a part of geographical Afibika into Eubopa in a futile effort to exclude Afibika from sharing the glory of inventive genius and from being their cultural and racial ancestral home. In short, they have been engaging in the promotion of another oxymoron: claiming the existence of non-Afibika that is Afibika, belying the truth, and disclaiming their Afibikan origins from Afibika for their vain, racist, self-glorification.

This unfounded sense of super self-worth is well illustrated in an interesting and revealing anecdote related by a friend who witnessed the following scene: A group of deviant young browns would have been in serious trouble for surfing a moving train if they had not flattered one of these bossy buffoons (pink ticket examiner) by addressing him as their king and god and asking him to give them one more chance to correct their misdeeds, whereupon he let them off with a stern warning, and they in turn thanked him profusely with more flattery, catering to his self-importance as their *baas* (boss). Once off the train and safely out of danger, they proceeded to heap scorn and curse him in the most revulsive terms, obviously very pleased with themselves for having made a fool of this dolt who thought that he had the whole world at his feet. Obsession with his pinkness and self-importance exposed him to flatter and made an absolute fool of him, as it always does with all of them. But that is the failing of people who pretend to be what they are not, whose lives are a lie to themselves and to those they wish to deceive with their assumed importance. They always end up holding the short end of the stick, undressed, with egg on their faces and their grotesque forms exposed to the light of day.

The inhabitants of Eubopa have also arbitrarily, and for their own selfish convenience, divided the population of twin world into pink and brown tribes, an invention that serves them well in their untiring efforts to trample on the other tribes for their exclusive survival Such division is intertwined with stratification that implicitly reduces browns to subordinates of pinks, with no homan rights, and merely destined to be perpetual hewers of wood and drawers of water, while pinks are destined to be the rulers of twin world by their vapoury criteria, although they are trying hard to make everyone believe that this setup comes about naturally by divine decree. On this basis, every brown is expected to know her place, to remain in it, to be happy with her assigned lot, and to eschew communist agitators and "terrorists" who want to disrupt this profitable but fiendish design where browns may not aspire to scale the ranks of ethnocentric pinks or carve out their own destiny in the history of nations.

These fools forget, or they do not know, that while they wantonly sacrifice the lives of their pink citizens to terrorize and subjugate browns, their victims terrorize them reciprocally and sacrifice their own lives in their struggle to achieve the lofty ideals of freedom and tribal honour against the disrespect, hubris, hegemony, and serfdom that pinks dish out to them; they do not aggress, they only retaliate. Besides, their nauseatingly vaunted pink superiority is nothing more than an empty shell rooted in the brownness of others, because without relegating them to an inferior position by lying to themselves and to them about what they are each worth in their contrived world, they cannot continue to wield their pinkness as their entitlement to superiority or *baasskap* (literally translated from an African language styled Afrikaans, it means "bossness"). Therefore their pinkness is parasitic on the brownness of others without whose ongoing existence as such, in their forcibly assigned inferior status, it cannot survive. No parasite survives without its host, not even the lowest of parasitic species with which these self-styled superior beings are competing in many respects.

One of the most unfortunate outcomes of this abiding parasitic relationship is the successful infusion of a paralyzing, self-repudiating slave mentality into most browns by pinks, to the sad extent that they are not willing to respond to many efforts meant to encourage them to emerge from the mental bondage that has been imposed on them and aspire to a better mental and material life. They have accepted a false definition of who they are, and they have become so accustomed to eking out their life of empty contentment with just enough to get by that they find it an onerous burden to strive for a fuller mental life, even if they may still be lacking in material possessions. If anything, they rather prefer mental slothfulness and the hollow opportunity to rise far above the level of others of their tribe in their possession of the inconsequential material things of twin world to forgoing them for the things that stimulate and feed their minds to think like a free people. Thus, they incapacitate themselves from pursuing the rights to which all free people are morally and legally entitled and which are being withheld from them by persons who have no respect for others and their duty toward them as holders of rights, and who count them with their marketable commodities whose labour can be bought cheaply in sweatshops.

This failure to free their minds from the serfdom of yesteryear has proven to be the root cause of the impediment to upward and forward mobility in brown development. They refuse to acquire a vision for new ventures; instead, they are content to mark time, doing the same things over and over again, going through the same humdrum motions every day like the inimitable, mythical Sisyphus who spends days on end rolling a huge stone up to the top of a hill, only to see it roll down, and then rolling it up again and watching it roll down, then rolling it up many more times and seeing it roll down each time, so that at the end of it all he accomplishes nothing. The end comes, of course, when he collapses or dies from exhaustion and other calamities, crowning a wasted life that did not benefit him or anyone else, as is sadly the case with many brown lives under the yoke of pink oppression, dispossession, and dehumanization.

Amidst this mélange of similarities and unseemly aberrations of behaviour and the refusal to acknowledge, among other things, their possible origin and the fountain of their civilization from a part of their world in which they claim not to have had their roots and from which they would rather dissociate themselves as non-Afibikan Afibikans, these wretched souls can still not resist the lure of wealth from the cornucopia of natural resources inherent to this alien land that has possessed them so much that they have scrambled to colonize and exploit it since they became aware of its rich stores of plant (rubber, timber), animal (ivory, skins, zoo specimens), minerals (diamonds, platinum, gold), oil, and people (slaves counted with goods and used in the payment of debts). Their behaviour is no different from the reported behaviour of our world's colonialists who from November 15, 1884 to February 26, 1885, when "spheres of influence began to crowd each other"[13], met in Berlin "to sort things out", like thieves who caucus to share the spoils of their marauding, dividing other people's homeland among themselves (14 of them) to facilitate their systematic and protracted (to date) plunder of the varied wealth of the African continent and to enslave and trade its peoples in the marketplace like common commodities. Just in case anyone should think that this was an aberration in behaviour that belongs to those times, the same pattern of purloining is still being practiced today: "they passed laws allowing foreign companies to own 100% of these resources, . . . and within two years, Indonesia's natural wealth—copper, nickel, hardwood, rubber and oil—was being divided up among the largest mining and energy companies in the world."[14] Also, pariah states of Southern Africa became magnets to them when treasure-troves of diamond fields were discovered there recently.

This oxymoronic, almost schizophrenic contrast in behaviour exhibited by the pinks of twin world is the product of chance and greed. By sheer happenstance they have been able to achieve what the other peoples of twin world have not had the opportunity to achieve, and these fortuitous and contingent results of circumstance have intoxicated them with belief in superiority of their homanity, which happens to be no different from the homanity of all the other peoples of their world. Even the vulgar morons among them regard themselves as more homan than the most accomplished members of the other tribes of their world, not on the basis of the sizes of their noses, ears, hands, brains, or feet, let alone cognitive ability, which has been tried unsuccessfully as a criterion present in them but lacking in others, but on the stupid basis of their endowment with less pigment. The less pigmented, the more homan; i.e., less is more and more is less or "more fewer", to quote some local authorities.

These unfortunate, inane attitudes have also enslaved the minds of enlightened pinks to a sad degree; they who should and often do know better by virtue of the evidence from their own sense of propriety and from their scientific and biological discoveries, which have shown that all persons possess equal intrinsic homan worth that entitles them to equal standing, and that if any deserve denigration of their homanity, it is strictly on the basis of their individual conduct and not their tribal origins. They should be able to edify their less cognitively endowed tribesmen that the rogues of homanity occur across continental divides without limitations by religion, education, political affiliation, culture, economic status, or skin colour. Some of the most devoutly religious, most highly educated, most politically influential, most cultured, or most economically secure persons have been the worst bigots and haters of other persons for no other reason than the colour of their skins. That has also made them the kinds of detestable homans that are distinguished by their inhomane attitudes and practices, and by their racist envy of the slightest efforts of browns to improve their own lot. They are, indeed, paragons of unmatched oxymoronic contradictions.

The prevailing attitude of pinks, on the international, national, and personal levels, is that brown (sub-person) rights depend on their discretion as the only real persons in twin world. As we have already noted, this attitude of denying the personhood of another is meant to infuse doubt into him about his personhood, and to make him finally accept his non-personhood as drilled into him by the oppressor who also wants to convince him of his worthlessness to all of homanity. With this attitude of mind, he will not question any acts of dehomanization directed at him, since he is already a non-homan homan who can therefore not be dehomanized. Pinks also hope that the goofy disconnection between pink theoretical professions of universal homan rights and their practice of depriving browns of those rights will not attract criticism from his supposed non-homan intellect, nor from any other intellect, thus leaving them free to abuse these deprived and visible minorities (as they style them) who still remain largely invisible to them. Another oxymoron? No. It is true that they can look right through browns, as if the substance of their visibly coloured bodies does not present a physical impediment to their (pink) vision, even if they know them well enough to be able to recognize them. When it does not suit their whims to acknowledge the existence of a brown, she does not exist in their world at that moment. The ultimate oxymoron is that these invisible visible minorities constitute the majority of the population of twin world. They are the majority minorities; so, pinks beware this oxymoron,

All in all, the virtues of sincerity, kindness, and the promotion of harmonious relationships with other persons appear to be foreign to these immodest persons. To suggest to them that they are one side of the same coin with the people whom they despise forming the other side of that coin, is to imply that they are equal to the other persons, which is tantamount to insulting them. They cannot appreciate the fact that one side doth not a coin make, because the "whatness" or being of the coin resides in the unity of the being of its sides, without which it has no significance and no conventional value. A coin with only one face has yet to come into circulation and be accepted as legitimate currency to discredit this comparison. For now, that is the nature of coins (and paper money), which is as undeniable as the need of browns to complement and complete the barren being-with-the-otherness of pinks that they arrogantly refuse to acknowledge, although browns have readily and without any qualms admitted the interdependence of all homans (*ubuntu*).

Pink homanity, if they have any, can't flourish without the aid of the homanity of browns, and they know that; otherwise they would not be so dependent on them to fulfill those functions in their economy and society that they think are below their dignity and for which they can't hire animals or harness robots, the latter of which have rendered superfluous the hitherto callously exploited manual labour of browns in other areas where they found the few jobs that they needed desperately for survival, if they were not preferentially given to pinks. Still, they deceive themselves by thinking and acting as if they have no need of the inferior homanity of browns, thus becoming incomplete persons with inhoman propensities and behaviours that they use to achieve their most ardent desire in life: to control and misdirect the destiny of their world to ultimate disaster. Besides, some of them, like some in our world, daydream brazenly that they are divinely chosen and guided to dictate to the rest how they shall live. They quote from this world's scriptures fictitious passages conveniently written to shore up this brand of arrogant self-regard and entitlement: "The LORD your God will set you high above all the nations of the earth."[15] "You shall rule over many nations, but they shall not rule over you."[16]

So what is the point of praying for salvation from predestined homan bondage? Browns might as well write their own scriptures to inspire their people to cast off the onerous yoke of serfdom to pink supremacy. But, perhaps, they should study the intricacies of this wonderful, all-empowering pink religion that has given them so much power, and learn from it how they can also pull off the same hoax on their oppressors to share a spot on the pedestal that they occupy. After all, when they brought them their religion, they told them that it would teach them how to live well with their neighbours and how to prepare for entry into a world beyond twin world where there is no evil, but only goodness, brotherly love, fellowship, cake, and sanctified—not to be mistaken for sanctimonious—eternal life.

Before we do so, however, let us consider some representative scenarios of the attitudes that we have been discussing, if only to add substance to the foregoing conceptual analyses of the herrenvolk or master race mentality of the pinks of twin world. For the rest, since this essay is not meant to be a compendium of specific instances of pink inhomanity, but rather an exposition of the trends that illustrate their philosophy of tribal superiority and how it is lived and imposed on others, I will dwell on generalities, mentioning specifics only to illustrate the general concepts under discussion with concrete examples from every possible world, since these obscene attitudes that characterize pinkness appear to be universal. The universality of these attitudes defies any attempt to curb them, because they are innate characteristics of these people. Besides, to eradicate them will entail eliminating the bearers of those characteristics.

# Chapter 4
# Representative scenarios

In the first scenario strong man $x$, a heartless murderer posing as a statesman, assaults, victimizes, oppresses, and dehumanizes weaker man $y$ by denying him political and civil rights, restricting his movements, taking his property by force and settling on it with impunity, wantonly and indiscriminately killing his family and demolishing their homes, schools, and hospitals with bombs and bull-dozers, shooting his children in cold blood, and maiming many of them with chemicals. His lack of concern for their welfare militates against any tendency to ever show compassion for their resultant suffering; so it is ironic that he should be seen shedding tears of contrition for the victims of his truculence, like some in our world. But he does put up public appearances where he is seen shedding loveless crocodile tears for those of his victims who hold embarrassingly high international profiles, or those whose massacre has aroused general ire of proportions that cannot be ignored. Like those who weep over their emerging visual infirmities, but still continue to broadcast evil lies and spew venom from their foul mouths, or those teary-eyed politicians who achieve their own dreams but blithely thwart the realization of those same dreams by others, his oxymoronic display is a tatty facade for his deep-seated inhomanity and his driving desire to liquidate the other under the pretext that her mere presence near him constitutes a serious threat to his esteemed survival.

$x$ and his ilk are elites of homanity who take their own right to exist for granted; it is the other people who have to produce to them, as the supreme beings, sufficient and stringently defined proof to justify their right to exist, beyond the fact that their existence is already a *fait accompli* that just happens to offend the sensibilities of their self-styled superior tribe by its uncomfortable proximity to them; hence their perennial efforts to try to eliminate them. In his self-sufficiency and refusal to recognize the personhood of others and its influence on him, $x$ repudiates the concept of being-in-the-world-with-others; he strives to be alone, far above them, but he also foolishly refuses to acknowledge that in their absence he has no one to lord over and whom to use to rouse and feed the dormant, dominating depravity of his character. His lack of common decency, which is astonishing for the highly "civilized" person that he claims to be, and his arrogance, which befits his concept of himself as the superior being, impel him to refuse to recognize and acknowledge the interrelationship and interdependence of homanity that he misuses to place himself above others, instead of relating to them as equals in humanity and realizing the fulfillment of his life in theirs. His entire indecent demeanour betrays a pathetic lack of what decent "primitive" people have called *ubuntu*.

Ultimately, because all chickens love to come home to roost, $x$'s chickens also come home to roost in the form of retaliatory strikes from $y$ in response to $x$'s continuing, shocking, and awesome acts of violence toward him. $y$'s acts of minor violence meant to express his displeasure at being abused by $x$, and intended to make him feel the pain of being the victim of constant assault, even if it is to a very minor degree compared to the vile harassment and unwarranted massive punishment that $x$ is meting out to him and his family, elicit further violence from $x$ who also responds by claiming to the whole of twin world that $y$ is constantly attacking him for no reason at all. He unleashes his superior fire power against $y$ and his entire family, claiming that he has the right to defend himself against $y$'s repeated and unprovoked attacks by murdering $y$'s family in a savage form of exemplary, collective punishment, as if $y$ did not also have the right to defend himself against $x$'s attacks on his person and property in the first place, which is more often than not how the conflicts begin.

Murder, as wanton slaughter, has now acquired the new usage of "defence" in the hands of $x$, replacing the old usage of "defence" as driving danger or attack away from oneself, leaving us all confused. $x$ has pitiably wrapped himself in his fabricated robe of supremacy, acting as if his rights supersede the rights of everyone else. He even has the audacity to acknowledge that he launched "a war of choice", attacking $y$ for the sake of gratifying his hubris and racism. In spite of the efforts of $y$ and his tribe to coexist peacefully with him and his tribe in their original homeland, on homanistic terms, he has continued to pillage $y$'s property and steal his lands (killing him in the process) with impunity and with the connivance of his buddies in manipulated governments and the puppet news media of his world. They cheerfully disseminate a barrage of captious opinions that have been artfully crafted by collaborators to create the impression that they are the disapproving opinions of recalcitrant elements, and they couple them with responsive lies about their efforts to resolve the impasse that they are perpetuating, when it is clear to anyone that they have no such intention. Hence it is that some people can put allegedly fictitious words like the following in the mouths of these rascals purporting them to be true, if only to portray the scurvy duplicity with which they operate: "Thanks to such methods we shall be in a position as from time to time may be required, to excite or to tranquillize the public mind on political questions, to persuade or to confuse, printing now truth, now lies, facts or their contradictions, according as they may be well or ill received, always very cautiously feeling our ground before stepping upon it."[1]

The reader will encounter many more oxymorons used by $x$ and his ilk to whitewash themselves and mischaracterize $y$ and his tribe, lending support to the view that where truth is lacking, confusion and contradiction will remain as the only available media through which to portray unstable, crumbling situations founded and built on lies, selfishness, homan inhomanity, and hypocrisy. Besides, pinks of twin world have been known to inflict harm on themselves for which they have incriminated innocent other persons on whom they wish to exact revenge for their own victimization by persons who have no relation to their newly found scapegoats on whom they wish to impose their unfettered authority, simply for the sake of dispossessing and dehomanizing them. $x$ and his tribe can't set aside their hubris and narcissism to recognize the ludicrousness of their endless self-pitying remonstrations and reprehensible, retributive actions when they are the known initiators and perpetuators of the cycle of violence and aggression. They just don't get it, and as long as their shallow, self-deluding, ideological attitude does not change for the better, so long will they continue to live illogically in the depths of their cocoon of compelling, self-serving lies that is impervious to reason and truth, condemning everyone and the many attempted peace initiatives to endless strife, while spelling only death and ruination for $y$'s family.

In this scenario where $y$ realizes that events do not change of their own accord, he embarks on efforts to also "defend" himself more vigorously from attacks by $x$ at the risk of being labeled the aggressor by $x$ and his hypocritical buddies. These same sponsors and buddies of $x$ urge him on to batter $y$ and his family, because he has the right to defend himself against $y$'s "unprovoked" attacks with oxymoronic "measured" excesses of his own. Meanwhile, true to the adage that the cruelest lies are often told in silence, they either look on in silence, pretending not to see the genocide that $x$ is perpetrating on $y$'s tribe. Their biased, cheer-leading, habitually conniving, corporate-controlled news/myth media, whose expertise is to act as echo chambers of the cacophonous knavery and buffoonery that issues from the sacred chambers of political power, unabashedly distort and suppress these and many other recurrent inhomane catastrophes perpetrated by these callous butchers, and they even sink so low as to misrepresent them by also blaming their defenceless victims. All of them have been well schooled by the aggressor-owner to believe that he is the victim of aggression and to serve as his propaganda tools. Their aversion to truth is equaled only by their egotism and racism. Everyone who has the power and the leverage to intervene in halting these systematic genocides that have been going on since the day that the one group decided that they are the superior persons who must own everything that belongs to the other people has been mesmerized by the flow of money from agents of these butchers who also claim to be their Gudd's chosen people, the most intelligent of all the tribes, destined to save their world, wherever they are to be found in it. Their pressure tactics to have their agenda carried out include a firm grip on the running of the national governments of some states. Are they standing on the threshold of sovereignty over twin world and over all empires? They now control them like puppets and dictate to them whom they will kill on their behalf (while they stay out of the fray and its aftermath to save their butts), what they will say or write, and how they will conduct themselves in all matters affecting them and those that they represent, if they seriously want to win their contests to accede to or stay in their chosen jobs of power and also avoid being black-listed. Those who do not toe the line will be harassed until they and others who are like-minded get the message. Such is the power that some pinks wield over other pinks and browns in twin world.

    The thought of all these powerful persons being held captive by a few recalcitrant, self-serving, hard-line, arrogant, and racist fiends who are using them to do their dirty work is discomfiting. It is enough to generate despair and gloom in the future of the victims of this joint skulduggery who can only vent their wrath in feeble strikes. The only response that will deter them from their mischief is a torrent of fully merited harder strikes, coupled with rampant and violent revolt which matches the cruelty that these fiends are force-feeding them, but this possibility was rendered almost unachievable by the presence of quislings who are content to sell out their people to the oppressor for small favours and mere pittances as rewards. When it seems as if the tide is turning, to the gratification of most concerned browns and others, along comes a moron, so-styled by those who know him, to muddy the waters with controversial and thoughtlessly irresponsible pronouncements that turn the clock back.

    The hypocrisy that attends the attitude of pinks to browns is astounding in the light of historical events. When $x$'s tribe was living under foreign domination in a state created for it by its benefactors, some of its then heroes and subsequent leaders (rewards for heroism, alias terrorism, to use their unfortunate terminology that has now become the denotative reference to any dissent with their repressive governments) perpetrated acts of terrorism, viz., assassinations and bombings of buildings owned by their oppressors; but these were euphemistically termed gallant acts of freedom fighters. The same kinds of acts, carried out today by less favoured persons who are oppressed by these same quondam victims of murder who are now the butchering "heroes", are glibly labeled unequivocal terrorist crimes deserving of inhomane and, more frequently, lethal collective punishment prompted by self-pity of their oppressors.

The warped and hypocritical trend of reasoning is as follows: First, pinks brand browns as incorrigible terrorists (for resisting oppression); so all their acts are automatically and designedly labeled and condemned as terrorist acts for which pinks are given the unfettered license to liquidate them summarily and without mercy for their gallant struggles for survival aimed at pink inhomanity, because terrorists can never do any good, every speech and act of theirs is a self-fulfilling confirmation of their violent nature. So, what the same category of speech or act is called and how it is rewarded depends solely on the tribal/racial affiliations of the perpetrator. That's how people are silenced in twin world, hypocritically, ingloriously, and terminally. "Never again" has become empty rhetoric from their lying mouths as they continue to sacrifice lesser beings, alias collateral damage, in their quest for the material goods of twin world and the pursuit of their misguided ideology of pink supremacy.

In the second scenario, which is a virtual repetition of the first one, another pink bully, $\varepsilon$, wields his might to dispossess brown $\omega$ and his tribe, killing hundreds of thousands of brown civilians (babies included) and plunging his own state and the rest of twin world into economic chaos. For his recklessness, he wins accolades from his cronies and besotted citizenry, making him feel like a big boy who is standing on top of twin world and all its inhabitants like a mighty conqueror of Napoleonic proportions. In the pink view of twin world, the hero is the one who can oppress and dispossess browns better than anyone else. After his ruinous escapades, however, his tribe rejects him and his cronies, and they even opt, in their despair, to settle for a saviour, $\psi$, a brown leader from one of the despised tribes. But being of vile nature, some of their ilk fail to curb the habitual indecency that is integral to their low lives by heaping all kinds of scorn on him and thwarting his every effort to lift them out of the gutter where they live.

Some of their insignificant females who hail from the gutters of an obscure hamlet in twin world and who also lack a quarter of his wife's academic qualifications give vent to their felt inferiority, jealousy, and inane racism by deriding her and calling her an "ape in heels" (they have apes in twin world too, but these apes can't strip; their covering hair won't let them) while also expressing their delight at the advent of a classy(?) and dignified (?) substitute, who was not native to the country like the "ape" but an illegal immigrant at the time of her arrival in that country of twin world—ironic from the present standpoint.

When it becomes apparent that $\psi$ will succeed in cleaning up the rot created by $\varepsilon$ and his cronies, some of $\varepsilon$'s tribesmen display their typical jealousy and lack of class by hurling venom and ordure at him, using spineless poster-boy brown tools to attack him and lie about him to lend credibility to their racially prompted onslaughts on him. They lampoon him in the hope that besmirching him will help to demean him and enhance their execrable personalities to make them look less like traitors and more like heroes to their cloddy constituents. They vociferously reject his redeeming fiscal initiatives, but secretly seek aid from them to ingratiate themselves with these dolts, betraying disgusting duplicity that is motivated by their despicable racist hatred. Regardless of their gambits, and to their utter dismay, he remains unruffled by their sleazy verbal assaults, while they continue to wallow in the self-service and corruption that was responsible for their neglect of the affairs of state, allowing them to degenerate to a level that left the majority of citizens in financial and emotional ruin.

Driven by their intransigence and blind desire to pursue the same ruinous course, and rejecting every nation-saving effort mounted by more rational persons, they succeed in inciting the racist sections of the citizenry to bow to their ploys and behave like hooligans who betray their inability to reason and to discuss common matters in a decent manner. Their slogan: if you cannot reason and you are losing the argument, make a noise, be rude, be obnoxious, and make a fool of yourself. Question everything about a brown leader: his place of birth, education, patriotism, etc., (no such questions for mediocre or other pink "leaders" of infamous racist lineage who indulge in unmistakable treasonous actions) in hopes of discrediting him. Only bigoted fools believe that foolish talk and lies can undo hard facts. Other foolish pink citizens oblige by becoming pawns in their own exploitation by selfish persons who appeal to their racism in subtle ways and incite them to reject programs that are meant to help them, until they realize what their bigotry will cost them in health care. They also realize that slogans and nastiness won't put food on their dinner tables; they still have to line up for free food rations, while the instigators and their corporate friends are jetting around and gorging their pot-bellies in the comfort of their mansions and milking them for their own free health care.

This toxic frame of mind underlines one of the basic principles of pink operation: never to pass up any opportunity to bash brown successes in their myth media, and to deny them further successes in areas where they themselves messed up and failed miserably before them. To them, the oxymoronic belief in negativity and inactivity is the best and only fitting means of positive productivity. Some of them are victims of the sore loser syndrome, because they could not succeed in piling enough dirt on their brown competitor to convince their racist kith to write him off as a potential leader of their state. So, rather than see a brown succeed, they prefer to sacrifice what is left of the faded glory and integrity of their country to their decomposed self-images that were never there to begin with, although they tried hard to foist them on all and sundry. The delight of causing the failure of a brown in his devoted service to his countrymen and women infinitely surpasses any commitment that they claim to have for the welfare of the citizens and the country that they claim to be serving; after serving their vain egos, of course. Racist jealousy consumes them and deprives their actions of any semblance of rationality and humanity. Little wonder that they are offended by the emergence of a brown who devotes himself to championing the cause of all humanity and a better life for those who have been left dispossessed by their irresponsibly racist policies.

Meanwhile, many of their hired howlers continue to wallow in their less than adequate circumstances, which may be far better than those in which browns are struggling to survive, but are nowhere near the comforts of wealth in which their instigators are bouncing, while they pretend not to be aware of the hardships that they have imposed upon those over whom they have political and economic authority and advantage. The best they can do is continue to preach their infamous failure-promoting inactivity as the only cure for the ills that they have brought upon the citizens, while also hankering after reckless ventures in search of states to conquer and dispossess to assert their might at the expense of all efforts by others to change the habit of belligerence and bullying that has continued to be their trademark. They are ready to trade peace for war, and friendship and co-operation for antagonism at any price to boost their puny egos, regardless of the suffering that they cause, because they worship domination and despise peace activism. In their eyes, peace activism is an unbecoming mortal sin that is only fit for weaklings.

What is most flabbergasting and unnerving, as already indicated, is the implicit faith of some of the citizenry of twin world in this kind of buffoonery as they stand poised to buy into this claptrap without any qualms. Equally amazing is their gullibility in falling for the ploys of so-called leaders whose expertise in leadership consists only of engaging in *ad hominem* attacks on the infinitely less impeachable characters of the critics of their rancorous policies for proposing feasible solutions to national problems, instead of responding with plausible, substantive, justificatory arguments why they will not abandon those policies. This tactic of demonizing and responding to reason with physical violence is typical of these small minds that cannot hold their own against facts and logic. They also do not hesitate to distort the facts to suit their nefarious intentions, uttering lies with which they then erect straw men that they can easily and maliciously attack to deflect fair public criticism from their ruinous policies, as if their critics ever uttered any of the mythical statements that they fallaciously attribute to them. The only genuine response that these despicable types are capable of is a continuation of their active display of ineptitude at dealing with the economic and other serious problems facing their states and cities that have been brought on by their greed for power and their irresponsible and reckless "leadership", some of which is further tarnished by drug addiction and wanton high-ticket spending of tax payer dullams on self-promotion trips and advertisements.

The third scenario is a highly regrettable one where "leaders" of brown states of twin world that have recently been emancipated from the weight of the oppressor's boot are now pursuing their own agendas of amassing wealth in their fiefdoms and trying to achieve fame and international status. They have developed blind spots for the plight of their citizens who wallow in poverty and the modern diseases of their world. Denial of the facts that attend situations that threaten and decimate the lives of millions of citizens is their stock in trade, not because they are too stupid to appreciate the damage that they are causing by yielding to the evil schemes of corporations and some of the economists who control them behind the scenes, but because these lives mean nothing to them, and they don't care about second, third, and fourth class "citizens" who are counted with live stock, as long as they are profiting from the rape of their people. People suffer and die needlessly while their inhomane, greed-driven "leaders" are pandering to their racist mentors and stealing from the coffers of the state to feed their greed. As some of these filthy rich low lives are reputed to have said while pilfering public funds, driving around in expensive cars, and living luxuriously in several mansions that they call home, "I did not join the struggle to be poor." Elsewhere, others have brazenly promised the people "floods of [their own] blood" for trying to slough off the autocratic and corrupt domination to which they have subjected them for decades.

This scum of inept dolts is the same bunch of so-called heroes of the struggle for freedom who have conveniently forgotten that they were not alone in that struggle. The heroes who remained at home and endured torture at the hands of pinks or died in the struggle are never acknowledged, as if their sacrifices are not worth a fraction of the comforts that were enjoyed by the elite of the struggle where they were roaming, some of them living in luxury on funds collected in the name of the people's struggle, others of them cavorting with Eubopan females on the same monies. It is true that a few of the exiles made great sacrifices and fought gallantly for the liberation of their people, but it is also true that many more who remained to face the wrath of the oppressors and their guns fought just as gallantly and perished. Still, their names are never mentioned by the egotists who want to shine alone in the spotlight of history and have relished the erection of monuments to eternalize only their own names.

They have also forgotten where they came from and the people that they have left behind as they prance with enslavers of the people and do nothing substantial to eliminate their agonizing poverty. Instead they delight in adorning themselves with despicable labels of the worst oppressors of their people to prove that they have arrived, and they think they are elevating themselves to positions of honour by so doing. Who ever heard of a brown conservative? Conservatives of twin world, neoconservatives and religious bigots, are haters of poor people, who are mostly browns; they love only themselves, their close families, and their rich friends. They dislike and fight against any attempts to improve the lot of the poor that they exploit for their own comfort, which they earn from squandering surplus funds that they inherited from liberal governments. They undermine and suppress their educational and economic advancement, deprive them of basic health care and social services, and continue to tread on them in their lowly status of deprivation. Unlike their patronizing liberal analogues who show their true pink colours only when their security is threatened, they succumb readily to their vile hatred of browns, and will, in unguarded moments, utter prejudicial statements that they fumble insincerely to explain away, but will not retract. Hence, the thought of a brown conservative who is, on this view, a self hater, is another oxymoron that defies logic and decency.

These sybaritic leaders who cling to power for decades depend on the support of taser-and-trigger-happy police and the army to maim and kill citizens for criticizing their misdeeds, proving that they are greedy frauds who only came to plunder the coffers of their states. They dope committee reports that reflect unfavourably on them and their unceasing executive efforts to usurp the functions of the legislature for entrenching their positions and diverting public funds from hatched up purchases of unnecessary commodities, e.g., arms, for their personal enrichment and for rewarding their cronies. They reward their attack dogs with cabinet posts and other positions of power, firing those lapdogs who pose a threat to their devious schemes of stealing state monies, and they viciously malign or order the assassination of those who expose their inhomane policies. As one casualty of their cronyism observed, quoting words from our world, "When you look at allegations of corruption, you find investigations are extremely selective . . . if you are perceived to be a friend of the President's or within his political circle, the less likelihood there is of being investigated . . .".[2] The author concludes his studied insider observations thus: "[His] presidency was a tragic failure. His autocratic, paranoid leadership style and vindictive Machiavellian politics fatally undermined the culture of [the organization]."[3] Unfortunately, that can be said about many, if not all the "leaders" of Afibikan states (kleptocracies), giving ammunition to racists who are guilty of the same misdeeds, which they magnify disproportionately when they are committed by brown leaders, as they do with every common homan foible of every brown.

Details of the rot that goes on within these governments have been recounted by several authors from every corner of twin world, but it (the rot) has also been captured for us by the authors of books that are available to us in our world, like "The Arms Deal" (Paul Holden) and "After the Party" (Andrew Feinstein) to mention only two of the thousands. The principle is the same everywhere in twin world: get into government, steal, and amass as huge a fortune as you can, before you croak (sorry, can't take it with you!) or are replaced by others who are hungry for the same loot and want you out so that they can have their turn at stealing and fortune building.

Readers know and can find many more instances of the kinds of oxymorons mentioned in this essay anywhere in any world to fill pages of endless narrative with these troubling examples of the concept of homan inhomanity. But what is the use of a collection of narratives, if they will not do anything to soften the heartless hearts of liars, oppressors, killers, and thieves who can subject a one year old to interrogation in a court of law? They have turned off their consciences and are cruising on brutish meanness that crushes even the humblest of supplications for mercy coming from children. Any adult who kills children (directly with bombs, or indirectly through willful neglect or wrenching them from their parents and locking them up in internment camps) for the sake of the ideology of pink supremacy or to gratify his vain ego, racism, greed for money, oil, or diamonds, is an inhomane brute who will understand and respond only to violent confrontation. This type of despicable creature is not hard to find anywhere in twin world. Browns should resist their assaults with every sinew in their bodies, otherwise the brown tribe will be doomed to perpetual serfdom and eventual annihilation.

In the pages that follow, I will discuss the principles, trends, and some illustrative examples related to inhomane homan attitudes like those referred to above to highlight the depravity that underlies and drives them and their bearers: the people who have arrogated to themselves the prerogative of deciding who dies and who lives, as if they are the creators of other people's lives with the undisputed right to terminate the objects of their creation at will. They exercise this prerogative everywhere in twin world; hence their evil deeds can be readily anticipated in every part of it where they make their odious appearance. Do browns have to wait for Armageddon to find the ultimate solution to this menace in their lives? Perhaps Krustans, in their goodness, will bring the joy of salvation before the advent of that horrific event. Their religion is replete with ethical canons that can make the most depraved of this infamous camaraderie of thieves, liars (including habitual pathological liars in high office), and venal, exploitative oppressors forsake their contumelious ways for the ways of the real master of grace, respect, forbearance, compassion, love, and fellowship who founded that noble religion.

We shall now, therefore, pay heed to what the Krustan Religion has to offer to browns with its magnanimous moral directives; but we will go even further to analyze the deeds of Krustans that conform with or belie those communications about browns. Perhaps, just maybe, we will light on a glimmer of hope that will illumine the depression and despair that browns are compelled to endure physically and intellectually in their misery-filled lives.

# Chapter 5
# Religion to the rescue
(making the devil the saviour)

Twin world also has hypocritical believer communities that read their holy bubels (bibles) up side down, like some of the infamous Christians of our world, and who believe in a deity, Gudd, whom they own and worship once a week as Krustans, named after their mentor, Krust. They believe in a home called hivana, which they will inhabit after their deaths, if they have led upright lives, which include putting and keeping browns in their place. But it turns out that these Krustan types are not like the honest, principled, and just bible-clutching Christians of our world who exude impeccably high moral scruples, and who never deviate from the virtuous standards set for them by their mentor, Christ. Anyone from another world who is expecting to find exemplary humanistic behaviour on par with what she is used to in her world will be sorely disappointed by the goings among them. Their inhomane ways of treating browns are a far cry from the humane ways in which we treat the equivalents of their browns in our world, without regard to the disdained skin colour or their religions that are infinitely inferior to our Christian religion. When these Krustans have tried to duplicate our illustrious way of life, they have always corrupted it so extensively that we shudder to imagine their impious and inhomane ways being adopted as the norm in our singularly pious and humane world.

The Krustans of twin world have entrenched their pink tribally discriminatory laws in their civic statutes, and they even interpret their bubels in a manner that supports the malignant tribal prejudices with which they have been raised. A case in point is their Pink Reformed Church, a pink church that preaches and practices a vicious kind of brown maligning and hatred as the prelude to a ticket to hivana for its members. They have also constructed merciless civic governments on tenets of mercy, while they promote racist hatred on tenets of love, engage in the murder of the millions that they wish to dispossess on tenets of abundant life, resort to lies and intrigue on tenets of truthfulness and sincerity, and flout their arrogance against tenets of meekness. In short, their relationships are piloted by a complex of oxymorons that psychiatrists would characterize as schizoid, the operations of split minds trying to construct the picture of a coherent reality out of contemporaneous inconsistencies and contradictories. It is no wonder that twin world finds itself in the global mess in which it is wallowing today, because it operates with contradictories, which implies that nothing that is done in it will make any sense to rational minds. The precariously constituted personalities who are driving it and have assumed sole control of it are dominated by corruption, xenophobia, and insecurity. They also lack of self-confidence in their ability to hold their own in fair competition with those whose aspirations they have vowed to suppress, but on whom they depend to prop them up against the self-induced disintegration that seems to be their inevitable lot under the misguidance of their uncontrollable greed and rabid racism.

It is no wonder that rational thinkers have rejected religion's demand on them to perpetrate inhomanities on oppressed, dispirited persons by offering them "illusory happiness" to soothe their misery, instead of radically redressing the sources of their woes. In this context religion assumes the role of "the opium of the people" as Karl Marx said, by inducing oblivion to the ills of society that are borne by some, but not by those others who have inflicted them and are guilty of the most heinous and hateful crimes committed against all of humanity. These Krustan types who claim to be promoting the gospel of their saviour, bringing light and salvation to those who are still in the shadows of darkness where this marvellous soul-saving hoax has not yet reached them and enslaved their minds, have successfully used their religion to subdue, dominate, and corrupt their world. To characterize this Krustan religion as a hoax is not to engage in blasphemy. One only has to take stock of the murderous actions of Krustans through the ages, as will become apparent in the pages that follow, to realize that this purported bastion of homan service and salvation is a tool for killing, exploiting, oppressing, and stealing from unsuspecting believers who have not taken the trouble to question the bona fides of religious charlatans who are using religion to boost their puny egos, feather their nests, or gratify their varied carnal cravings with the lure of celestial mumbo-jumbo. It is also a handy tool for controlling the masses of people who are forcibly disabled from exercising their freedom to pursue their chosen individual and collective happiness as they see it, within the legal limits and moral values of their societies, purely on the basis of secular reason and evidence, without the intrusion and imposition of religious bigotry, which is based on so-called divine revelation, and which lacks reason and evidence.

So intoxicated with their false religiosity are the pinks of twin world that some of their secular states are founded on vacuous, ostentatious religious sentiments that make complete nonsense of the secularity that they claim for them. They might be paying lip service to the separation of state from church, but they have not yet learnt how to practice that separation as enshrined in their constitutions. To them, state and church are separate but one—an oxymoron on par with that of homan inhomanity—and church must always dictate its religious dogma and bigoted policies on social life to state; e.g., secular schools and governmental gatherings must start and end with prayer to their Gudd, not the (inferior) gudds of the non-Krustans who are a legal part of those assemblies, and government policy must always bow to the wishes of the Krustan right, if they expect to govern in peace. One would expect these children of Gudd to be peace-makers as their bubel commands, but they are the ones who are always fomenting strife and killing to promote their religion (and egos). So, why lie about separation and even constitutionalize it when they know that their state is the slave of their bigoted church?

In addition to their other terminology, which we have already noted closely parallels our own, e.g., 'homanity' and 'inhomanity', other words in the vocabulary of twin world, spelt like our earthly words, e.g., 'evolution', 'creationism', etc., mean the same there as they do here. So when we talk about the viperish contest that is raging between advocates of these latter two concepts in their world, the discourse is not lost in misapplication. We understand fully what it means for them to impose the extreme religious values of pressure groups within their societies on the daily lives of the rest of the population, restricting and taking away their freedom of, and from, religion and religious dogma by ensconcing religious canons in secular state legislation. Hence their persistent efforts to outlaw open-minded instruction about scientific, evidence-based evolution in the science classes of their children in favour of closing their minds to rationality by promoting mythical, unscientific, and faith-based creationism.

We also understand their violent efforts to surreptitiously impose constraining, controversial, self-indulging abortion laws on persons endowed with freedom of choice and self-determination; their with-holding of public funds from organizations engaging in birth control counselling (which includes abortion); the arrogance that impels them to impose on physicians' expert clinical judgments laymen's religion-based directives on the resuscitation of disabled infants; and the hubris with which they impose on scientists (in the hypocritical guise of showing respect for the homan dignity of an embryo, in contrast with the ignominious indignities to which they callously subject autonomous brown homan beings) a multiplicity of prohibitions against research on trashed embryos slated for destruction, when they are really pandering to the inane wishes of and pressure from holier-than-thou "pro-lifers". Their pious regard for trashed products of conception that are destined for undignified destruction exceed by far their concern for the persons whose lives those embryos could be saving, as long as their bigoted wishes prevail and they can score points as the real pro-lifers, as if other persons are anti-lifers (living anti-lifers, another senseless oxymoron, because anti-lifers should not be struggling against their own alleged weltanschauung by staying alive). So who is the true pro-lifer, and who is the real anti-lifer or fake pro-lifer? The one who selfishly withholds help for the afflicted with trashed materials, or the one who salvages these materials to save other lives, including the lives of the same selfish, ideological types who are driven by crass irrationality to oppose the utilization of discarded products of conception for the benefit of homankind?

In some of the leading democratic states of twin world the people are subjected to deleterious manipulation through their governments that have been systematically infiltrated, if not taken over, by the meagre, bigoted religious right, which acts with impunity as the paradoxical minority that terrorizes the majority (it used to be that the majority terrorized the minority; not anymore), depriving them of their Gudd-given liberty to realize their cherished aspirations to their own satisfaction in untrammelled ways. They literally dictate to the rulers and foist their own agenda on the nation in their quest for dominance and the promotion of their selfish, ideological interests at the expense of the common good. These self-serving bigots will kill and lie to exercise control over the lives of people who do not in turn strive to impose their ways on them. They call their odious ways the ways of the religion of Krust. In the same democracies also, it is the pink minority that tyrannizes disenfranchised browns, or the few "democratically" elected Krustan "leaders" who tyrannize the masses of citizens with the aid and direction of their think tanks and highly sectarian lobby groups that hew out the direction and details of government policies at the expense of an electorate that is powerless to have its will executed by the persons who solemnly offered to carry out that will if they are elected into office. They have allowed themselves to be vassals of pressure groups for a price.

Such blatant imposition of theocratism must be strongly rejected on all fronts. Religious fascist states use it as their cloak for pursuing selfish ends in the name of a parochial, devalued brand of religion that is being rammed into the throats of those of other religions by sheer hubris, under the groundless pretence that that is the universal and only authentic way of inculcating moral values into people and taking them to hivana. The protagonists of this point of view assume without foundation that morality based on divine command, which is entirely a figment of their sterile imaginations, does not require personal interpretation by the standards of daily living in their world; and judging by their atrocious deeds, anyone would demur at entrusting his precious life to divine commands that they hear and follow, and to their vile manner of treating other people.

Moreover, even in a world with their kind of religion, with its uncertain promise of a future life of eternal bliss and with its practitioners who are no better than rapscallions, moral decisions have to be made by mortal beings in terms of what obtains in their world; decisions don't descend on a platter from the clouds with every detail written on it; they have to be made by persons. Every person who is confronted with a moral problem has to make her own decision about how she will resolve that problem. Appealing to Krustans to help solve these problems is like asking the wolf to be the shepherd or the devil to be the guide and saviour. Many of these people live by valueless, inhomane moral codes that even the most depraved of non-krustans would shun, and which they are always trying to impose by force on those who live by comparatively noble codes. So how can they be classed as raisonneurs of the virtues of their religion when all they display is a complete lack of virtue, good reason, decency, and homaneness? What they do is what they are.

Krustans preach sanctification of other persons through suffering, but do not and will not set the example by subjecting themselves to that suffering; they love the good life. They say browns should, *a la* David Lawrence, forgo the "loaf of common bread" to which they are entitled in their world for a slice of "the most marvellous cake" in hivana, while they are devouring the bread and gorging themselves on the cake in the same world at the same time; they will not wait to go to hivana to indulge themselves. The questions posed by a study of the works of William Jones *(Is God a White Racist?)* and Charles Mills *(The Racial Contract; Blackness Visible)* are as relevant for twin world as they are for our world: Should those who want to inherit eternal life in hivana bear suffering alone with docility and quietism, despite its amount, intensity, duration, and unequal distribution among the tribes of twin world? Why should an entire tribe of browns bear the suffering of all of homankind when the curse of original sin that Krustans blame for the suffering of homankind was not limited to them? Why should the burden of punishment for it be the preferred destiny of browns, as if they were the only original sinners? Is Gudd being partial to pinks at their expense because he is a pink, or do browns suffer more (vicariously) because they dominate his cosmic plan for the liberation of homankind? Do they want to pay such a heavy price to take a chance on living indefinitely (how boring) hereafter? What if there is no hereafter? Even the ones who are promising it to others don't know and can't prove that it exists; they only surmise that it does and fear that it doesn't, and that is why they are having their cake right now. On the other hand, James Cone's treatment of oppression in his *God of the Oppressed* is too conciliatory to apply to these rascals of twin world. They are already getting away with too much.

To emancipate themselves from this untenable situation into which they have been cast by their creation, the evil devil, and to explain the purpose of their Gudd to their homankind, as John Milton tried in *Paradise Lost* to "justify the ways of God to men"[1], Krustan theologians have concocted an explanation or theodicy why their Gudd permits the perpetuation of evil oppression of browns by pinks, hoping to pacify them into submission and acquiescence in their own dehomanization. First, they sold them their dubious religion as the authentic word of their Gudd; then they tried to convince them that it is his will that they serve him happily in their state of subjugation and privation for handsome rewards in the life that awaits them after this one. Therefore, they should do nothing to try to change their present situation, but leave everything in the hands of the Gudd of pinks who ordained their role in this unbalanced state of affairs and has promised rich rewards with more of the same suffering for their endless and fruitless perseverance and for their foolishness for believing these tricksters.

Meanwhile, pinks are not doing anything to find their place in this enviable circumstance that promises such magnificent rewards to browns in the oblivion to come. One would think that they would be eager to swap places with them so that they can earn those rewards, since they have proved themselves to be extremely selfish, always wanting everything that is good for themselves only; but they will have no part of it, because they know that they are lying when they tell others that the price for going to hivana is suffering silently in the temporary residence called twin world. Their theodicy thus compels them to try to skirt the logical inconsistency presented by the contemporaneous combination of challenging statements like 1, 2, and 3 below, where 1 and 2 are incompatible with 3, and asserting 3 will defeat their concept of their Gudd as defined in 1 and 2.

1. He is omnibenevolent; opposed to this and all the other evil that is occurring in twin world.
2. He is omnipotent; he has the power to eliminate it right now.
3. The evil still exists, in spite of 1 and 2.

So why the impasse? Is he being malevolent, or is he just impotent?

On the same subject, one theologian from our world says "God has the right to allow humans to cause each other suffering . . . still, limits there must be . . . and limits there are . . . provided by the short finite life enjoyed by all humans . . . one human can hurt another for no more than eighty years or so."[2] That kind of argument is cold comfort to the brown inhabitants of twin world who are destined to suffer under pinks for eighty years or so and then die without enjoying the short finite life enjoyed by pinks. Coming from those who are privileged to escape the suffering of oppression, it confirms the characteristic lack of empathy for and the insensitivity to the suffering of the oppressed that they have learnt to expect from the master tribe. Pinks can afford to rationalize suffering from which they profit, because they don't feel the weight of the burden; they don't know "what it is like for a bat to be a bat. . . . The best evidence would come from the experiences of bats, if we only knew what they were like."[3] They also do not understand why browns fuss about being limited to sycophantic gratitude for meaningless favours, but not afforded the freedom to exercise the civic and moral rights that are due to them as citizens of the same states as their counterparts of a light skin colour.

Looking at the situation from within, and failing to realize that it dehomanizes them for participating in it as much as it does its victims, pinks also fail to muster up the objective perspective that will tell them how iniquitous it is and how guilty they should be feeling for supporting it and allowing it to continue unchecked. They have failed to see the inhomaneness of their system that neglects the welfare but condones the abuse of its victims when it is staring them in their faces, because it has no existential meaning for them; they do not live it. Instead they preach from selected texts like our own world's biblical texts to lull browns into docility and submission, since they and their religion have decreed that they are the masters and browns are their eternal subordinates: "Servants, obey in all things your masters according to the flesh, not with eye-service, as men pleasers, but in sincerity of heart, fearing God. And whatever you do, do it heartily, as to the Lord and not to men, knowing that from the Lord you will receive the reward of the inheritance; for you serve the Lord Christ"[4]. Inheritance? I beg your pardon.

To compound the weight of oppression on the less privileged, the author of "eighty years or so" goes on to say, "God plausibly exhibits his goodness in making for them the heroic choice that they come into a risky world where they may have to suffer for the good of others."[5] The choice of vicarious suffering for one group hardly seems fair coming from an omnibenevolent being, but it fits in well with the agenda of flagitious oppression promoted by those who preach it to justify their assumed superior homanity; the same ones who bomb the houses of worship where browns pray to the same Gudd whose fatherhood they are supposed to share (that's what their religion claims). Are they trying to bomb out this commonly shared Gudd, whom the browns use for claiming equality with them, and to replace him with the inferior, detestable one that they created specially for inferior browns, a deaf and powerless one who is more appropriate for their more dehomanized status, since he will not hear their cries for mercy and will also lack the means to rescue them from poverty. He is not like their own superior pink gudd of money who listens to and serves only them. One thing they do realize is the mistake they made of introducing them to a Gudd of mercy, fairness, love, and brotherhood, qualities that are far removed from their own natures, but which browns have come to expect from them as the professed apostles of that Gudd, the one that has been basic to brown worship through the ages, anyway.

So far, therefore, religion as practiced has failed to uphold truth without oppression. In typical Machiavellian fashion, it has become such a handy political tool for rationalizing oppression as part of its take on truth that it has become irrelevant in the lives of many of the thinking people of twin world. Somehow the version of truth on which it has come to rest by catering to the egregious hegemony and superciliousness of the hubristic minority over the majority and to the spread of dubious pink values of violence by atom and smart bombs and by hate, in violation of the true Krustan values of peace and love, is incompatible with the universal version of truth that is still eluding all others. For them truth is an abstract concept that can be manipulated to suit the expediency of the moment; but for browns it is the very lives that they live. And for thinking browns, the popular homan pictorial representation of Gudd (who happens to be a spirit) and his angels as pinks is a direct affront to Krustan browns who are allegedly also made in his pink image (pink browns) but are still victims of this kind of shameless, double oxymoronic bigotry wrapped in promises of hivana and enjoyment of life everlasting. Even Krust and his crew are represented as pinks. So where do browns fit in? It seems as if the entire structure has been created to finally convince browns that they have no status in this hierarchy above that of servants and slaves. Even their bubels are permeated by mendacities that purport to portray pinks alone as their Gudd's chosen people. Obviously, browns have no place in this disreputable holy propaganda that attempts to emulate Greek and other acknowledged mythologies of our world with their tin gods and masterful men. The only purpose served by this arrogant fiction is the justification of self-elevation over the rest of homanity and the brazen promotion of the odious practice of squelching browns.

The poignancy of this calculated insult to the brown image is highlighted by pictorial representations of the fiction known as "the devil" as a brown. Are pinks trying to impress upon their children the other fiction, that browns are not real persons but some caricatures of the persons that pinks are, if not subhoman creatures? As one astute observer remarked, "The Ethiopians say their gods are snub-nosed and black, the Thracians that theirs have light blue eyes and red hair. If cattle and horses or lions had hands or were able to draw with their hands . . . horses would draw the forms of gods like horses, and cattle like cattle."[6] So how can anyone expect any good from a religion that lacks so much authenticity and that defies the authority of its jealous Gudd by promoting the worship of its own graven image of him in the gudd of insincerity, money, and greed, which rests on supporting pillars of murder and inhomanity; one that misuses his homan creations as the tools of its proselytizers who have proved themselves to be no better than ravening wolves in sheep's clothing? Pinks can keep their religion.

Their new god of money has proven to be a curse on the homan species, so much so that if there were a way to deconstruct money, it would result in the relief of the species from much of its besetting misery; and that would be a blessing. Money happens to be a mere contingent homan invention or construction created to facilitate trade within and among the nations of twin world, not a vital constituent without which homan life could not exist. But it has become the ultimate goal of life, although life in that world can continue to exist and its people can function well without it. There is not a facet of life where the evil influence of the curse of money does not assert itself. People rob and kill for it; they exploit and oppress others from their positions of trust in government and from their control of cartels that impoverish poor states with the trade and other burdens that they impose on them for it; they betray friends and family for it (thirty pieces of silver); they use the pulpit and the bubel to entice others to hand it to them by cunning, including lying to them that Gudd will take them away if they don't give them several millions of it by a set date, as if anyone cares if Gudd takes them away, leaving twin world with one less swindler. In any case, why should they be afraid of going where they have been promising that others will go, if they faithfully keep bringing them lots of money?

Some others literally steal it from retirees and others who depend on the little bit of it that they have saved to see them through their twilight years, while others contrive wars and destruction of other people's property, after which they move in to amass fortunes from snide enterprises of compassionate reconstruction of infrastructure and public buildings that they wittingly destroyed. This war ploy also creates steady sources of hefty income from manufacturing the evil weapons of war. Readers can easily enlarge this list from their daily experiences of the kind of evil that is wrought in the lives of the people of twin and other worlds by extrapolating from the ill effects of the same lethal pestilence that has taken possession of our world.

A brown author of twin world used a quotation from our world to sum up the kinds of questions that his pink brother will eventually have to answer for mistreating him and his tribe, even if he is evading them now:

> BROTHER, come!
> And let us go unto our God.
> And when we stand before Him
> I shall say —
> "Lord, I do not hate,
> I am hated.
> I scourge no one,
> I am scourged.
> I covet no lands,
> My lands are coveted.
> I mock no peoples,
> My peoples are mocked."
> And, brother, what will you say?[7]

The only problem is that these people do not consider themselves his brothers; they claim to be his superiors, his masters, the owners and controllers of his life in the ghettos, reservations, locations, tribal homelands, enclaves, and wherever it is easy to poison him and his tribe en masse with dirty water etc., and where he and his tribe can be easily rounded up and shot at will. In these geographic political, economic, social, and educational enclaves established under pink justice, they have little or no say in their local government, and therefore none in successive levels of government, because restrictive decisions are made for them at every level. Clip the bird's wings, and it won't be able to fly, but blame the bird and smear it with epithets of laziness, lack of initiative, etc., for not using its natural, but artificially disabled, ability to fly.

Every reader must also know directly or indirectly of others who have been subjected to similar abasement by contemptuous caitiffs of other worlds who are always hiding from the truth, because they are too scared and insecure to face it, as if it is the black plague. The only toxic atmosphere in which they enjoy their false security is one in which they are well padded and sanctified by manipulative lies used to pacify everyone to whom they are lying, and where the purity of truth cannot contaminate and corrupt them — what a pathetic crowd.

# Chapter 6
# Religion indicted

So far, it seems as if we have been heaping blame haphazardly on Krustans and their religion with irrelevant narrative. But that is not the case, as we will discover, if we ask for answers to a few pertinent questions from this incorrigible breed of self-righteous miscreants.

1. If there is a hivana that select believers (Krustans) go to after their deaths, are those who have never come into contact with this choice religion barred from entering hivana, regardless of their exemplary lives born of upright characters, compared to the bubel-carrying monsters who profess Krustanity and show it off while they are perpetrating untold inhomane harm on other homan beings for self-serving reasons and sheer hubris? The firm answer is NO; even a child knows that. These hypocrites hold their religion superior to all other religions, arrogantly propagating the lie that any who have not been touched, or rather, contaminated by it are doomed to everlasting damnation. What is more likely is that those who have been defiled by it are in dire danger of suffering that fate, unless they can quickly decontaminate themselves before it is too late to do so, as Friedrich Nietzsche discovered when he said he had need of washing his hands after contact with religious people — true killers of truth — while calling religion "the immortal blemish of mankind".

2. Is the religious (Krustan, etc.) stance so critical to the survival of individuals, who are, in any case, free to exercise their choice of how they will live, that these religious zealots should maim and kill them for not succumbing to pressure to follow the religious path that they espouse. Does this religion not have enough intrinsic, universal value to attract all and sundry spontaneously, instead of being forced on them at gunpoint? One would have thought that it has, but its adherents make it appear barren, or else they are probably just using it to achieve other objectives of a selfish nature that have (relative) value for them only and not for those on whom they are forcing their religion. These should not be too far to seek; i.e., power and money.

3. If their religion urges them to make peace so that they can be called the children of Gudd, why are they always fomenting war

on the pretext that other people want to kill them? Why do they always see the enemy in Gudd's other children? Why the paranoia? These hating Krustans invariably resort to violence, instead of resolving differences peacefully. Are peace and co-operation alien virtues to Krustanity? Can their religion not knock some peace into their perturbed minds? If not, of what good is it? Besides, why would they incite others of their herd belonging to a different faith to persecute and kill innocent men, women, and children of other faiths that they label as inferior? Why would they provoke others of the religions that they hate to acts of violence in response to extended periods of violence that they inflict on them? They claim quite impudently that religions of others are violent, and yet it is their religion, culture, and societies that are violent. They are the slave-masters, the hit-men who eliminate rulers and leaders of other states that they disapprove of, the uniformed enforcers of unjust laws and arms bearers who invade other (mostly brown) states to change their regimes, pastors who openly threaten heads of states with execution for being uppity or for not bowing to their warped ways of thinking, and constant preachers of oppression of browns against clear commands from their bubels that they should love one another. They encourage usurpers to expel people from their habitats so that their usurper friends can own those lands under the pretext that bubel texts that they conveniently wrote to suit themselves proclaim that their Gudd promised them exclusive possession of those lands—unadulterated fabrication and malarkey.

4. Whichever way they interpret the commandment with which browns are more familiar than they are: "Thou shalt not kill"[1], whether they say their Gudd forbids killing because it is wrong or killing is wrong because Gudd forbids it (except in genuine self-defence, and only when personal life is in grave danger; not as a pre-emption of conveniently contrived, nebulous danger), they still have the audacity to act contrary to the teaching of their religion and to the dictates of common morality when they wage wars for personal gain at the expense of the lives of innocent men, women, and children of other nations, and also of the men and women that they send to die under the mistaken impression that they are making the ultimate sacrifice in defence of their country while promoting and defending the selfishness and lies of these sods from phantoms. Hearing all of them gauging their worth by how many people from other tribes they have killed, one would think that they were responding to the command from their holy book to kill so that they can enter hivana with the blood of millions dripping from their hands. Perhaps it is thus written in their bubel; the rest of twin world

is just not aware of it, because it cannot interpret their depraved scriptures.

5.   As for those pious hypocrites who kill others because they oppose or refuse to bow to their authority, or because they criticize their sectarian faith (everyone wants to be the quintessential prophet who will save homanity and twin world, as long as they bring him money), they can stop pretending that they are alone privy to the truth in all matters of homan salvation. Many of them are fatheaded rubes who are trying to define their absent egos by using unwary believers, or else they are bigots in scholarly garb, and all of them are wolves vying for the biggest slice of the worldly cake of luxury and comfort. If they were all genuine representatives of the one Gudd in whom they are urging everyone to trust, they would not be fighting amongst themselves for the supremacy that comes with running off with a bigger piece of the pie or forming the hundreds of existing and ever burgeoning religious but mutually hostile sects that are all competing for the same loot. They would belong to one organization that does not divide people into warring factions in support of each one of them in their respective fiefdoms where the gudd of money has displaced the Gudd of their bubels. So, no one should be gulled by what they preach when it is quite clear that their cherished aspirations and deeds do not match their words, because their talk is as cheap as they make the lives of other people. These pious types are always the most putrid apples in the basket, and the people of twin world know that their ploy is to confuse them by saying one thing and doing the opposite. Some of their churches are their businesses, with succession confined strictly to the family.

6.   These highbrow moralists talk about the fear of their Gudd as the beginning of wisdom, leaving us to wonder if it is just that, fear, rather than an expression of their respect for the one that they claim to be worshipping and following devoutly, one whose commands they claim to obey with reverence, but for all of whose creation they show no respect, including the many whose lives they terminate at will. There certainly does not appear to be any wisdom in the rudeness, arrogance, hubris, and callous disregard for other people with which they act most of the time, including their disreputable behaviour towards veterans who fought their wars of hegemony for them. They also think that they can command the rest of the world to do their bidding by belching impatience with what they consider their tardy decision-making on matters of common interest, because they are looking at dullam signs; that's all they see. Besides, their overwhelming sense of entitlement and grossly imperious behaviour and actions whose purpose is to dispossess and

devalue others, all of which are guided by greed, do not qualify as worthy hallmarks of wisdom that any person can envy, leaving nothing to emulate in these and other Krustan attitudes and actions.

7. If they are guided only by fear, then they should be afraid of causing harm to other persons who are also made in the image of their maker like them, because such harm eventually reflects their disrespect for the one who made all of them equally in his image. But they are too arrogant to be tied down by the moral prescriptions that place them on par with all the other creatures who worship the same Gudd and with whom they are in perpetual strife over their own superiority and that of their particular religious dogmas. They will do as they please, and as the gudd of their making has directed them, not as they claim that the Gudd of all religions has commanded all homans to do. In their pink world, only their religion must prevail, the religion of eternal life in the violent deaths of browns.

8. Yes, they say, although the text quoted in paragraph 4 above prohibits killing, the prophets of our Gudd who are his messengers have conveyed to us alone his commandment to kill: "Now therefore kill every male among the little ones, and kill every woman that hath [carnally] known man. But all the women that have not known a man [virgins] keep alive for yourselves."[2] To do what with them? The answer should not be too far to seek when we read accounts of how savagely and immorally invading Krustans and pink settlers of other religions abused the women of the tribes that they attacked, conquered, and killed. In all honesty, can anyone take that kind of religion seriously and swear unwavering allegiance to it? The only ones who are ready to obey these commandments of the self-made gudd that they manipulate at will are the diabolical Krustans who crafted him. (See page 47, reference [4]). They have also provided him with many prophets to issue inconsistent, unethical, but politic directives that are designed for some heinous purpose, such as the homan carnage that is related on pages 98-100 and in other sections of this essay.

9. Amidst this rank selfishness, how do they respond to the inordinate amount of good that is being done by non-religious persons and by those of religions other than their own, which they like to discredit in everything they do? Their religiosity conceals the worst kind of baseness, which manifests itself in the constancy with which some of them set out to perpetrate evil. It seems as if they were made only for that. Twin world looks in vain for deeds of love and compassion from them, but all it sees is spite, smallness of mind, and arrogance laced with brutishness born of racist prejudice and disrespect of other people's cultures and religions, all of which

prompt them to intimidate and terrorize them so that they can impose their own superficial, hollow, kitschy, and amoral cultures and religiosity on them while they wreck their lives with their unguddly actions. These persons (men and a few women) live for nothing else but evil, but they are also cowards who seek out defenceless nations that will be easy to victimize and reconstruct after their own corrupt prototype. In the process, they display their dazzling might to extract ready obedience from onlookers, ensuring success in their endless efforts to establish universal dystopia. These Krustans might as well be busy paving their way to the fictitious product of their imaginations styled hallum (hell) with which they have tried to scare the rest of twin world into Krustan subjugation.

10.  If their religion commands them to sell all that they have and give to the poor, why would they want to take away from the poor the very last morsel of food that she and her children have and leave them to die of disease and starvation, or force them into lives of crime, depersonalizing drug dealing, prostitution, etc., in order to survive in the mean world that they have created for them, while they feast sumptuously on the spoils harvested from robbing these poor people? In their search for scriptural passages that help to justify their deviant natures, they have deliberately overlooked the injunctions of the holy books of our world against greed-driven practices of hoarding at the expense of poor people: "Lay not up for yourselves treasures upon earth, where moth and rust doth corrupt, and where thieves break through and steal: But lay up for yourselves treasures in heaven, where neither moth nor rust doth corrupt, and where thieves do not break through nor steal: For where your treasure is, there will your heart be also"[3]. One only has to look at the obscenely opulent lifestyles of the preachers of twin world to know where their hearts repose. They repose in the private jets, fleets of expensive cars, and vast estates and mansions in which they wallow, while they exhort the people to live lowly lives and never forget to keep the flow of money in their direction. Why don't they follow their own preaching by giving up some of what they own to help feed the foolish poor who made them so filthy rich? Does their religion teach them to take unfair advantage of ignorant people who are buying security in the life to come that they promise them, but on which they are themselves not taking a chance? They prefer to sink their hearts into the riches and pleasures of twin world, rather than in the imaginary, gilded streets of hivana. They are not stupid.

11.  If their religion requires that they do (good) to others as they expect others to do (good) to them (different from doing it to others before they do it to you), why would they persist in harming

them, but reacting violently to being paid with their own coin. They terrorize, but they do not want others to fight for their rights and freedom from their tyranny and terrorism. When they have been suppressed they have responded to suppression like true "freedom fighters", but when others respond to them and the terrorism that is operated by their terrorist governments that invade other states for cooked up, illegitimate reasons, the others are the terrorists who have to be exterminated. They are not ready to relish the goodies that they dish out to others for their forced enjoyment. What's the matter, don't the goodies taste as good in their own mouths as they are supposed to taste in the mouths of their victims? Perhaps their mouths are foul.

12.  Why have they, from time immemorial always persecuted scientists and others who would not subscribe to their ignorance-driven dogma, idolatry, and narrow-mindedness by burning them at the stake, while the scientists never burnt them alive for their views. Why would they still perpetrate virtual violence on them today for holding and expressing evidence-based views that are contrary to their unfounded, trumped up, and greed-driven propaganda? As one author from our world has so aptly stated it, "Those lower down on the totem pole, who say they were directed to do the dirty work—that is, . . . the control of the spoken and written words of scientists—always received such orders orally . . . in the absence of other, potentially troublesome witnesses . . . "[4] in order not to leave any incriminating paper or electronic trail of the malicious misdeeds of lay persons audaciously tinkering with highly technical information and scientific results, arbitrarily adulterating them, and distorting research facts with fictitious, ideological drivel before releasing the prostituted misinformation from bureaucratic high priests of spin and their superiors in higher places to the citizenry of twin world. Why obliterate your tracks, if you know that what you are doing is right and honourable? Only scoundrels do that, not honest Krustans.

13.  These evil doers lack the hard facts to support their trumped-up case against the best information available to science about how their greed for money is polluting twin world's atmosphere and terrestrial environment, because their lies cannot stand up to truth. Their only hope of scuttling scientific evidence as we know it, and against which their lies cannot prevail, is to undermine those who are striving to use it truthfully by either committing outright fraud on their work or muzzling them through vicious pressure exerted by governments whose business sessions hypocritically always start with prayer—to the devil? Their watchdogs against dissemination of climate information sedulously

prohibit scientists from giving press interviews to suppress access to dissemination of evidence-based information about the ultimate lethal effects of global warming on their planet. Their line is that their world's global warming is an uncertain theory about the cause of melting polar ice caps and weather upheavals, and they cavalierly and arrogantly spread this disinformation and other lies about the lethal harm that they are abetting, such as claiming that global warming is good for boosting agricultural productivity, in defiance of authentic scientific data. At the same time, they pretend to champion protection of "endangered species" in the frigid zones of their world, which they are rendering uninhabitable for these same species via the timeworn ploy of saying one thing and doing the opposite. Mark Bowen calls these tactics of our world "the gory details of the possibly criminal and certainly immoral campaign that special interests have waged to obscure the true science and prevent any effective action against devastating climate change."[5]

14.     Other deniers of science in twin world who are also poisoning citizens with their money-generating wars have admitted secretly to themselves that "Doubt is our product, since it is the best means of competing with 'the body of fact' that exists in the mind of the general public."[6] This despicable policy of ideological insincerity and skulduggery against oodles of scientific evidence is common to the world's criminal bedfellows: industry, government, and religion. Where are the Krustan morals that would dissuade them from sacrificing the lives of so many people for money? Is that the Krustan way, the way of truth, or the way of hypocrites and of their gudd of intrigue and money? By the way, scientists who do not toe their ignorant line, or who dare to tell the truth about the known effects of global warming live in constant fear of being fired from their jobs by these ruthless frauds, after being subjected to extensive vilification by them and their superiors with the help of their puppet news media. Who ever heard of fiction ousting factual evidence in determination of state policy, except in these pigheadedly denial Krustan states. We might well ask what kinds of heartless fiends delight in expending all their energy in constructing death traps for the rest of the citizenry at the behest of their corporate paymasters by poisoning their habitat. Such behaviour is best expected from unprincipled muggers of truth and science; the ones who are worse than common criminals who rob only one or two people at a time and receive severe punishment, while these unscrupulous, self-licensed, white collar criminals do not receive any punishment for brazenly destroying many people's valued lives.

15. Their religion admonishes them to be merciful so that they can also obtain mercy, why would their church deny AIDS sufferers the means of protecting their partners from contracting the virus and passing it on to their children, condemning the innocent little creatures to short lives of pain and misery? Is that the merciful way of Krustanity, or is it the thoughtless way of ideological foolishness and disguised bigotry of Krustans whose love forced indigenous peoples to accept and submit to the pink supremacy teachings of their churches or face death? These angels of death have brazenly avowed the extremist view, borrowed from our world, that there shall be "no equality between white and black in church or state"[7], implying that Gudd does not recognize equality among the homan beings that he made of one blood, as the scriptures say; not of superior and inferior bloods. Other holier-than-thou racists of twin world have taken similar reprehensible steps of also borrowing and adapting passages from the reported sacred texts of other worlds: "that they might not be enticing unto my people the Lord God did cause a skin of blackness to come upon them. . . . I will cause that they shall be loathsome unto thy people, . . . And cursed shall be the seed of him that mixeth with their seed."[8] Somewhere else, another one of them has brazenly re-iterated an odious exhortation to Krustan oppression, again borrowed from our world: "We must adopt a system of despotism such as works so well in India in our relations with the barbarians of South Africa"[9], implying that what works for these Krustans is only inhomanity.

16. If their religion commands them to love one another and to let brotherly love continue, why do they hate homosexuals (so they tell their world) and any who are not of their creed or lineage when they also engage in homosexual activity or shield those who do so at all levels of their brotherhood? They should not be having this so-styled "objective disorder in the structure of human existence" in their holier-than-thou ranks from whose repercussions they seek refuge by hiding behind time-limited civic laws, which are not the guardians of the timeless morality that the church espouses. Their evangelists and priests are among the worst sex offenders, but also the worst of hypocrites who stand behind pulpits or on platforms to denigrate and denounce gays and their life-style, while their equally hypocritical, gay civic legislators cockily champion the enactment of laws against these persons or try to pretend that they do not exist by avoiding any mention of them in state documents, unlike the quiet majority of the people who are not trying to appear holier-than-thou or are ironically poised to cast the first stone, but are ready to accept and live with everyone as they find her.

17.     Which sensible person can heed the entreaties of a lying hypocrite who is doing exactly what he is preaching against, or even give him the time of day to display his foolishness and his audacity to solicit money from her so that he can pay for his deeds. And who in her right mind can vote into office a professed Krustan, a hypocrite and a liar, who spews venom out of one side of her mouth at the "socialist" (meaning? Only a buzzword) health system of one country in twin world for the sake of appeasing her naive audience, whilst singing its praises out of the other side to conciliate another doltish audience, but also tells a completely different story to a third bunch of dupes, leaving anyone to wonder where the truth lies in these inconsistent accounts of the same event. Only the dupes are taken in by this brash act, because they fail to realize that the architect of this impossible jigsaw puzzle is an inveterate liar whose game is to promote her maturing ambition for money and her blind ambition for office. Her pacified votaries, like her, pretend to live by standards that they consider to be the measure of paradigmatic morality, but are actually examples of the familiar unprincipled gutter amorality of expediency that has proved itself, on analysis, undeserving of any respect.

18.     If their religion teaches them that all the tribes of twin world are made of one blood, why the tribal discrimination on the basis of "one drop" of blood from those of a different tribal group? Would anyone of them refuse a life saving blood transfusion (more than one drop) or organ transplant from someone of a different tribe to gratify their bigotry at the expense of their lives? How many of these bigots have more than one drop of contaminating blood circulating in their pure, wretched bodies to which they will not admit? If ever there was an indisputable monument to stupidity and the height of oxymoronic thinking, this is bound to be one such. Only a fool can dare to utter an inconsistent statement like "I am not what I am" (being denying its being or determinate nature), and still succeed in deluding a few people who are dolts like him by claiming not to be who he is or claiming to be who he is not, solely on the basis of appearances. But to deny his essence as opposed to the trappings that make him look like who he is not or not who he is, is to utter contradictions and inconsistencies that amount to saying nothing, which is not out of character for fools, but happens to be anathema to thinking minds. The dull minds of these Krustans appear to have fallen victim to their religion, which is truly acting as an opiate on them, although it was intended to dull the minds of others to render them manipulable.

19. If they had control of the gates of hivana (assuming that there is such a place), would they (if they ever managed to steal or force their way in there by blowing up the gates and rebuilding them afterwards, as usual, with their own contractors and work teams, to the total exclusion of local labour) exclude from that paradise other people of different skin colours (blue, brown, yellow, red) or religions as they have been doing in twin world? They have thus far made it impossible for these others to ascend to high offices at all levels of administration in government, education, social, and economic spheres in many ways, unless they need a token brown to use to impress onlookers with their sham support and promotion of equal opportunity and rights. They also do not hesitate to use browns as mouthpieces and tools to attack successful browns and to attract unwary browns to their ignoble ranks; but their puppets dare not attack the pink sowers of trash from their rabble without being vilified and castigated for their uppityness. So what are they doing using a brown hatchet man against his brown brother, making him utter oxymoronic contradictions to his own aspirations? They use similar tactics against any who insist on brown economic empowerment by pretending to make it possible, while they contrive behind the scenes to place it out of their reach, and they think that they are duping everyone. Their lucky brown pawns get special treatment for committing the same crimes for which other browns are harshly punished by these hypocrites who claim to be "tough on crime", e.g., possession of prohibited substances, drunk driving, etc. Meanwhile they are content to squander billions of tax dullams on erecting enormous jails to confine other browns and anyone else who poses a threat to their unbridled power trips. To justify their wanton, costly decision, they decry impeccable statistics that support falling crime rates and substitute phantom statistics based on spurious high numbers of unreported crimes in a calculated move to confuse the citizens and pull off their ruses by befogging the entire issue.

20. If their morality is based on true divine commands (which are inflexible), they should be living different lives in keeping with the unbending will of Gudd who has issued a commandment like the one found in the holy books of our world: "Ye shall not make with me gods of silver, neither shall ye make unto you gods of gold."[10] But because their morality is man made, it can be violated at will to suit their selfish desires without offending against their gudd and the religion that they profess. Do they still need the authentic Gudd and religion in their lives? Apparently not, since they are their own gudds who implicate the real Gudd in the execution of their agenda of greed and racism and then turn around

and lie to the rest of the people that they are preaching Gudd's word. Somehow, they have blurred the boundary between the gudd that they worship (of greed and all that is evil) and the true Gudd that they sold to those worshipers that they overran and oppressed. So while these are still holding tightly on to that Gudd, they have moved on to worship their new gudd of silver and gold. But with the lines of demarcation between Gudd and gudd obliterated, they now appear to be the same person, if only for their own pecuniary and other convenience. That difference between the two gudds, which is as clear as night is from day, has now magically disappeared.

21.     So, if they can create their own tin gudd in their own image, one who caters to their bigotry and malevolence, one whom they can easily manipulate and instruct as if in supplication to damn "the enemy" and bless them with triumph over him, one who is ready to absolve them of their unguddly deeds against their neighbours, they should also have the power to create a pink life of bliss to come, where they will not have the rest of the people that they hate to share their special eternity with them. But they are as powerless as the rest of the people are to ensure that kind of eternity for themselves, and they have to invoke deity to insure their uncertain future, in spite of their cockiness and cruelty to others in this life (again assuming that there will be another life for them after this one). They use passages from their bubel that echo the controversial passages from the bible of our world, which have been constructed to discriminate against certain tribes and to favour their persecution and extermination: "The Lord will have war with Amalek from generation to generation."[11] "Now go and smite Amalek, and utterly destroy all that they have; do not spare them, but kill both man and woman, *infant and suckling*, [my emphasis] ox and sheep, camel and ass."[12] "You shall blot out the remembrance of Amalek from under heaven; you shall not forget."[13] Those are scary instructions that cause anyone to pause and ask if this is the kind of Gudd that the rest of the people should accept, one who is ignoble, vindictive, unforgiving, and murderous. Perhaps they have an acceptable explanation to offer for this kind homan malevolence that is unbecoming of a gudd, unless these words are the product of their collective miserable, evil minds that they attribute to the gudd who happens to be the graven image of their contemptible selves. Krustan browns have seen these terrifying injunctions applied to them, proving that they have fallen into wrong company. Krustanity is certainly not for them.

22.     If their religion forbids them from bearing false witness against their neighbours, why would they engage so freely in

shameless lying, fabrication, misinformation, disinformation, and slander, especially the political animals among them who will gain an advantage over their competitors at all costs, including gutter tactics? They are infamous for their scurrilous assassinations of the characters of their critics and for their habitual lying to discredit dutiful, honest, truth-telling malcontents (disgruntled employees!) who expose their evil deeds. What are they afraid of, if they are so powerful and so morally correct in their Orwellian behaviour that they can arbitrarily and audaciously lie about others and dispense harsh judgment to them?

23.    Why would they torture the "enemies" that they have made on the basis of the lies that they have concocted about some of them for the sake of exacting revenge for "unprovoked" attacks against them by these others, when the whole of twin world knows that they are the aggressors who are out to colonize other people's lands for the sake of denuding them of their wealth? All of these cowards will vehemently deny that they and their agents have been involved in the torture of other homan beings, directly or indirectly, to save their careers and their butts, instead of boldly admitting that they ordered or condoned the torture and ruined the lives of many browns to teach their defenceless non-Krustan scumbag victims the lesson that they should never forget, that Krustan pinks are the bosses; they wrote the book on the methods of torture that they deny using.

Meanwhile, their racist pink supporters reveal their bankrupt morality by cheering the callous actions of their leaders, instead of pulling them to order for violating these basic principles of homan decency. But who cares how a brown is treated? The same leaders taunt one another at the expense of their victims: the pinks who are being held accountable for these misdeeds by their pink brothers display their characteristic depravity by asking them if they value the welfare of the brown scumbags more than that of their pink Krustan brothers and sisters. Of course, they don't. So they shut up, or "shut the f--- up", as thy have been so wisely, or unwisely, advised by some of their ilk, unless they want to incur the wrath of their king and suffer all kinds of punishment from losing funding for their organizations to losing their jobs unceremoniously. But this king guy is not really a king; he is only an elected citizen who fancies himself as, and conducts himself like the king of the castle, obsessed and intoxicated with power. So perverted is his mind that he also takes to snooping on university professors who display "lefty philosophies"

24.    If they believe that Gudd is the one and only Supreme Being who made possible the existence of all homans, why do they

think that their worship is closer to him than that of other homans? Why would some of them consider it sacrilegious for their fellow Krustans who do not belong to their "prestigious" denominations to partake of the blood and body of Krust (ignore the absurdity of this concept)in holy sacrament with them, and why would they scorn marriages to persons of other sects? What is so special about their persons and their denominations that sets them apart from the rest of homanity, including their chauvinistic bias against female priests? These elites of Krustandom have yet to show the grounds for that pomposity; but surely not the paltry grounds of their chastity, moral uprightness, and empathy with sufferers from diseases like AIDS, or justice and fairness in their dealings with other homan beings. That would be a joke. Twin-worlders know far too much about their barren, vaunted saintliness and their pervading unholiness to be taken in by their vain display of purity that is steeped in impurity and celibacy that revels in licentiousness. Enough with those phony mortal sins that these hypocrites toss in their faces.

25. If their bubel teaches them that the saviour of homankind came to twin world not to kill, steal, or destroy, like the colonialist thieves who killed browns, stole their lands, and destroyed what they could not steal, but so that they might have life more abundantly, why would they rejoice when natural calamities decimate browns, claiming that they deserve these tragedies for having kicked out their devilish pink oppressors, which, their all-knowing pastors claim, is equal to making a pact of mutuality with the devil of their pink religion, if that makes sense? True Krustans empathize with, and exude compassion toward, those who are suffering, and they go out of their way (which should be their natural response) to help those who have been incapacitated by their suffering. They do not rejoice at the misfortunes of others. Only the evil minds of hypocritical preachers prompt them to assume that kind of unguddly demeanour. One could spend a lifetime asking questions about what the folk in twin world should believe about the disconnection between the teachings and actions of their Krustan neighbours. But that is a luxury they cannot afford; they need a saviour from this crushing Krustan hypocrisy right now. Are there any volunteers?

# Chapter 7
# Religious inhomanity

The answer to the call for a saviour will probably come from some humble non-Krustan who is not as self-conscious and as perfect as the Krustan who vaunts his hollow piety and from whom most of twin world is seeking salvation; one who recognizes her homan frailty and inadequacies and is always trying to make a better person of herself; one who knows that even as she is made to feel inadequate, she has an intellect and free will that is equal to that of any other person, and she has the liberty to exercise her free will and interpret the moral code in terms that are different from those self-serving ones that the Krustan would like to impose on her by claiming that they have been decreed by Gudd (lying again); one who knows how to be truthful, compassionate, respectful, peaceful, and honest in her dealings with others, without pretending that she is the superior Krust-like being who is really nothing but a parody of what a Krustan should be, sacrilegiously mouthing fake holiness when she is not slandering and lying but still perpetrating heinous crimes against homanity in the name of her Gudd, her Krust, and her religion; one who is unlike the perfect Krustan whose actions are prompted by ideology, cowardice, hubris, and bigotry, and who detains, terrorizes, and assaults weaker tribes, sacrilegiously quoting from his bubel (the equivalent of Romans 13: 1-5) to justify his inhumanity in the name of exercising his gud-given authority, but purposely pretending not to be aware of the real issue which is "I was a stranger and you did not invite me in."[1]

In the true spirit of homanism, however, the non-Krustan avers that honest, homanist-oriented, and faithful Krustans among these villains have done much good: promoting and sustaining education in poor, unenlightened countries; cultivating the spirit of mutual tolerance; advocating civil rights and political equity; establishing and maintaining health care facilities and providing sustenance to prevent untimely deaths from disease, which is in turn caused partly by the poverty and hunger imposed by Krustans; and promoting fellowship and peaceful coexistence for the benefit of the entire homan community. At the same time, she is aware that religion has ruined many people's lives by threatening them with celestial wrath and eternal damnation for denouncing the unsavoury practices that characterize Krustanity, because their refusal to tie themselves down to Krustan dogma and take everything for grist that comes to their mill from Krustanity undermines the control that the holier-than-thou Krustans want to wield over them. She also warns against avaricious charlatans, devils behind the cross, who are hungry for power to manipulate unwary believers by promising them everlasting life in hivana in return for their liberal monetary contributions to their capacious pockets, insatiable greed, and as part of doing Gudd's will.

It is, however, difficult to convince oneself on the basis of logic, rationality, and empirical evidence that a select place named hivana exists. True, the people of twin world talk about the hivanas, but that is only figurative language to refer to the vast swathe of unprobed, awe-inspiring space that they "see" when they look up into their sky, especially at the stars, the milky way, and the galaxies; but ignorance and dread of this immense mysterious abyss does not justify the gratuitous postulation of a fictitious abode where they will enjoy endless bliss in the presumed life to come, only if they have been good Krustans in their present life. Moreover, non-Krustans believe that if the people who are proselytizing this hivanaly abode are the same ones that we have been asking questions about, then they can keep their hivana, because going there will amount to no more than exposing them to an extension of the same vile indignities to which they have been subjected in their present abode by these same gyps. Experience has taught non-Krustans that their Krustan analogues can never be trusted to convey a true and intrigue-free representation of many situations, including what they claim to be reading from their bubels. So they can't take a chance on the bliss that these rascals claim is awaiting them on the other side. They have seen them taking oaths of benevolent service to homanity with their hands on their bubels, enacting and committing a sacrilegious symbolism to which they have subsequently paid only lip service, because they failed to uphold the wise admonitions contained in those holy books, and because they were already scheming evil and murder as they took those oaths. Little wonder that non-Krustans have taken the logic-defying inductive leap from doubts generated by such occasions to the paralyzing, counterproductive attitude of universal skepticism about all the pledges of their dishonest Krustan brothers.

They have also seen clear signs that this worldly oppression and inhomanity is destined to endlessness, because Krustans brainwash their children well in the art of perpetuating their legacy of bigotry. They also try to spread it in the classrooms, through their myth media, through their legislative statutes, and even through their courts of law, which claim equality of all persons before the colour-blind eyes of their inclusive, liberal, colour-seeing pink laws that still manage to victimize persons of dark skin colour selectively, especially if they happen to be highly successful in life. Is this another one of those scores of oxymoronic situations that demands from browns justification of their worth to be respected and treated like the rest of pink or "real" homanity, but simultaneously rejects it on the basis of skin colour? So how do they qualify for respect and fair treatment if they bear the unjust burden of having to prove themselves at every turn, while their efforts are selectively rejected, unlike their pink counterparts who do not have to prove anything, because they automatically qualify for a host of privileges, rights, and protections by virtue of their skin colour rather than by merit?

Pinks foster narrow-mindedness by insisting that students be taught creationism, in any of its myriad forms, as the only authentic means by which homans came to be, forcing on their system of secular education a type of religion that unfairly uses tax dullams to promote the irrational ideology of religious fundamentalists who arbitrarily reject the rational and open-minded teachings of science. They insist that the dogmatic bubelical view of the origin and nature of the universe is the only correct view; but instead of operating their own schools where they can teach dogma and narrow-mindedness, they cash in on public education systems to spread their propaganda, rejecting the exposure of students to evolution by natural selection. They reject the logically reasoned scientific facts on which evolution is based to make room for the fanciful, unscientific, and unsupported opinion that twin world was created in six days and is now 6,000 years old, because their theory can't survive rigorous scrutiny when it shares the stage with evolutionary theory. They claim that existing forms of life in twin world are descended from the paired remnants of each form of life that survived a great deluge that engulfed their world some several thousand years ago. In all these wild claims, they ignore fossil and other physical evidence of the evolution of life and homanity in twin world in favour of mythology. In short, they want to impose their despicable bigotry and dismal ignorance on everyone.

What is evident from these bigoted opinions held by religious fanatics for whom truth begins and ends with them, is the inability of these Krustans to maintain the level to which they are supposed to have evolved as members of the homan species. We have to assume that the instability in their cognitive constitution, resulting from their precipitate one-day creation at the end of the entire humongous process, perhaps as an afterthought, tends to drive them into reverse gear, so that they head in the direction from which all other people are courageously struggling to emerge, viz., into the depths of ignorance and inhoman behaviour. If we assume primordial matter from which plants, animals, and homans were formed as end-products (in that order, as postulated by evolution and progressive creationism), it is easy to understand how some homans can reverse the process of evolving into the better homans that they claim to be and regress to acquire the pre-homan amoral characteristics that they so arrogantly attribute to browns and lower forms of life. They are simply reverting to their origins, and they want to take the rest of humanity with them, instead of going alone to their favourite haunts.

That is the price that other homans are made to pay by people who interpret allegorical scriptures literally, without imagination, and without any inkling of an ability to fathom the mysteries of life, but rather choose to believe on faith what goes against scientific and other rational evidence and knowledge. Science proposes pragmatic and economical theories to analyze and explain observed phenomena and to speculate rationally on unobserved ones, but it also recognizes that its assertions are not final pronouncements; new evidence often brings new perspectives, unlike the eternal truths (fictions) espoused by Religion. Its data, when politicians have not been tampering with them to convey their squinted points of view in the hope that the unintelligent garb in which they clothe them will pass unnoticed, are factual, value-naked, unbiased, and hence more reliable than the ethereal, emotion-clad, and slanted fabrications that attend religious dogma and idolatry without explaining anything.

It may be true that evolution does not refute religious belief or disprove Gudd's existence, but it provides another and more credible viewpoint on the origin of species and the ascent of homans. Like true science, it tells only how things happen, which is why they happen, not what or who is behind them as religion so dogmatically claims, because these things could have originated as spontaneously as the causeless cause without need of the postulated ultimate cause. In this respect, evolution serenely undermines both the argument from design and the cosmological argument that depend for their ultimate justification on an imagined divine, uncreated creator to explain the complex constitution of living things that has defied complete comprehension up to now.

As Mortimer Adler argues in his book *The Difference of Man and the Difference It Makes*, evolutionary theory also confirms the fact that homans of twin world are part of the environment where they live with other animals from which they do not appear to be different in kind but only in degree. A common evolutionary history connects them, but it does not entail possession of an unfounded, elusive soul whose point of dawning on homan lives will always remain a mystery. The minor and almost imperceptible differences that were present among them at the start of the evolutionary process have multiplied through countless generations with slight but progressive variations in the form and function of offspring from their ancestors and from each other. The result is that species that are not really different in kind appear to be so, because the intermediates that might have connected them by a continuous but graded series of complexity in constitution are absent or missing. These missing links in the chain are believed to create only the appearance of a difference in kind between species, without vitiating the firm evolutionary principle of developmental continuity as proved by fossil evidence. We have, therefore, yet to see in what way the pink species of homans is more evolved than the brown species, and why they are postulating the being of a Gudd to whom they are closer than the rest of homankind.

On the other hand, it is clear that all homans differ in kind from animals, because, unlike animals, which possess only perceptual thought, homans possess conceptual thinking, which manifests in their ability to use propositional language, e.g., expressing the desire for justice, a feat that animals are incapable of attaining. Justice is widely defined in twin world as treating each person fairly on the basis of her homanity, which is equal to that of every other person, regardless of sex, size, looks, habits, life-style (religion, sexual orientation), financial ability, or formal education. The caveat that Krustans have introduced into this concept is that "person" refers only to pinks; the rest are non-persons or $3/5$ persons who also earn $3/5$ of pink wages for the same work. Thus, the notion of treating equals equally and unequals unequally in proportion to their relevant differences leaves some at the mercy of Krustans who have made it their business to stipulate the nature of those differences in keeping with their racist prejudices born of sheer ignorance. They have distorted this concept to suit their own ends by claiming the existence of hierarchical differences in kind among tribes in an attempt to establish the superiority of their own tribe and to justify their unequal treatment of moral equals without reasonable grounds.

The existence of differences in degree of endowment among different people right across the tribal spectrum is not in dispute, but these differences are not the preserve of certain tribes. Nothing in this situation justifies any difference in treatment on moral or any other grounds of superiority of one group over another in defiance of the dictum that we should never treat persons only as means to our own ends but also as ends in themselves, and that if we treat them as means, it should be with their acquiescence, and only after they have been fully informed of the noble purpose and the absolute need for treating them like that. Some Krustan churches have tried to justify discrimination on bubelical basis to legitimize contravention of this dictum by them and their racist governments, but their efforts have resulted in dismal failure, and they have eventually come to partly acknowledge their mistake, although grudgingly and only after perpetrating the most heinous crimes against homanity in the name of their religion. Other bigots have promoted vicious, separate and unequal development of the citizens of their countries that is reminiscent of the discreditable "apartheid" system that is still being practiced in parts of our world where rights are so artfully defined as to apply only to exclusive sections of the community with specified ethnic lineages. The rest of the inhabitants (browns) do not even have birthrights; they are mere items in these "ethnocratic" states that have fierce, vote-pandering apologists in notable western states.

Twin world also has sections that live in the shadow of their bigoted predecessors, like Hagala, from whom they inherited the temerity and hubris to denigrate brown religions, calling them superstitions, although close examination of their religions reveals an intensification of the practice of other forms of superstition and witchcraft, like believing in devils and evil spirits, and engaging in bizarre rituals of exorcism and séances. Hence the question: If, as the great thinkers of our world have so wisely proclaimed:

> our own conception of religion tells us that it requires that man should recognize a supreme being which exists in and for itself as a completely objective and absolute being or higher power; this supreme being determines the course of everything . . . Religion begins with the awareness that there is something higher than man"[2],

how is it that their religion has given such absolute power to devils, evil spirits, and other spirits to control the lives of homans on par with the control that should be exercised exclusively by this supreme being? How many supreme beings are vying for control? Are they now denying their claim of the existence of only one Supreme Being by admitting to the existence of these others? Where lies the real truth in this religion of expediency that they use to denigrate browns and elevate their own breed with contradictions?

As for Hagala's claim that all men in Afibika are sorcerers by virtue of their religion and of his prejudicial assertion borrowed from our world that "the African arrogates to himself a power over nature, and this is the meaning of his sorcery"[3], one can only observe that

Afibikans would not be so arrogant as to allege that that they know that all men in Eubopa are sorcerers on the basis of only their biases (reciprocal) against Eubopans, as the learned men of twin world are so bold and arrogant to claim about Afibikans. If "God thunders, but he is not recognized as God"[4] by Afibikans, how is it that they who recognize more than the thundering of their Gudd don't live in peace and charity with their neighbours but arrogate to themselves power over nature and all its creatures? They are the ones who "see nature as opposed to them"[5]; they are awed by its powers and their lack of full control over them—hurricanes, tornados, floods, droughts, and earthquakes devastate their habitations without regard for their tribal affiliations or self-assumed superiority; the fury of nature whelms them, and "its powers fill them with fear"[6] as it does the Afibikans who accept nature as it presents itself and try to live with it as best as they can, perhaps in their tested, primitive way.

We do not need to discuss proofs for the existence of Gudd as the architect and executor of his creation versus evolution and blind purposeless natural selection in shaping twin world's homan origins, favouring only those genes that are slated for survival, because these discussions can be found in many didactic text books; but we should be aware that for some twin-worlders to say that they know that Gudd exists because he has told them that he does, as many expositors of their holy books maintain, is as presumptive as it is circular. They assume the truth of what they are supposed to prove, and then use their assumption to prove its truth. Appeals to unusual religious experiences like believing that they hear his voice, that they have seen him in visions, or that they have had mystical experiences of him are not self-authenticating or intersubjective; they still qualify as figments of the imagination, and like miracles, they still have to be subjected to rational interpretation. Many, if not all, of them are mere hogwash and unfounded wishful thinking, no more rational than a child's fanciful belief in Santa Claus; others are like being subjects of a magician's sleight of hand, being just plain stupid and gullible, or being in states of rueful irrationality induced by aberrations in brain metabolism caused by emotional frenzies, illness, or the influence of drugs, as argued in chapter 11 of my book *Our World and its Values*.

As a follow up on this kind of credulity, it is amazing, perhaps amusing, but disappointing, that some people actually believe a charlatan, perhaps an ignoramus as well, who professes and tries to impress them with his miraculous powers when he tells them that he instantly restored the sight of someone born blind by applying a mixture of his sputum and soil (yuck!) to the subject's eyelids. Any person with common sense, let alone a basic knowledge of science, listening to this piffle that I once heard from a preacher should feel intellectually insulted that she is expected to believe it and incorporate it into her repository of knowledge. Others assemble a host of programmed imposters who act as patients with chronic disabilities that they cure with a push on the forehead and a few nonsense utterances, while their co-conspirators line up behind the victims to catch them, so that they are not injured as they make themselves fall; and the gullible audience believes that the charlatan has performed a Krustan miracle. Despite all these ardent, phony, and faith-demanding performances of the exhorter (or prevaricator), whose only goal is to promote his self-serving financial agenda, lack of proof of the existence of this unknown Gudd or of the justification for belief in him outside the domain of influence of Krustanity on its converts will always fail to convince thinking people in other domains of *his* existence — ascribing masculinity to a spirit.

It seems, therefore, that the faith that guides Krustan belief rests on the shaky ground of ignorance and needs firmer ground on which to repose. Religious beliefs, like other beliefs that lack objectivity, are subject to variation with changes in the circumstances that have generated and tended to perpetuate them. Contrariwise, knowledge based on objective scientific discovery and evidence can withstand all kinds of subjective opinions and the pluralistic beliefs on which these opinions are often based, as well as all the uncertain truths and realities that such beliefs generate. Hence the adage: "It is wrong always, everywhere, and for anyone, to believe anything upon insufficient evidence"[7], although the apostles of faith claim that the illuminations that come from the practice of spirituality cannot be apprehended by means of the rational model argument alone. They claim that the relevant experiences are not available to us during the times when we forsake faith for rationality. To this irrational piece of sophistry, the reply is simply that faith should rest on evidence and reasons that make the existence of this $x$ a plausibility approaching certainty. I cannot claim faith in my car's ability to carry me to town without authentic, reliable, and assuring evidence to justify the belief that it is equal to the task, even if I lack indefeasible evidence for it. Using irrationality as a precondition for apprehending rationality is foolish; it entails an unwarranted infinite regress of irrationalities.

Nevertheless, irrationality occurs widely in twin world where these credulous Krustans are being marshalled by imperialists of all stripes to terrorize and kill people who do not subscribe to their faith, claiming that they are terrorists, simply because these people object to the economic and other burdens that they are being made to carry for the comfort of the greedy few who wield power. In fact, the present age has pushed the killing culture to its limit under the technical auspices of the strongest and hitherto most respected Krustan nations of twin world that murder people outright or make them disappear before they murder them. Relationships are no longer based on the promotion of the homan dignity of all people, but on militarist imperialism and the use of brute force to take from others what one wants, instead of negotiating and paying a fair price for it (diamonds, land, oil, etc), or else by using trickery and intrigue (cartels for trade in commodities and produce). Some Krustans within the ruling circles of certain states in twin world have said that they will not allow other states to control resources which they need for driving their own economies, but they will find ways of taking over the control of these resources, even if it means killing innocent men, women, and children in war to achieve their self-serving ends. They have clearly exhausted the feigned decency that they put on when they entered into agreements of trade with other states, in the same way that they reneged on land treaties entered into with the aboriginals of the lands that they now inhabit and rule, treaties that they never intended to keep, because they could not curb their greed to be in possession and total control of all the fertile and mineral-rich lands on which they found them living. Instead, they huddled them into arid corners of the country (e.g., reservations) where their only prospect was just what they had planned for them: annihilation.

The result of this attitude is a nation-wide orientation toward a war mentality and glorification of this ignoble pursuit promoted by so-called Krustan leaders, whose worth is gauged by their hatred of browns and the poor (who happen to be the same people) rather than by their devotion to improving the economic, educational, and social levels of the people who are caught in the midst of severely floundering economies. These people who claim to have emerged from the primitive culture that exists in uncivilized states where there is perpetual "War of every man against every man"[8], have now become savages and wagers of war against all in their efforts to expand their empires and grab all the riches of the world to satisfy their insatiable greed, bequeathing hunger, devastation, and death wherever they go in search of worldly fortunes. Meanwhile, they are telling everyone that their Krustan religion teaches them to be like real Christians and "seek . . . first the kingdom of God, and his righteousness; and all these things shall be added unto [them]."[9] But that teaching is good for others, not for them. Their motto is: do as I say, not as I do. (During a reading lesson, a lisping teacher is reputed to have instructed her class: "don't thay thea ath I thay thea; thay thea ath the book thays thea." Interpretation: don't say sea as I say sea; say sea as the book says sea. How were the poor tots to know what the book said when all they could hear was what she was saying?)

Motivated by fear or blind faith, the people allow themselves to be taken for a ride by Krustan warmongers who waste money on butchering defenceless peoples of other tribes and religions with sophisticated and unmatched weaponry and fire power, instead of feeding them, as their bubel instructs them to do: "feed my sheep." Defenceless men, women, and children of other tribes are sacrificed on the altars of greed, grudge matches, assertion and maintenance of superiority, and control of other states by violence, while the sick and hungry at home and in other lands are wailing for help to deaf ears that are listening to and hear only their own greed-driven voices yelling for the loot. Similar weaponry is used against a handful of native peoples who are still protesting violations of their lives, rights, and territories by these evil bullies who pride themselves on their homanity in the midst of the atrocities that they are perpetrating.

When the people are living peacefully on their lands under their traditional chiefs who resist the efforts of the usurper to dominate them, they depose the chiefs by applying their pink laws and using force to install their own puppets who will do their bidding for a few pieces of silver. Together they dehomanize the tribe and destroy its traditional ways of life and anything that will remain as a reminder that the lands that the usurpers claim to have discovered belonged to the millions of people whom they murdered with their superior fire power. In the process, they stole their lands with phony treaties that they designed to give them an unfair advantage over the browns who did not understand the legalese in which they were written. How does anyone discover lands on which other people have been living for eons? They also stole documents that proved ownership of these lands and that were acquired with the help of the very few good ones among them who recognized the rights of other people to their life and property, although they might not commit themselves to admitting equality with them. These sympathizers of twin world still earn the derogatory nick-names equivalent to those of "kaffir-boetie" or "nigger-lover" (enemies of pink supremacy) bestowed on them by haters and harmers of the brown peoples of our world.

These thefts have been facilitated by their virtuous laws of justice and fairness, freedom, and equality that applied and still apply only to themselves as persons, while all others are slaves who have no rights and inferiors or sub-persons who do not qualify for just or fair treatment under their pink laws. If sub-persons are deceived by the presumed universality of these virtuous laws, they have the rug simultaneously pulled from under them by imposed economic, social, educational and other ceilings that keep them from availing themselves of the security that they offer; and that is called playing on a level field, one that is heavily weighted in favour of the usurping class. One would expect that the archangels of Krustanity among them would be the champions of the rights of the aboriginals, but it was the racist leaders of the racist church who sold the people out to their Eubopan countrymen, earning a serious indictment for the church, Krustanity, and those who proselytize their warped virtues through this instrument of vile oppression. Most of the time many of them pretended not to see what was going on, to soothe their guilty consciences, allowing evil to triumph unopposed; but that inactivity alone still renders them as guilty as the active perpetrators of these evil deeds on all browns.

As usual, evil triumphs when so-called good people do nothing about it when they see it, but instead look the other way, or tell themselves that there is nothing they can do about it, or that it will be over and forgotten in eighty years or so, however destructive it is to the people on whom it is perpetrated, as long as it does not spill over and affect them directly. They forget, or they are probably not aware, that rich people or those in positions of power will listen to them and consider their pleas on behalf of poor browns and others to whom they do not care to listen, provided that they assure them that they are not trying to make browns their equals or to make it possible for them to become their masters. For those in power, there is no point in heeding the pleas of the oppressed to have the yoke lifted from their backs and to have their injustices redressed, because to do so will place them in the oxymoronic situation where they oppresses, but also simultaneously relax their oppression in response to the loud and long-drawn-out squirming of the victims that they are trying to eliminate. However, their ilk might successfully persuade them to exercise a limited degree of mercy on their victims to ease their suffering, as is occasionally the case in some notable situations.

The question now is: Amidst all these unguddly doings, how can people repose their trust in the Krustan religion and its preachers when they engage in arrant treachery, inhomanity, insincerity, and lying? How often have they not been heard belching racist hatred, lies, and murder from their pulpits to their equally racist audiences that should be censuring them for their unkrustan behaviour, but instead applaud them for spewing vitriol and death threats to all ranks of browns from platforms that should be used for spreading love, homanity, and fellowship? Isn't the church supposed to be a refuge for browns and those who are persecuted like them, instead of a willing participant in the despicable language and acts of murder to which they are subjected? How do we separate chaff from chaff when the church has reduced itself to chaff by being the instrument of the inhomanity and evil preached and perpetrated by some of its depraved leaders and their followers who participate in the political gutter morality of inciting murder? Separating grain from chaff is easy when the church is the grain and the secular "rulers" and the mob are the chaff; but not when both are chaff.

The racist societies that constitute these churches, thus making them foci of immoral enterprise, also fan the flames of iniquitous oppression and dispossession by their gross and willful ignorance of historical facts. They arrive in the country where their brothers are practicing the most ungodly and immoral forms of discrimination, inhomanity, and dispossession, and they foolishly take sides against the owners of lands on which they are squatters by virtue of the intrigue and brute force of those who took land that did not belong to them in the first place. They then engage in stupid talk about being inconvenienced for a few days by the protests of the locals who have suffered through many decades of exploitation and dehomanization under the thumb of the very people who can't bear to have their comfortable way of life disrupted for a few days by protests against exploitation. They clamour for more force to settle legitimate issues of the aboriginals' rights to stolen lands that have been shelved by their brothers for decades with insincere promises and lying about trying to restore those rights over decades of neglect and inactivity when the matter is unequivocal and they know very well what to do—play fair and just, and do not dispossess others.

Instead, they invent all sorts of evasive moves; as one of the leaders of twin world admitted, in language attributed to our world, "we have taken their country. It is true [our] God promised it to us."[10] Their country that your God promised you? What was he thinking? Well, they say, the answer is in the holy books for all to read: "the land which the LORD swore to your fathers to give you."[11] That is why they play games like uttering insincere regret, while holding their noses to swallow the bitter pill of apologizing audibly (to themselves, not to browns), for the loss of their homes that they bulldozed, because they were an eyesore of "blighted houses and dilapidated structures", without basic amenities, in the midst of their upscale homes on lands that their Gudd promised them during their fits of auditory hallucinations when they heard him pledging other people's lands to them. That is the propaganda that they have been spreading through all their myth media in twin world, including the bubels that they have printed for consumption by the unwary who are being led to believe that pinks are the chosen people. Twaddle!

Of course they will say that they were not the actual thieves, but they know full well that they are enjoying the fruits of the theft that was initiated and perpetrated by their forebears, and that they are perpetuating and compounding the wrong by not redressing it, but instead continuing to steal more land from the little with which they have left the aboriginals, so that they can settle their own pink brothers and sisters on that stolen land. What happens to the owners of the land is not their guddless concern; they can find their own brothers and sisters who are willing to accommodate them, or be content to reside in the homan zoos or reservations in which they will be placed and then provided with bottle stores where they can purchase liquor to keep them perpetually inebriated and cloud their minds to quash their motivation to pester the usurpers about unjust and unfair treatment. If that is not dirty Krustan trickery, what is?

In the practice of dirty tricks, the church of today, like the corrupt church of ages past, does not fare any better, since it has become the fiefdom and money generating factory of some greedy pastors or guardians of the flock who fleece their sheep thoroughly to swell their bank accounts and expand their already enormous real estate holdings that far exceed the modest celestial abodes that they have turned down for the relish of these obscene pleasures of twin world. Each one ventures out to found his own religious sect, convincing a good many dolts to swallow his bait and follow him like the sheep that they are, until some of them also decide to go off, in fractal fashion, to establish their own religious communities where they can claim sole authority on the spoils that they amass from these ventures. It's all about being the boss and having sole control of the loot that the poor, bamboozled followers bring in. Hence the rampant hypocrisy of the leaders of these religious sects who preach dogma and scriptures in which they do not believe, and which they do not practice. They recite their prayers and credos like automatons, and because their epistemic content lacks meaning to them, they readily infringe their vows with the least amount of guilt for the suffering that they are causing to those who believe their pious lies.

Such is life under the domination of Krustans who are governed by lies, racism, hubris, hypocrisy, duplicity, and inhomanity. We could fill pages of discussion about these Krustan types and their practice of their religion; but we have to move on to consider a question that is begging for an answer: why and whence this racism?

# Chapter 8
# Emergence of racism

Pinks operate under a weird but convenient logic that protects them from a truth that they find to be traumatizing: the truth of the equal worth of all homanity that does not confer a special status of superior homanity on anyone. No person has more privileged moral claim to the primary rights to life and subsistence from which all other rights follow and from which he might like to exclude other homans. However, they unjustifiably embrace the false belief that all browns cannot be treated equally with them, since they have set themselves apart as the unequalled standard of homanity to which everyone should aspire, and so any browns that they encounter cannot be their equals. We have already seen that this distorted logic is prompted by the desire for unimpeded political and economic advantage and power, the same desire that undergirds the illogical contradiction that we have encountered before that says all homans are created equal, but some are created more equal than others—if the oxymoronic concept of unequal equality makes any sense—and the more equal ones have natural rights and liberties that the less equal ones do not possess in the inferior status to which they have been relegated by the more equal ones with their non-natural pink laws. Giddy? Racism itself is giddy with its structural contradictions.

But, of course, it does make sense if you are a Hagala, one of the renowned thinkers of twin world who believes (without foundation) that browns are things or animals that still have to emerge into personhood, and with whom interaction does not have to be guided by ethical principles of justice, decency, and guddliness. He borrows prejudicial expressions from our world to convey the racist biases of his world against browns, claiming justification for his "civilized" tribe to exercise rights that they deny the barbarians, [as browns are described], because "their consciousness has not yet reached an awareness of any substantial objectivity . . . in which the will of man could participate and in which he could become aware of his own being"[1]. So, the concepts that apply to persons do not apply to them, because they have not progressed beyond their immediate existence where they live, "in a state of savagery and barbarism . . . [as examples of] animal man in all his savagery and lawlessness,"[2] that is ruled by passion. In this state, he alleges, it is as difficult for pinks to feel themselves into the nature of browns as it is to feel into the nature of a dog, because pinks can only feel that which is akin to their own feelings of reverence and morality, which is lacking in dogs and browns (presumably entities in the same class; hence posted prohibitory signs like "dogs and browns not allowed"). How can anyone share moral feelings with a dog, a homan dog? This is the poison that he fed his university students and his readers who believed every word of his slanderous verbiage. His execrable legacy and disreputable tradition perdure to this day in the conduct of his tribe, and it will survive into the foreseeable future, if the delusion of pink supremacy is not stamped out.

However, Leon Maccas, the author of the book *German Barbarism; a neutral's indictment*, depicting the "barbarism" of some in the twin tribe of our world that matches the tribe to which this castigator of browns belongs, paints an extremely gruesome picture of their own beastly inhumanity of gross proportions. How much credence to attach to Hagala's racist, ranting diatribe directed at browns against this background is epitomized in his adaptation of words borrowed again from our world: "As to the African character, it is still unknown to us, because the Europeans have not yet penetrated sufficiently far into the interior; Africa still remains cut off."[3] So why rant and rave against what you do not know and understand, unless you are just unleashing vile prejudice based on racism and the blind desire to show off your assumed superiority, betraying a prejudiced lack of ability to appreciate the self of the other that is not your self like some notable narcissists of our time?

Hagala saw slavery as a civilizing and justifiable form of allowing Afibikans to eventually become a part of homan history, from which he claims that they are excluded by their origin from and sojourn in a dark and mysterious continent. Once out of it, they can lose their limiting identity by aping Eubopans, and thereby become civilized, even in the hot climate of their habitat that he claimed inhibits cognitive development, and even if he has already labeled them as "intractable". He exposes his dismal ignorance of them by suggesting that these people who live with *ubuntu* are the ones who should learn it from the selfish, bigoted ones who have enslaved them; the same ones who think that everything in twin world is about them, simply because of their skin colour. In any case who would want to lose her identity for the sake of acquiring a decadent, money-worshiping civilization that disrespects other homanity?

Where are the Krustan feelings of love and altruism, and where is the moral consciousness of persons who oppress others and deny them their homan rights and freedoms, dehomanizing them every day of their lives? Perhaps they are to be found in words that reportedly come from our own world and reverberate in twin world:

> Every Englishman is born with a certain miraculous power that makes him master of the world. When he wants a thing, he never tells himself that he wants it. He waits patiently until there comes into his mind, no one knows how, a burning conviction that it is his moral and religious duty to conquer those who have got the thing he wants . . . he does what pleases him and grabs what he wants: There is nothing so bad or so good that you will not find Englishmen doing it.[4]

What further proof does anyone want of the arrogance, immoral conduct, and religious hypocrisy displayed by some representatives of the pink society of twin world, and what does the rest of their society have to say about these injustices that are being perpetrated in their name? Some, only a few, have objected at the risk of their own lives, because the hatred of pinks for browns will not brook interference by anyone, not even their own kind; but the majority couldn't be bothered. Life goes on for them, and it goes on much better with browns marginalized and not constituting a threat to their insecure security. Thus inactivated, there is no way that they can be a threat to pink survival, because their ruling brothers have ensured their inhomane subjugation and harassment in many ways. They have also designed an education system that will ensure the enslavement of all browns for generations to come, and they are feeding their brothers' anxious minds the lie that the enslavement will go on *ad infinitum*. (Interestingly, when slavery was abolished, pink slave masters were compensated by their pink governments for the loss of their property and currency, the slaves, but the slaves were not compensated for the erstwhile loss of their freedom).

Needless to say, this low down arrogance is as prevalent now as it has ever been in twin world, and is of the same order as that espoused by another great thinker of that world, Lacka, who also believes without foundation that browns are not persons or self-conscious agents, because they lack a rational faculty that can make them eligible for the homan rights that are enjoyed by pinks in their own liberal tradition. He brazenly claims that they fall into the same category as stones and trees, which also lack that faculty. Hence they can be arrogantly and arbitrarily dispossessed, krustanized with pink "krustan names" like my own high school contemporary whose given (heathen) name was replaced with a so-called christian name by arrogant missionaries who thereby disrespected his parents and the entire brown tribe while doing nothing to replace non-biblical names given to so-called "whites" — show me a St. Cody or St. Zoe from the bible. They can also be enslaved, or else "assimilated" and made dependent on pinks, if not killed with impunity for resisting control and subjugation to Krustans and their churches. Nothing could be more insulting to browns and to the irreproachable Krustan religion that pinks proudly flaunt in their faces than to be made victims of these inhomane deeds that only prove how pinks have fashioned Krustanity — their superior religion that should rule their world and efface all other religions — into a sordid tool for perpetrating evil on browns. (A fuller discussion of this kind of outrage is found in chapter 9 of my book *Our World and its Values*).

Similar irrational blather was spewed by a concatenation of other thinkers of twin world, including most notably Humono who boldly uttered the unwarranted and foolish statement that the natural inferiority of browns to pinks makes them unable to rise to levels of distinction and eminence that even rude and barbarous pinks can achieve, because browns lack scientists, artists, and ingenious manufacturers. Meanwhile, he claims, uneducated pink riffraff have distinguished themselves in every profession. Every profession? (But see page 125). That is the wild, racist, non-empirical conclusion of an empiricist (whose reputation is founded on his postulation that knowledge comes from experience) that one $x$ that he has heard of as being a $p$ makes every $x$ that exists a $p$, even if he has not met a single $x$ or all existing $x$s, past, present, and future to be able to take the inductive leap from "some" to "all", as we noted on page 7. And yet, he is reputed to be the quintessential critic of the inductive method of argument. Racism does indeed make fools of wise men.

In his pitiably racist mind, which has overtaken and eclipsed his illustrious logical mind, ignorant pinks are smarter than all the brown intelligentsia by virtue of what: intellectual endowment, rationality, or skin colour? The shocking answer is: skin colour. Hearing of an accomplished brown, the best comment that this respected intellectual can make is to compare him to a parrot whose slender accomplishment is to speak a few words clearly. This empiricist ignores all the empirical evidence of brown achievement throughout the world and rather prefers to live in the fairyland of racist make-believe where he can spin his yarns of bias freely, since they cannot be confirmed or denied empirically as his philosophy demands of the assertions of others. He is no different from today's chimerical leaders or from self-opinionated liberal pinks who believe that a brown can ascend to prominence only if he speaks like them, because he inherits 50% of his constitution from them. If he spoke like the rest of his folk, he would not be eligible for emergence from the pit of misery in which all browns belong.

Their liberalism is of the same phony order as that described by Susan Nathan in her book, *The Other Side of Israel,* where she portrays leftists, so-called, who play the ostrich in the face of injustices that they see perpetrated on innocent victims, and rather than fight for the rights of the underdogs, choose to pacify them by effusing vain sympathy on them, advising them not to rock the boat. In other words, "shut the f… up" (see page 62), let things be, and try to survive as best as you can. This brilliant solution to a lethal problem is typical of pinks of all stripes; they relieve browns of their burden only if it is in their own interests. If all sympathizers went a step further to empathize with the victims of racism, they'd realize that more is demanded of them than mere lip service to nebulous, idealistic liberal goals. Admittedly, it is not easy to be subjective about an objective situation, but they can still involve themselves in brown situations by allowing deep, empathic feelings of concern to replace their gracious, sympathetic feelings of detachment, and thereby effect needed changes to pink barbarism and inhumanity. As I have noted throughout my book *Philosophy for Medical Students and Practitioners,* empathy is an essential element in holistic doctor-patient relationships. Quite often patients are treated like objects or foci of constellations of signs and symptoms waiting to be knitted into some diagnostic category for mechanistic treatment, without regard for their whole personhood and the circumstances that surround it. Their feelings are left behind, because they were never taken into consideration, and they end up as mechanically sound specimens, but emotionally still wrecked persons.

Kantono, another authority on nature and the superior gifts of pinks, first lays down the requirement for anything to be a moral being as the possession of rationality, then he goes on to extol the humanity that exists in its greatest perfection in the pink tribe by virtue of their skin colour, implying that no tribe of a different skin colour is greater or better than it, and categorically apportioning a decidedly smaller amount of talent to all the other tribes. From these unfounded premises, he concludes, by a vicious logic, that the other tribes do not possess rationality, and hence do not also qualify as moral agents worthy of respect. He opens the way for them to be used as means to the ends of the perfect tribe (see reference [4], page 144), and to be treated worse than animals by prescribing the means of disciplining them like children, but also inflicting the maximum amount of pain with a split bamboo (to slash their skins?), instead of a less traumatizing whip, displaying sadistic, racist malice that runs contrary to the utilitarian principle of maximizing the happiness of all persons, and to his own Categorical Imperative of moral duty to other human beings, to which browns are not entitled by his twisted logic. What a pity that wise men should assume such unbecoming, grotesque mental contortions to gratify mere racist prejudices.

Indeed, to confirm his deviant, colour-coded reasoning, Kantono further went on to say (like Humono and Lacka) that their cognitive deficiency barred browns from acquiring the moral status of ends in themselves, and so moral laws did not apply to them and they could, therefore, be used as means to any end that pleased the whims of pinks, thereby exonerating pinks from responsibility for the heinous crimes that they are committing against browns. So his postulated universal imperative of duty is a mere colour-coded sham that has limited and bigoted application to pinks, based on the wider assumption that browns do not (on purely moral grounds) have the rights to justify recognition of their tacit claim of duty toward them from pinks, and that they will remain eternally inferior to pinks, simply because they are of a darker skin hue.

This disrespect of brown dignity is a universal pink bane. As some indigenous peoples of one of our world's ostensibly liberal, Christian states said about their humiliation when their conquerors forcibly moved them from their habitat into the tundra, "I was E9-551. We were treated like dogs. We were just numbers, not humans. . . . They didn't think we have feelings too."[5] At the same time, aboriginal women of twin world who married pink men lost their "Brown status"; they became non-browns, according to the law that is imposed on them by pinks. They were also not pinks by virtue of their marriage to pinks (which is obvious); they were still browns (aboriginal) by birth, but not "Brown" by status. So what were they? Who cares? No pink cares about the personhood of browns. They are items like all the other inanimate items of twin world, and that's why pinks never stop to think about the illogical, nonsensical laws that they impose on them, laws that they would never impose on their women. The only difference, though, is that the systematized natural laws that regulate inanimate matter are not as asinine as the pink laws that are crafted by these rapscallions to dehomanize browns.

To further amplify his disdain for the other people, Kantono says that the feelings of browns cannot rise above the trifling, and their views are stupid, simply because they are expressed by browns. The same views expressed by pinks would be wise by his logic, because they have a different complexion—pink views. This is regrettable piffle coming from a reputed thinker who chooses to colour-code people's views and to equate their cognitive ability and moral worth with their skin colour: brown=stupid, pink=wise. Highly respected logical thinkers of twin world like Kantono have defied logical principles by declaring that all views expressed by members of other tribes are stupid, implying that they have taken a census of all such views, past, present, and future, all over twin world to be able to say that they are all stupid, without exception. It is only a warped logic that can besmirch all with the deeds of some, and only a deplorably prejudiced mind that can impute stupidity exclusively to one group while pretending that the other (privileged) group is totally exempt from stupidity. Great minds like Humono and Kantono should know this as well as any child does, unless they are consumed by a baleful herrenvolk mentality, as evidenced by their reference to all browns as ugly, vice-ridden savages who seem to constitute what one ancient encyclopedia defined as a new species of homankind (with whose women they habitually cohabit and even raise families, producing another species of homankind?).

These are people who fit the description that has been applied to the Aryan races of our world whose impact, in pre-historic times, was "to lower, rather than raise, the level of civilization"[6], and who have also been described as "disgusting savages" and "wreckers". (Ouch, that hurt!) Nevertheless, Kantono, one of their learned men, borrowing language from our world, referred to his pink tribe as the "most beautiful people on dry land"[7] [who are] "more intelligent than any other race of people in the world"[8]. He forgot to add that they have used their intelligence to control others by incinerating them with weapons of mass destruction, while neglecting to name those sites of inhomane incineration "holy ground" for their victims.

As intelligent as they are, these intellectually barren saps are still being misused by special interest groups and immoral legislators who push them into resorting to hooliganism to offset their inability to win policy contests with logical arguments. These poor gulls are tools of the adequately-catered-for and the greedy money-grubbers who use all of them to do their dirty work of opposing progressive ideas that restrict their chances of making more money on the backs of poor people who are trying to ensure that they are prepared to meet the hard times of their lives when illness and other adversities have struck. They shoot themselves in the foot by acting like driven cattle to shout down schemes that are meant to benefit them, because the benefit will be extended to browns too, but they don't see that they are being made patsies. Their talk is as irrelevant and ignorant as that of some of their mushroom leaders who spew drivel in their misguided quest for hollow popularity and the highest political offices of their states, which they will most likely achieve in the prevailing toxic, racist atmosphere of ignorance and negativity founded on intense, uncontrollable hatred of brown authority over them. They falsely believe that only they can take charge, even if they are messing up and have insulated themselves from criticism with emergency laws meant to muzzle citizens and to feed their hungry prisons that they also use to house mentally ill persons, because they blow 23 billion tax dullams on war toys and not on appropriate rehabilitative facilities for them or on many pressing community needs that languish into decay through negligence.

So where did these paragons of morality lose the moral high road and respect for the dignity of persons, replacing it with respect for mere colours? Sadly, these distorted opinions prevail widely in twin world, as evidenced by those who would create an inferior system of education for browns, enabling them to follow the instructions of their pink masters, but not to enter into discourse with them, because homans do not discourse with subhomans. (See page 144, references [3&4]). They call their policy one of separate but equal development, lying to themselves and to those they want to oppress with their discriminatory and dehomanizing policies and actions by labeling their heinous, bigoted, racist actions as non-racist. To show how foolish racism can make one appear, Lacka thinks that he is mocking the religions of browns by claiming that they consecrate common objects with a few words, thereby making them objects of veneration and invocation, in the same way that a wafer of bread undergoes transubstantiation into the body of Krust when Krustans like him recite their incantations. What's the difference? The skin colour of the performer? Modern-day pink torturers of browns also descend into the same gutter in their efforts to break the morale of their imprisoned victims by mocking their religions in the hope of enraging them and simultaneously frustrating them, because their physical and mental shackles render them powerless to retaliate for their shameful humiliation. That is the Krustan way.

But that inconsistency, which is deadly to any set of allegedly rational philosophical propositions is not the end of this illogical pink venture; one other pink of twin world disgorged the pitiable and ignorant claim that that he picked up from our world: "they [browns] secrete less by the kidneys, and more by the glands of the skin, which gives them a very strong and disagreeable odour."[9] This stroke of physiological genius may be appropriate for fictitious twin world, but it certainly does not have application in our world where all healthy, human kidneys and skin glands, which lack colour coding, function alike, and where deodorant-antiperspirants are not made specifically to suppress the products of some sweat glands and not others. All stale sweat exudes the same disagreeable odour, which also lacks colour coding. Only a fool would believe that pink sweat exudes a sweet aroma, while brown sweat stinks disagreeably.

Another of their renowned anthropologists, taking his cue from one Johann Blumenbach a disciple of the botanist Carolus Linnaeus of our world who was the first to categorize humans scientifically, tried to set his tribe up as the prototype of the homan species, while debasing browns to the lowest imaginable level. Others displayed their prejudice by claiming that browns exhibit more sensation than reflection and are incapable of "tracing and comprehending the investigations of Euclid"[10]. All of them are uttering these fabrications to pave their way to justify the unjustifiable belief that leads them to the false conclusion that browns "are inferior to [pinks] in their endowment both of body and mind"[11], from which they can with audacity classify them with non-homan animals that they can misuse and control at will. Their evil designs and deeds defy all bounds.

The preceding reference to Euclid can be dismissed as a further attempt by pinks to degrade browns below the lowest level to which they have already reduced them by wildly implying that all the untutored of their pink tribe are natural geometricians. It may be true that the pink slaves of the Ramonos of twin world excelled in science and were "employed as tutors to their masters' children"[12], but the lowly crowd of twin world pinks that we know is hardly the type to indulge in such lofty pursuits; they are an ignorant, shallow rabble who lack the capacity to think before they quickly embrace and practice the cheap clap-trap coming from the mouths or pens of their reputed thinkers (and morons) as indisputable gospel, because it feeds into their own unfounded, ignominious racist biases, phony religiosity, and, most of all, their goofy ideology of pink supremacy, which all of them espouse and promote unashamedly every day of their lives. This perverse ideology has become their real religion, except that they dress it in glittering Krustan garb.

At any time and in any place, personal, national, or tribal pride could be a laudable sentiment, as long as it is not based and does not thrive on malicious derogation of other people, and as long as it remains cognizant of the truth that this insanity about the superiority of one tribe over another is the delusion of insecure minds that are trying to suppress the relevance of the pertinent but nagging question of the centuries: how many of these superior pink beings have brown blood running through their veins? The oxymoron was crystallized by another deluded individual from a recognized hybrid tribe who did not want to be classified with other browns when he remarked that his kind should keep their tribe pure, venting the pitiable *ignis fatuus* born of the arrogant pink dream of maintaining the "purity" of their tribe by keeping brown blood at bay, but failing to curb pink male desire for brown females!

In other respects, and confirming their lack of class, pinks have built their golf courses over the graves of browns, while they also continue to celebrate their thefts (so-called discoveries) of occupied lands that they claim their Gudd promised to give them. They stage offensive anniversaries in which the surviving victims of their planned but failed annihilations are expected to participate joyfully, even as they continue to suffer oppression, torture, humiliation, dehomanization, exploitation, and attempted annihilation. As one of our world's oppressed persons said about one such celebration,

> I answer: a day that reveals to him, more than all other days in the year, the gross injustice and cruelty to which he is the constant victim. To him, your celebration is a sham; your boasted liberty, an unholy license; your national greatness, swelling vanity; your sounds of rejoicing are empty and heartless; your denunciation of tyrants, brass-fronted impudence; your shouts of liberty and equality, hollow mockery; your prayers and hymns, your sermons and thanksgivings, with all your religious parade and solemnity, are, to him, mere bombast, fraud, deception, impiety, and hypocrisy—a thin veil to cover up crimes which would disgrace a nation of savages. [13]

Their best witless response was to recognize the intelligence that he owed to his *white* blood, and to regret the *black* blood in him that cost the world a genius. So, what is it about skin colour that confers either preference for or discrimination against some people when all people share and differ in so many physical and psychic attributes? This is the same question that we often do not care to pose about what makes us call all the various shades of one colour by the same name, like all the shades of orange that blend imperceptibly into red at one end of the spectrum and into pink at the other end. The other question that we should ask is why people think that the gene for the pigment of skin colour (melanin) is the same one that controls and varies inversely with aptitude, so that those endowed with more pigmentation have less aptitude than those with less pigmentation; i.e., the more any person has of one, the less she has of the other. This biologically baseless categorization is woven by bigots into the fabric of homan society where it enjoys the distinction of forming the basis of the unequal, differential treatment that is given to its members; hence the odd logic of a positive designation, *x*s, for less pigmented persons and the negative designation, non-*x*s, for more pigmented persons. Those idiots who are deluded into superiority by their skin colour are confusing the incontrovertible fact of the reality of colour with a groundless, fabricated, and absurd belief in a hierarchical gradation of colours that would allow them to say that the pink colour is superior to the brown colour and claim that as a fact of life. These dolts have to be taught that there are no superiorly and inferiorly constituted colours in the light spectrum. Only ignorant, arrogant fools like them would think so. What more can one say?

A pink tennis star of twin world was taught that lesson in humility by two brown aspirants to tennis stardom after they had outperformed all their initial pink competitors. He said they would never advance in the tennis world, implying that their performances were meteoric flukes. He did not advance a rational basis for his statement, because he did not have any, but it was quite clear that his motivation was the usual pink racism compounded by the jealousy that always prompts the derogation of brown successes, which often far outshine pink performances. The brown stars are still twinkling; his star ceased to emit light many years ago (which theirs will undoubtedly do with age in years to come, but not in the few hours of glory that he in his arrogance had allotted them).

In other domains, pink intellectuals and professionals have designed aptitude tests based on their own privileged cultural setting and have used these to try to prove that browns are less intelligent than pinks, because they did not do as well as pinks in those tests, which is to be expected, since they come from underprivileged societies that have been created for them by the same rascal pinks. So what have they proved? Not the ineptitude of browns, but the extent to which their lying will stretch to force the issue of their spurious superiority. There is no end to dirty tricks in the racist agenda that tries to force racially neutral genes into its mold, so that fabricated genes for aptitude, moral worth, and humanity can be denied to browns and remain the preserve of these self-righteous reprobates. With the advent of gene patenting, there is no telling what they will do next to ensure that browns end up with all the deleterious genes. Their stratification of races is nothing more than a prostitution of natural differences among differently complexioned peoples to ensure contrived pink supremacy that is enforced with such cruelties as imprisoning and torturing them without just cause, infecting them with syphilis for experimental study, vivisecting them while they are alive (Maccas), and murdering them barbarously. Even though the questions raised by all these considerations have not yet received rational answers, and in spite of what has been revealed about the demeanour of the privileged classes of twin world, it might perhaps be less challenging now to understand how racist attitudes arise and prosper among them and their fearful cousins in their attempts to ensure the perdurance of conditions that maintain their privileged positions in society; also why they come into office to maliciously destroy the good that has been done by their brown predecessor to erase his legacy. Morons, they don't know that they can never wipe out a legacy. History will always reflect it, especially against the sordid background of their ineptitude and hurtful racist practices.

So let us first define "racism" as it is understood in our world. Racism differs from raciology, which only studies factual physical differences of the races of humankind without pretending that they signify superiority of one particular race over others. Racism, on the other hand, consists of serfdom to beliefs derived from distortions of these differences into criteria of the intellectual and moral inferiority of groups selected at the whim of the dominant group, anxious to protect its self-assigned privileged and power-wielding status, and lacking the intelligence to realize that physical characteristics don't entail mental and moral attributes, just as skin rashes do not entail mental deftness or torpor. Lacking genetic and biological bases for race, they used a socially constructed concept of race to satisfy their prejudices and efforts to maintain their decadent superiority and normativity. But this substitutive manoeuvre failed to justify their case or convince eliminativists who reject the concept of race but are still powerless to deconstruct it or eliminate its persisting heinous effects that target browns exclusively.

It is well known that variations in genetic and biological makeup are greater within races than they are among them[14] (85.4% versus 6.3% for blood groups), and that no meticulous analysis of genes will determine decisively that their owners belong to different races, even though their non-genetic characteristics might do so; but even they don't delineate superiority or inferiority. They are simply differences among individuals and groups of them until evil minds attach their own immoral import and devious hierarchical values to them as indicators of superiority of one and inferiority of the other who are falsely believed to be incapable of attaining cultural par with them. In the end, however, it does not matter whether race is real or a mere construct, institutional fact, or convenience in the same sense that money is a convenient instrument for trade and marriage is another type of convenient construct for cohabitation, as posited by John Searle in his book *The Construction of Social Reality*. Both are not natural processes like breathing and the circulation of blood through the body without which life cannot go on; life can go on quite well without them. As regards this fabricated entity, race, it has brought untold suffering to millions of people at the hands of the few who have used it to assert themselves as masters over entire, successive generations of others who are of a different skin colour from them and whom they have exploited and humiliated most unscrupulously.

So it is as naïve to think that we can ignore race as it is to say that we can ignore money; both are sources of misery and death to their victims as the racially privileged sacrifice the disadvantaged on the inauspicious altars of their social constructions: race and money. Those who are perpetuating the concept of race, not colour, as the basis of their racism are not impressed by scientific arguments that purport to discredit the concept as otiose; to them race remains the flexible criterion (see pages 148-149 "Chinese...") that they use to ensure their survival by differentially suppressing the aspirations of those who belong to races other than their own—which detracts from their own bona fides that survive only by denying others their chance to compete in the survival game and share a place in the sun.

Meanwhile, the pinks who are held captive by these warped beliefs also act with the same vulgarism, making no effort to critically examine the "facts" with which they are presented. They are content to sacrifice the truth by ignoring rationality and expert objective evidence pointing to the absurdity of their beliefs in favour of pledging their faith in the depraved personal prejudices inculcated into them by charlatans and xenophobes. Granted, we cannot verify every opinion that we accept on trust as fact, because we do not have the time, means, and breadth of universal knowledge to delve into the authenticity of every opinion that is presented to us as factual, but people often do not make any effort to at least wean their beliefs of their foundations of bias and the lure of their ignoble intentions before they embrace them. So, most of the beliefs on which they act are short on evidence, but lavish on faith and blind trust. That is a given of life in our world, and it seems to be the same in twin world.

People of twin world tend to believe crafted anthropological, genetic, and other such evidence presented to them as gospel coming from the mouths of self-proclaimed oracles who have postulated that race is real and natural to homanity on the basis of shared group and racial genetics and the distinctive physical features that genetic endowment generates among homan groups. They also appeal to their common anthropology as manifested in their ancestry, sojourn, language, and customs, and in their restricted breeding. That being the case, they maliciously make them believe that the races have to be kept "pure", since that was the original natural intention of the creator who stationed them on different continents, ensuring their separation until (they forget to add) pinks decided to invade the habitations of others to make them and their women folk their own. Their claim is supposed to be based on their selective interpretation of the statement from their bubels which states that their Gudd "made from one every nation of men to live on all the face of the earth [twin world], having determined allotted periods and the boundaries of their habitation."[15] They conveniently ignore the first part that makes all homans cousins, and they emphasize the second part that justifies their attitude of enforced oppressive separation.

All these arguments can be seen to be flawed by their selection of only one criterion (skin colour) for stratifying people, to the exclusion of all other commonly shared homan characteristics. They also end up being mere rationalizations, because all racists and others who claim not to be racists use only this silly, arbitrary criterion to classify others as belonging to one race or another, while some among them will declare anyone who belongs to the despised and enslaved race an outcast, if she has even one metaphorical drop of blood from that race, although her skin colour is no different from theirs. They clutch at straws to save a hopeless situation resulting from miscegenation instituted by their failure to curb their voracious sexual appetites, and they pretend to forget that no one can have just one drop of blood obtained by way of procreation, and no one can distinguish with certainty between a person with one drop and another with no drop to be able to tell who is a brown trying to "pass" (trespass) as a pink for survival in a pink-dominated world. The architects of this idiotic concept thought it was a clever device for demarcating those who should be enslaved from those of the master race who should be the enslavers, but it is not a credit to their intelligence or to that of those who are still perpetuating the ludicrous tradition. Rationalization is not equivalent to justification; it is only a denial of the truth of their own prejudices and a confirmation of their bad faith in them, hoping that others will buy into their self-deception and follow their fatuous example. We have to wonder what they themselves become after receiving a life-saving blood transfusion of millions of drops of blood or donated organs that are transplanted across colour lines from one of these persons that they despise; brown pinks? It seems that the oxymoron comes back to bite them in their tails.

So, let us ignore for a moment the nitwitted concept of "one drop", face facts rationally, and confine our analysis to its motivating compatriot: skin colour. Can the racists tell us the racial identity of hybrid offspring? How do these zealots delineate this nebulous concept to be able to calculate the amount of pigment (or lack thereof) that she inherits from each parent to make her one of their chosen race or one of the inferior races, seeing that none of them can claim racial purity (if they believe their bubels' tale of "one blood", not "one drop") and the margin of inheritance cannot be known with any certainty? Is it 15%, 35%, 60%, 95%? By some fuzzy logic, they reason that pink+pink=pink; brown+brown=brown; but pink+brown always =brown, never =pink. Does that mean brown is dominant over pink, and that is why pink is for ever trying to suppress and oppress the natural dominance of brown? It seems that pink can define itself fully only in terms of brown, whereas brown is able to define itself, regardless of the presence or absence of pink. But if pink can define itself only against the backdrop of brown, not its absence, that alone renders it void. Pink thus becomes the true negative entity, non-$x$, in this relationship, defined as what is not-brown, although it speaks of browns as non-pinks, non-$x$s, in an effort to dump its negativity on browns. If these loathsome browns were to oblige by evanescing from twin world, how would they define their pink selves in the absence of their brown door mats and backdrop?

A clearly failed attempt to debase browns is the one meant to describe their rulers as licentious, as this blooper borrowed from our world so clearly illustrates. A twin world author quotes from one of the authors of our world thus: "The king of Dahomy, for example, has 3,333 wives"[16]. Unfortunately, this far-fetched example does not stand up to logical analysis. To service them at the rate of one a day, he will have to execute the impossible feat of spending time with each one once in 9.13years (3,333÷365). But to service all 3,333 of them daily, he will have to spend 25.92secs (24÷3333x60x60) with each one, and during that time he will also have to take care of all his daily chores, including duties of government and self-care. This is another absurd example of racism that leaves its author with enough egg on his face to feed on for the rest of his miserable racist life.

Apologists can forget trying to excuse this kind of bigotry by claiming that it is not fair to judge obviously colour-biased opinions of the 18th century by the standards of the 21st century; (like judging a boy from big city gutters by the lofty standards of conduct of other people) to which I reply that colour biases of all the past centuries placed browns where they are still being kept by the added colour biases of today. Colour bias retains its ugly head and far reaching tentacles through the ages; it is a blight that transcends the limits of time and is sustained by its entrenchment in the beliefs, morals, laws, and daily practices of the people whose scrupulously protected racist institutions are its execrable monuments of oppression.

Nevertheless, the reality of the glaring disparity in physical features of homan constellations from diverse geographical regions of the world resulting from selection of genetic traits induced by sojourn in those specific regions can't be denied, despite the subversion of this constitutional difference for evil intent on the basis of the skin colours of the affected persons by evil minds. This truth is exemplified by the sporadic appeals to persons from specific ethnic groups for donors of compatible bone marrow to transplant into other persons who stem from their socio-cultural groups and geographical regions for whom matching donors cannot be found among other groups. In this regard one can argue that common ancestry, culture, and physical traits, not skin colour, are a necessary and indisputable part of the individual's distinct categorization, but they do not define or determine her moral and intellectual personhood, except in the minds of moronic bigots.

At the same time, it is noteworthy that the incidence and prevalence of apparently "racially" confined medical conditions like the bone tumour Ewing's sarcoma that has a marked predilection for pink youth, but not their brown counterparts, and Sickle Cell Disease, which affects mainly Afibikan browns, provide cold comfort to exponents of race theory, because these conditions do not respect the limitations of skin colour; they affect persons across colour lines who share ancestral genes or habitats, a fact that racists prefer to shy away from. In addition, skin colour racism meets with difficulties when it has to deal with the case of the pink who has a condition known as Addison's disease where the amount of skin pigment is increased, or the one who is the subject of an atavism that makes her look like a brown. Both are condemned by their kind to the life sentence of being second class pinks or browns, unless they can fight their case to be included in the select racial group. Nevertheless, these academic arguments do nothing to lift or even ameliorate the sorry lot of the real brown or the nondescript one (borderline pink-brown or brown-pink) in whose favour the dice failed to roll in this game that pinks play with other people's lives.

Lately, however, and in an effort to continue to justify the racist compartmentalization that is based on peoples' skin colour, the concept of race has been conveniently crafted as being derived from the individual and her fit and level of comfort in communities that share her customs, and of misfit and discomfort in those that do not share those customs. This way the discriminators continue to hide from accusation for their racism, which is based on phantom genetic and anthropometric parameters of skull and brain size, skin colour, and intelligence tests based on biased comparisons derived from unequal exposure to sources of privileged knowledge. Behind this socially constructed shelter and refuge from culpability from where they can justify neglect of brown education and promote their bell curve prejudices that insult browns with the impunity and arrogance of liars plying a supremacist agenda, racism still thrives unfettered.

The architects of this offensive but refined, propitiatory strategy of perpetuating the status quo (racism) in a less offensive manner to soothe their guilty consciences, instead of boldly condemning and outlawing it, know just so well that no practitioner of racism stops to inquire about the origin of race before instituting his (more often than her) hateful practices; the biologically (genetically) determined skin colour of the victim is enough criterion for all of them. They and other members of the race of privilege can afford to speculate endlessly about the desirability of eliminating talk about the biological foundation of race while toying with ideas of its socio-institutional constructionism to take the wind out of its sails, because they do not have to endure the indignities that are suffered by those who are racially discriminated against. Those ideas are mere airy flights of fancy that do not alter the reality, vulgarity, cruelty, and inhomanity of the forced burden of racism on its victims.

Ultimately, however, the whole concept of race as practiced in twin world for purposes of discrimination and oppression becomes an exercise in absurdity, because every aspect of it proves to be an irrationality that eludes even its architects, many or all of whom will surely trip up when their ancestry is investigated and exposed, like the holier-then-thou gay-bashers whose own gay ways have been exposed to the light of day, much to their chagrin but comeuppance ; or the squeaky clean who accuse others of being soft on drug dealers, until they are caught with or doing drugs; or the self-professed animal rights activists who secretly wear fur coats while they vent venom on seal hunters and fur wearers; or philanderers who claim to promote family values against the backdrop of their clandestine wolfing activities; or cowards who are compelled to uphold laws against discrimination by their professions, but still don their evil masks and bed-sheet attire and display other luminescent symbols of oppression in the privacy of their world of darkness and homicidal deeds—lately they have discarded that apparel, and they now show their ugly faces boldly with encouragement from national leaders of twin world who belong in the same gutter as these low lives.

One would like to think that this racist insanity will end some day soon, but all indications point to its escalation under the unholy influence of religious and other bigots of twin world. We will therefore explore a few more areas where it is expressed before we can begin to evaluate our hopes for its overdue demise.

# Chapter 9
# Social inhomanity

And so the saga of self-contradiction still endures. In one breath, pinks espouse equality and entitlement of all persons to inalienable rights and justification of the continuing enslavement of some on the basis of their colour and warped pink views of their faculties. As some of that breed have stated blatantly, they are the master race that does not need to have empathic feelings for inferior races for whom any form of ill-treatment is befitting. They all subscribe to the fallacy of our world, uttered by a Supreme Court judge in regard to a colour-blind legal system, that browns are

> beings of an inferior order, and altogether unfit to associate with the *white* (my italics) race, . . . and so far inferior, that they had no rights which the *white* (my italics) man was bound to respect. . . . [They] were bought and sold, and treated as ordinary article[s] of merchandise and traffic, whenever a profit could be made by it"[1].

The author of these demeaning words is reported to have further said that those who framed the document of independence of his country knew that its terms would nowhere in the world be interpreted as embracing these inferior beings, as such a concession "would have been utterly and flagrantly inconsistent with the principles they asserted."[2] This frank expression of unadulterated racist prejudice is consistent with the current unabashed display of twin world's diehard racist pinks who vilify browns publicly, while others of their hypocritical brothers who want to present themselves as sympathetic liberals resort to euphemisms and racial cryptography to say the same things, much as they call the invasion of nation states to purloin their oil, diamonds, and other sources of wealth liberation. Con men who act like racists while claiming not to be racists think they can fool everyone by calling themselves nationalists—herrenvolk nationalists. History from the 15th century to date bears witness to the serious resolve with which all these vulgarities were expressed as the official attitude of these people, wherever they came and stole land and natural resources while enslaving the owners of those bounties, instead of dealing with them fairly and honestly according to their own laws that purport to advocate justice for all but should really be understood to mean justice for us ("just us"). So who are the knaves?   Some pinks of twin world have been greatly influenced by fittingly pontifical utterances and sentiments that they have imported from other worlds to express their conviction of pink superiority to other tribes: They have adopted and adapted such expressions as "The duty of the *white* (my italics) man is to conquer and control, probably for a couple of centuries, all the dark races of the world, not for his own good, but for theirs."[3] Theirs? They have also been impressed by insultingly racist statements of pink superiority like this one: "I do not agree that the dog in a manger has the final right to the manger even though he may have lain there for a very long time. I do not admit that right. I do not admit for instance, that a great wrong has been done to the Red Indians."[4] Today other racist public figures still call brown persons dogs and low lives—pathetic!

Regardless of authenticity and attribution in our world, all of these statements express the arrogant, insensitive, and offensive attitude that defines an unmistakable lack of regard for the homanity of other persons, and to say that no great wrong has been done to the millions of browns who have been mercilessly decimated by Krustan pinks is to betray abject callousness and depravity like that shown by those who have immortalized their depravity in war with photographs of their victims being humiliated by them, while they insensitively make fun of them in an arrogant pose of hegemonic triumph, with their boots resting on their victims' bodies.

Nevertheless, that does not annul the sensitivity of other pinks, such as that displayed in an utterance reported by Oakland Ross, quoting from an interview with a young soldier who admitted: "We have done some very, very dirty things"[5], occupying the lands of other people after decimating and displacing them; using them to inspect suspicious packages found in public places, so that if the packages blew up, they would be the casualties; terrorizing them and their families in their homes; burning down homes with their occupants inside; all done by "19 year old kids" (soldiers) from the occupying army who wield "absolute power" to occupy the homes of the oppressed for as long as they wish and to keep the residents as silent prisoners in their own homes while they murder people on the streets. When they have finished and left the home, they neglect to inform their strategically posted snipers who then shoot and kill the residents, "mistaking" them for insurgents as they go about their usual activities in their homes. Sometimes, as they say, they "see a man walking, he doesn't have to have a weapon", and they just shoot him. This is "the most ethical army" in twin world.

Elsewhere, others of them "burst through doors" shouting obscenities, shoot the persons that they encounter on every storey, and arrest and cast thousands of men into their many secret prisons. There they are subjected to degradation and torture like breaking their arms and skulls; water-boarding and sleep-depriving them in many inhomane ways like exposing them nude, electrocuting them via their testicles, and confining them to a solitary existence in tiny cells where the only sounds and lights are the loud noises and bright lights to which they are subjected continuously for days on end. Little do they realize that this despicable process of dehomanization helps to convert innocent people that they picked up randomly and detained arbitrarily into "terrorists" (their terminology). Their hollow licence for murder, conferred by their genocidal pink superiority that is based on hatred, spite, disrespect, barbarism and savagery coming from the most civilized tribe in twin world toward a poor, powerless people, is proof of their monstrous, fiendish inhomanity to which some of them admit indirectly, while others complain that these outrages are too soft to intimidate their victims. Meanwhile, they've denuded their victim countries of their professionals, literati, and common folk whom they murdered or else forced to seek refuge from their malice in neighbouring countries.

Echoing the sentiments of their elders who are reported to have borrowed from our world the derogatory remarks that they made about these browns, such as, "[They] are beasts walking on two legs"[6], these youngsters have also expressed their disdain for these people thus: our soldiers do not regard these people "as fully realized [homan] beings" and "After having such total control of so many lives, you can do anything you want to them. You can steal from them, sleep in their house, steal their car. You really can do anything. Anything. Anything."[7] This is the army that has been lauded as "the most moral army in the world"; the one that "shoots an elderly woman walking past them at a distance of about 100 meters" for no reason; the one that enters people's dwellings and throws all their belongings out the window on orders from their superiors; the one that is described by some decent others of its own as having "fallen in the realm of ethics" into the despicable pit of inhomane depravity. Ah, but they happen to be the fully realized homan beings. Those who want to dispute these accusations should provide good reasons why they create an atmosphere in which these things can and most probably do happen, judging from how else they treat these people. If the atmosphere were one of serenity and respect for the autonomy, personhood, and homan rights of others, these occurrences would be too remote a possibility to even imagine.

All of this is "the moral price tag of the occupation" as the soldier sees it, and as envisaged by its architects some 60 twin world years ago. Their plan was to damage the sources of livelihood of their victims: water wells, mills, etc., attack their clubs, coffee houses, meeting places, etc. Today they deny them free access to water, virtually forcing them to stock-pile it in buckets when they have been allowed access to their ration of it for a short period. Meanwhile, they enjoy copious, continuous free flow of water for all their needs, but they arrogantly, conveniently, and selectively disregard the drinking rights of others to the naturally flowing, common waters that they should be sharing equitably. The acquisition of water, which should be a basic homan right, is now being used by pink states as a weapon for oppressing brown states; but as one of the wise men of our world once observed, in the spirit of true humanity, when he was not justifying the dispossession of indigenous persons, "Nobody could think himself injured by the drinking of another man, though he took a good draught, who had a whole river of the same water left him to quench his thirst."[8] What these villains of twin world are displaying, however, is the double oxymoron of homan inhumanity at its best worst. (See chapter 9 of my *Our World and its Values* for a critical discussion of the distribution of material goods and my quarrel with this wise man's attitude).

Like some of the people of this world, their behaviour can be best described in the words used by Ilan Pappe in his book, *The Ethnic Cleansing of Palestine*: they cleanse and destroy brown villages by setting fire to them, blowing them up, and planting mines in the resulting debris, so that the erstwhile owners will be blown up when they return to rebuild them. They also circle their villages, expel the population outside the borders of their state by force, and then misappropriate their land. In this process during which they are forced to march without food and water, many of their victims die from thirst and hunger on the way. These and many other atrocities that continue to be perpetrated on browns bear stark witness to the homan inhumanity that exists in certain sectors of twin world. But who cares? Those that have the power to put a stop to these beastly deeds encourage them without shame, blaming the victims for their sad lot, in the same way that they have blamed the victims of their domineering and insulting behaviour for inviting the dirty things that they have done and are doing to them.

In an unparalleled similarity with events chronicled by Pappe from these same parts of our world from which they must have taken more than one page, the murderous gangs of twin world further make certain that they are accurate about their timing and place for perpetrating these crimes, and about those they hit, ensuring that they harm them without mercy, women and children included. They encircle their habitats, restrict their movements rudely and severely, and prevent them from making contact and trading with the outside world, thereby holding them at their mercy for supplies of water, food, medicines, and all the basic necessities of life, which they often deny them in a well calculated effort to decimate them. If that tactic does not work fast enough, they attack and kill them for no good reason, knowing full well that they have surrounded them and left them no route of escape from their evil acts of murder. And so it is that they will burst into any one of the villages and spray the houses with machine gun fire, killing many of the inhabitants. They then line up the children against a wall and spray them with bullets "just for the fun of it" before they leave, using a universal style of execution that is standard procedure for disposing of "vermin" and is being re-enacted wherever pink soldiers encounter brown civilians. Today they wrench them from their parents and lock them up (in seclusion) without regard for the permanent psychological trauma that they are inflicting on them—who cares if they are maimed; they are only brown children that we have the bubelical right to abuse, as amoral as it may seem.

Elsewhere in twin world, as Pappe's historical narrative relates about our world, "teenagers were shot with their hands tied behind their backs,"[9] and several hundred men of a village were shot while handcuffed. In another village more than 100 men were made to face the wall and shot in their heads from behind. The result of these heinous escapades was that over a period of 17 days 21 villages were destroyed, and during many of these murderous escapades young women were humiliated by being raped, as noted in the diary of the director of this entire operation who later became the leader of one of the new states of twin world. That is how new states are born in twin world, unjustly and with the connivance of all the big powers of that world who looked the other way while all these atrocities were being perpetrated by people who should have known better after suffering the same fate at the hands of another twin world tribe that wanted to wipe them off the face of the earth, in the same way that they are trying and succeeding to a degree to systematically get rid of these thorns in their flesh, as they describe their victims. But as fate would have it, they have not been able to get rid of these thorns, and that is why (ironically) intimidation, displacement, dehumanization, and wanton slaughter amounting to genocide are still going on today.

The foregoing events make it unmistakably clear that the ethic of happiness, individual and general freedom, and progress for all alike, irrespective of race or religion, as enshrined in twin world's statutes of coexistence in a spirit of tolerance and cooperation, is all cheap talk in the face of the overwhelming racism and arrogance that has gripped those who are parties to the formulation of these statutes. All over twin world those who have military power or are militarily empowered by their bully friends whose identities they do not hesitate to steal for carrying out their nefarious deeds, defy these statutes with impunity, and they violate the territorial boundaries of weaker states to steal their natural possessions and their lands. The bullies establish themselves as the supreme imperialist controllers of the economic resources of those states and regions containing them by their tactic of regime change. This hubristic aggressiveness and lack of respect for the other, coupled with his economic enslavement, is their illegitimate way of spreading democracy or securing their own borders against invasion of their state by them when they do not even present a palpable threat—a lot of hot air and fabrication to entrench their positions. Amidst this lawlessness, the club of hypocritical pink buddies remonstrates in unison, in stentorian tones, against those that they don't like for doing the same thing. They have defied resolution #4978653; they must be punished. All of them alike, or only some of them? Of course, some other members of the club who might not see things the way their bully bosses see them are forced to go along for the sake of retaining their favours as recompense for their sycophantic behaviour.

These usurpers dare to restrict immigration of browns to lands that they have stolen from them, preferring to populate them with other pinks to swell their own numbers and ensure that browns remain a "visible minority" that can be easily dominated. Brown sponsorships of family members take for ever, while those for pink families happen promptly. Now they speak of these lands as "our country" as in "our country is being taken over by browns", "they should go back to Afibika, etc., where they came from". And why don't they go back to Eubopa where they came from? They won't go back, because they are having a good time in stolen lands where their standard practice in these racist regimes is the promotion of state-sponsored assassination of any persons who openly oppose their imperialism, even if these others have been democratically elected and are running stable, productive, progressive, and non-aggressive governments. The dogs and the tails that wag them together conspire to punish this exercise in democracy by blockading such states and denying them exports of all locally manufactured goods to destroy their industries and impoverish them. Meanwhile, they are allowed imports only from the same oppressors who are trying to annihilate them, enacting vicious, racist, pink logic at its best worst.

On the other hand, those stooges who kowtow to their whims, even if they are running undemocratic, oppressive, and dictatorial governments that cut against the grain of what the imperialists claim to stand for, receive their total immoral and unfettered financial and military support and protection (even in their rigged elections), because they are pawns that are used to fight colonial battles for their masters against their own people for a taming price that buys their obsequious fealty, silence, and connivance. They are also allowed to export their goods to their benefactor states if they have a specified content of constituents from small states that use big states to retain their regional supremacy by throttling adjacent brown states. In the meantime, all of these superior beings are indirectly breeding and fomenting attitudes of resentment, revenge-seeking, and so-called terrorism (which is, in fact, freedom-fighting and logical reaction to centuries of racist provocation, oppression, exploitation, murder, and occupation) that history has repeatedly proved will ultimately result in the defeat of domineering pinks and their fawning pawns.

In case any present day pinks should be tempted to find fault with revenge directed at persons who are not responsible for past injustices, the browns of today's twin world wish to remind all critics that past racist pink policies and practices are still being perpetuated today on all browns by villainous descendants of the original villains. The historical indignities and assaults that pinks inflict on one brown at a time are only individual instances of the inherited, universal, state-sponsored policy of racist oppression by the ruling class that fully merits the mass response of equally violent rebuff. Their poignant significance cannot be minimized by invoking the excuse that they are incidental, mostly deserved, individual events that do not involve all browns at the same time, because they are firmly embedded in the existing culture of pink racism and they are the norm by which racists govern their lives and those of their victims, and by which the culture is perpetuated. Besides, pinks have state laws that protect and serve them and other laws that they apply prejudicially to humiliate and subjugate browns every day of their lives, while browns complain to their deaf ears about the raw deal that they are getting from them all the time. Colour consciousness and prejudice to "maintain the racial status quo", i.e., "the continued racial hegemony of whites in the subordination of blacks"[10] by the highest legal echelons of twin world are best limned for us in a different but parallel context by Linda Greene and other contributors to the same volume in which her article appears.

So it should not surprise anyone that browns react violently to the violence that is perpetrated on them by people who tell them to use constitutional means of changing their pitiful situation when all the cards have been artfully stacked against them to deprive them of the means of using those constitutional means to seek redress of their discontents. Pinks control all the constitutional avenues through which they ensure that legitimate complaints of browns are not heard, or, if they happen to be heard, that nothing comes of them, because to respond fairly to them will be tantamount to defeating the supremacist agenda of pink civilization. The only response they dish out is one of collective punishment of whole communities for the deeds of a few malcontents who dare to respond and react to terrorism from oppressors who now claim to be the real victims of terrorism. They think it is acceptable for them to react to individual acts of brown violence with mass violence, but not acceptable for browns to react likewise to systematic, sequential victimization of individuals and brown communities that is part of the pink universal policy of subjugation and repression.

This insecure, privileged class of people has always harboured fears of control of state and economic affairs by under-privileged browns who have for now been relegated to the shadowy fringes where they should be content to remain. Although it is not possible for all the members of their oppressing tribe to fill the few existing positions of power, they will not let browns fill them for fear of being outnumbered and losing their grip on power. That is why they refuse to see life from the brown's viewpoint, even twisting her expression of self-consciousness to mean the fostering hostility toward them. Browns may not express their frustrations with the existing system of oppression and exploitation; they should wait on pinks to determine what is good for them, even as they are stealing their lands and natural resources and enslaving them to labour for long, arduous hours in sometimes subhoman conditions. In this respect, the sorry plight of the Africans of the Congo that has been documented by Adam Hochschild in *King Leopold's Ghost*, like the equally heart-rending plight of the aboriginal peoples of the Americas that has been detailed by Ronald Wright in *Stolen Continents*, and like the beastly treatment endured by many aboriginal inhabitants of the rest of Africa and Australia whose lives have been largely decimated by colonizers, can be applied in their entirety to the fiendish situation in which the browns of twin world have also been forced to bear heavy crosses of torture and death. The following accounts of some of the events relating to the abuse of these peoples can, *mutatis mutandis*, be applied to the fate of the browns of twin world.

In parallel with what these authors have documented about

our world, pink brutes enslave them, chain them around their necks, and make them carry heavy burdens for miles and miles, over long stretches of time in what they call their journeys of exploration. If they complain or collapse under this strain, they are abandoned in the middle of nowhere, or else they are killed in cold blood for insubordination. Their right hands are severed and displayed in basketfuls to keep count of the untold numbers murdered, or as trophies, in the same way that their skulls are also misused as adornments on the stolen properties of their self-imposed masters whose litany of barbarous acts displays homan inhomanity at its beastly worst. These are the same dignified people who claim to be mature and civilized, and not the type to engage in such acts of barbarism, which can be perpetrated only by uncivilized, barbarous browns whose immaturity restricts their rights and disqualifies them from freedom but qualifies them eminently for slavery.

Taking another page from the brutality of the colonizers that Hochschild has documented, they also force them to gather rubber sap from vines in the forests of twin world under the most inhomane conditions, and they punish them with lethal floggings for failing to meet their daily quotas; they huddle them like cattle in holding compounds whence they fan out before the crack of dawn to descend into the bowels of the earth and dig out coal, gold ore, and other precious metals of their own land for the use of the pink usurpers. For this compulsory service they receive a pittance in wages that is designed to keep them in perpetual serfdom. In other areas of twin world browns are kidnapped and sold into slavery by Krustan missionary traders, especially if they are not baptized within their denominations. Their own unprincipled tribal chiefs also sell them for trinkets with which the invaders entice and reward them for the despicable act of merchandizing their people. On the international market men are sold for more money than women and children, and all are branded with red-hot irons like cattle en route to the market. (Lately the commodity value of women and children has multiplied exponentially as homan male depravity has intensified). Those who are near death resulting from suffering all kinds of deprivation are classified as valueless, since they cannot be used as currency for the purchase of commodities in the same way that live stock can be used as barter in the marketplace. Meanwhile, their lands and countries are traded in the marketplace without their knowledge, and they are evicted from them, or they are told that they are now the subjects of different masters on their own lands. The perpetrators of these unguddly acts do not see anything wrong with them, as long as they are being done to subhomans for their own benefit and for the benefit and advancement of the agenda of pink supremacy.

Available records of the atrocities carried out by the members of these vile occupying tribes, wherever they encounter indigenous peoples, vary only in locations of perpetration, but not in their sordid details. Everywhere people are chained by their necks while they are being marched from village to village (some dying of thirst and hunger on the way) where more of them are rounded up to be sold into slavery, for no other reason than that they are browns. They are whipped until they bleed from open wounds into which their depraved occupiers rub salt and pepper; used as targets for shooting practice; and have their heads cut off like chicken heads. Kidnapped women and girls are abused, and boys and able men are forced into the army. Resistance from any quarter is met with lethal force and humiliation by having the faces of resisters smeared with excrement, like perpetrating the ultimate insult on Muslim men held captive in Christian prisons by daubing make-believe menstrual blood on them.

Politically, pinks use the language of our world to vent their pig-headedness in denying browns recognition of their rights, e.g., "there is no question of granting the slightest political power to Negroes. That would be absurd. The *white* (my italics) men . . . retain all the powers."[11] Some others swear that "not in a thousand years" would they yield to brown majority rule, because that would be tantamount to committing political suicide, which no one in his right mind would want to do. So they devise the economic enslavement schemes referred to above, and they also take advantage of the prevalence of perduring poverty among the people, which makes them easy victims of bribery for the purpose of snitching on others. Those who don't toe the line are subjected to severe punishment and cruel death by shooting squads, lynchings, hangings from trees in public places, or decapitations. In the meantime, every pink state is trying to absolve itself of the heinous crimes that they are all committing by diverting attention to the crimes of other culprits in other parts of twin world while pretending to be benevolent in their dealings with browns "owned" by them. In the end, one has to again ask: who are the real savages? Those who are subjected to mass slaughter in many inhomane ways, or those who perpetrate these savage atrocities? Common sense says the latter are the savages, in spite of their efforts to shred and burn evidence that can substantiate these misdeeds, and in spite of peddling their degenerate civilization and religion that they have tried and are still trying to force down the throats of others who have their own civilizations and nobler ways of community living. Their selfish, confrontational, Krustan motto of "my way or the highway" in a world that offers enough room for people of widely varying opinions and beliefs to live side by side is a far cry from that accommodating and friendship-promoting motto of "live and let live" and *ubuntu* espoused by their victims.

Dependence on "savages" for menial and onerous tasks and utter dislike of them for the different people that they are generates the oxymoron of the wanted unwanted. Oppressors wish that these people were not here, because some of their own make them feel guilty about their treatment of them, but they also wish that they should be around to be used like homan tools and subhoman animals that cannot lay any claim to homane treatment. After all, who cares how tools are treated, but many people care about how subhoman animals are treated, and browns have been jailed for ill-treating animals, while many evangelical pinks still get away with killing animals or maiming and killing brown peoples. This is one of the many detestable double standards of twin world. Like the men of privilege whose atrocities were documented by Adam Hochschild, a pink who was brutalizing his brown labourers said that he did not care a d--- what anyone thought or said about his vile actions, because those who would judge him, if he ever had to face charges, were pinks like him; i.e., they would miscarry justice in his favour. Such things don't happen in our world; or do they?

But that sick attitude still prevails in twin world. In their police states or democratic dictatorships, kept intact by coteries of lawless police, some law courts, law-making machinery, army, and economy, pinks and their brown cronies do as they please, because they are beyond reproach and invincible, and the people have no power to change their sorry lot; these goons hold their lives in their murderous hands. If you have any doubts, they say, look at what our racist police can do to you with their guns, snuff you out fifty bullets at a time. We trade in legalized violence that we euphemistically style "law and order", and when it seems as if you are posing a threat to our superiority, we have no hesitation in unleashing a tyrannical reign of terror and violence against you in your misguided exercise of what you think is your constitutional right to universal freedom of speech and movement. Our brutal puppets, the trigger happy, lying, and fabricating occupying army of police, will dispel your dreamed-of freedoms in their sworn duty to secure our positions of power and superiority. Their motto is "to persecute and assault", to humiliate and strip-search browns for no reason and at any time that they appear to defy our authority or pose the remotest threat to it, not "to serve and protect" them. As they have been heard to boast, "we only shoot browns." Even when judges rule against them for violating your moral and constitutional rights by wantonly punching and kicking you in the head when they have wrestled you to the ground, and then unlawfully detaining and arresting you and lying about the incident to cover their butts, pinks continue to support their rogue tactics as one of the many ways of securing their tribal interests and buttressing pink supremacy—different "butts" at work.

All pinks wield vast victimizing power over browns simply by virtue of their vague degree of meagre pigmentation, compared to the ample amounts possessed by the people that they are oppressing, which makes one wonder again if quantitative advantage is in fact a disadvantage, or if more (possession) is paradoxically less (value) than less (quantity), or lack (of pigment) is qualitatively worth much more than abundance (of pigment). Mathematically and logically, that should not be the case, but nothing that these pinks do in their relationships with browns seems to make logical or mathematical sense. Degree of depigmentation, which matters so much to them, is at the core of their fatuous criterion of homan superiority. So what is all the racial fuss about when it does not even have a rational basis?

Those who harbour secret racist feelings, which they dissemble by decrying covert and overt institutional racism because it makes them look good, can stop consoling themselves; all forms of racism, covert and overt, individual and institutional, are based on the despicable attitude of denying the homanity of browns because of their skin colour, stereotyping them, and rendering them "irrelevant", as some "relevant" pink politicians brazenly said about a brown head of state and a "relevant" pink philosopher also said about a whole continent of browns about which he knew very little.

And those browns who delude themselves by also thinking that they are better than the rest, because they have arrived in the social stratum of pinks by marriage, companionship, or other ways of identifying with them by aping their ways and thereby qualifying for preferential treatment by them, can also start to face reality: they enjoy their preferred status at the discretion of those pinks who have allotted them a separate corner in their society where they must remain while the rest of their folk also remain shut out. To other pinks, they are still savage browns. In many situations they have become the tools that the oppressor uses to subjugate their own tribe, and they are always happy to oblige, so that they should not lose their pitiable position of favoured lapdogs. To show that they do not really belong and are tolerated as long as they toe the line that has been set for them, even those pinks who have recently escaped from despots in their homelands and are accepted into the pink fold as equals also discriminate indiscriminately, systematically, and bluntly against them as they do against all other browns. Their policy as a group is that browns must be taught and kept in their place, even if they pretend not to know it or think that they have risen above it. These considerations do not, however, nullify the genuineness of amorous and friendly relations that are sometimes established between persons of different skin colours, but they reflect the tradition and accepted practice in which such bonds have to struggle to survive. According to the racists, even intellectual pinks should not prefer to associate with intellectual browns when their racial duty is to associate only with those of their own colour, regardless of the wide gaps that might exist in cognitive and personal compatibility between them. The pink status of the intellectually and socially deprived of their tribe still qualifies them for a position far above that of the best brown minds in twin world. Asinine?

The beast named "racism" thrives on the existential helplessness and obligatory acceptance of their deprived status by its victims who lack the means to alter their lot for the better. It thrives on their failure to thrive by protecting pinks against competition from browns in jobs, housing, and the economy, since it makes the floor of the privileged class the glass ceiling of the underprivileged in all walks of life. It also renders their visible presence invisible (so-called invisible visible minorities), their stentorian screams against torture inaudible, and their concrete physical presence impalpable ("absent presence"), constituting a pathetic concatenation of oxymorons. Pinks have the power to make or break these poor wretches by bestowing their paternalism upon them or withholding it. And yet their fictive, irrational ideology of racial superiority can't maintain itself without acknowledgement by browns of the inferior status to which they have been relegated. We have seen this self-deluding, contrived superiority vanish like dew before the rising sun when they no longer exercise the absolute political power that enabled them to protect their simple, indigent brothers after the passage of government from them to browns. At this point their brothers have been forced to resort to the type of existence that was the sole preserve of browns while the pink *baas* (boss!) enjoyed the shelter from exposure that was provided by his brothers in government who spared no effort to sustain the lie of perfection that all of them had been living at the expense of browns. Today they are the pathetic panhandlers, while browns are still content to earn their traditionally imposed pittances with becoming dignity. They solicit sympathy from their pink brothers by showcasing the shanties in which a scanty minority of them live (versus the millions of browns who have always lived in shanties all their lives) as if to say, "look at how browns are treating us with they newly won freedom and rule."

Chickens should never be allowed to come home to roost!

In their cunning, pinks ensured that when they surrendered the reins of government to browns they kept economic supremacy, in effect still remaining the oppressors who are unwilling to share the fruits of the earth with those who saved their butts from a bloody revolution. Meanwhile the greedy and unprincipled browns, who now have their hands in the till, are sacrificing the lives of their own people on the altar of money by stealing what little monies are due to them to keep them afloat in a pink economy where their ancestral means of subsistence have been supplanted by an economy of trade based on money. What a pity that their concept of self-government cannot rise above the gutter level of irresponsibility, theft, and fraud to enable them to see through the snares that have been laid for them by their racist pink benefactors by appealing to their greed, which trumps their solemn duty to the people who made it possible for them to hold high offices by dying and suffering in "the struggle". These unreflective low lives are content to swell their pockets with money while the people go hungry and perish from treatable and preventable diseases, which they deny while they are selling the people's most precious inheritance—their land—to all and sundry who can swell their pockets further with more money. They have climbed into bed with recent oppressors of the people, and they have no shame in lauding them for reasons that others can only speculate about. But in their world of ubiquitous government corruption, the reason should not be farther to seek than the proverbial thirty pieces of silver rendered in multiples of the currency of their land.

The pink racial game is a crafty, evil cabal: first they concoct a delusional myth about the superiority of pink over brown; then they contrive evidence to bolster the myth, devoting their lives to the task of keeping it alive and never stepping back or allowing anyone to evaluate and question their domineering hoax, lest its barrenness should be exposed. They tell themselves the lie, and then impress it upon everyone else repeatedly until both groups believe it without adequate or any reason. This process of self-aggrandizement by stereotyping and debasing the other to make her always appear and believe herself to be inferior, has smothered their respect for universal truth and soothed their obdurate consciences into a false complacency with their own version of truth regarding the status quo; hence their expression of shock at the violent reactions of browns to the abuses that have been heaped upon them through the years by successive generations of pinks. The children learn the bad habits of their parents to trample on others for their survival, and they adopt the same kinds of inhomane and arrogant attitudes toward the homan beings that they have been taught to despise as a prerequisite to preventing the shattering of their racist myth of superiority. That is why when some of them hold political office they can call browns "cockroaches" with impunity—is the pot calling the kettle black? Their despicable parents even traumatize or brainwash them by dragging them along to watch the lynching and burning of browns for no good reason. They learn that the only way of dealing with browns and infusing pride into their parents is to despicably "kick some butt", humiliate, and torture, not to conciliate or negotiate in good faith. Nevertheless, when it comes time for using the athletic prowess of browns for personal gain or for the glory of their pink states, and when they steal art, music, philosophy, mathematics etc. from browns and claiming these skills as their own, they do so without shame and without acknowledgement of having stepped down the ladder of hubris to avail themselves of what they lacked, in their perfect homanity, from lowly brown ranks. What a shame that browns like the originator of the music and art of rock and roll and others in twin world whose tunes have been stolen and translated languished in relative poverty and obscurity, while those who stole their music and art acquired legendary status and amassed huge fortunes. Of course, no one in the pink camp acknowledges the theft; they say what they did was not illegal. But it was immoral.

Everyone in twin world is familiar with the sham *de jure* system of equality before the law, equality of opportunity to jobs and shelter, and equal access to educational institutions behind which pinks take shelter to escape censure for the *de facto* discrimination to which they subject browns every day of their lives. They deny browns admission to predominantly pink universities on "merit", in the face of odds that are always stacked against them, because their backgrounds have been deprived in all the respects that should qualify them for admission, such as their inner city schools that are poorly staffed and equipped—what with those in authority favouring parochial and other private schools. In this latter situation, even the bright ones among them have to depend on affirmative action strategies to secure places that they would otherwise be denied for lack of funds or simply because they are browns who don't have the rights that their pink counterparts enjoy. In the case of jobs, the standard transparent pretext for excluding them is that they lack the relevant job experience, e.g., Canadian experience, or they are overqualified for the non-professional jobs that they are prepared to settle for to ensure their survival in their hostile world; but pinks who lack the same job experience always end up getting the jobs and gaining that experience on the job, while browns are expected and required to acquire it magically before they start on their first job. In addition to this absurd and trashy exercise in brown frustration, colour coded job protection for pinks is applied rigidly at all levels to ensure their economic advantage over them, which in turn ensures socio-political advantage and the perpetuation of brown poverty and pink supremacy and pink domination for ages to come.

When the same people apply for accommodation, pinks end up acquiring the apartment that was denied the brown ten minutes earlier on the pretext that it was no longer available. As for justice, it might as well be colour-coded, because it was never and still is not colour-blind. Browns are singled out for compilation of information on them (styled "contact carding", which is our own euphemism for racial profiling) to track their movements in anticipation of the crimes that they are sure to commit, as is their wont. So catch and debase all of them before they offend, especially if they are seen walking in predominantly pink communities. Minor crimes by browns are trumpeted on the news screens all the time, while pink crimes of equal or even greater gravity are played down or kept off the screens to create the impression that only browns are the rotten apples. No one denies that there are rotten apples among them, just as there are among pinks of all ranks, including high office holders in their communities who enjoy the sympathy and protection of higher ranking officials who act as their apologists; but the effect of this biased reporting is to create the false impression and justify the illegitimate conclusion that all and only browns are criminals and must be profiled accordingly. Pinks claim that they are always doing something wrong. They alone do wrong? Always?

As we have already observed, the leap from *some x are p* to *all x are p* is an illogical mental and practical feat that can exist only in the prejudicial corridors of twin world. Besides, it is well known that the nature and severity of punishment for the same crime depends on whether it is committed by brown against pink, in which case it is harsh (death sentences are common in these instances); but when the order is reversed, the sentence can be as light as a slap on the wrist or a reprimand, if not complete exoneration; yes, exoneration for cold-blooded murder, especially at the hands of those whose duty is to serve and protect. Most of these vile manoeuvres are executed craftily without overtly breaking state laws, but they still remain a blatant defiance of moral laws and conduct.

Will these selfish, insincere, and unguddly pink attitudes that are so insulting to brown personhood ever change? Only after pink noses have been forcefully rubbed in the dust.

# Chapter 10
# More Social inhomanity

Some people believe that the brown-phobia of pinks is a mere expression of their irrational fear for anything that is other than "self", especially when it is coloured differently, and that is what helps to propel them into these illogical acts of stupidity. They magnify differences and minimize similarities and somehow end up with a formula that makes them better than and superior to everyone else in all the respects in which they differ. That would not matter much if it were just the thought; but the thought expresses itself in the immense suffering that they inflict on the "inferior" breeds who are thereby forced to develop mistrust and hatred of the evil deeds and their vile perpetrators. Strangely enough, some of these superior individuals appear to realize at some point that they are being irrational, but instead of yielding to their consciences and abandoning their indecent ways, they become the victims of "bad faith" by denying to themselves and to the world that they are acting like jerks and displaying abject hypocrisy by preaching theoretical care and compassion when they are actively oppressing others. Hence their idiotic talk that epitomizes arrogance, and their many invented reasons to justify their unjustifiable, opprobrious behaviour: pinks are destined by Gudd to rule and browns to serve as slaves, which explains why pinks want to be served when they have been elected into office to serve others; pink blood is pure and should not mix with brown blood, which will dilute it, contaminate it, and debase the entire superior pink race. (See reference [8], page 58).

They also try to stereotype browns before browns have had the chance to define themselves, etching out a stigmatizing image of them that then becomes the official one into which they rigidly huddle together all browns, regardless of the vast differences in character, cognitive ability, and social standing that obtains among them. Every member of the brown race is forced into the mold carved out by these scurvy racists, even if she does not fit the mold; they will forcibly squeeze her into it, lying to her and to themselves about her attributes to achieve their ignoble objective of creating the self-fulfilling prophecy of inferiority that they are inculcating. Hence their offensive use of unending lists of despicable and derogatory, but universally and indiscriminately applied terms to describe them, like: brutish, beastly, savage, ugly, lazy, immoral, stupid, ignorant, wild, and uncultured, as if anyone who has been actively practicing a culture for centuries can be logically accused of not being cultured. The illogical assertion is the customary racist and oxymoronic piffle with which pinks thoughtlessly tar browns. They pretend that it is possible for a community of persons to exist without a culture that knits them into a distinct tribe with an identity of its own, as long as they are not that uncultured tribe. Well, they might as well carry their absurd assertion further and claim the existence of persons without spatially locatable bodies, which they do in their ghost stories. They have assumed the right to decide on the attributes that they will assign to other people to define them, so that they can define themselves in contrasting glowing terms against their vulgar image of the people that they are trying to denigrate. Browns don't have a problem of self-recognition and self-worth; they are a problem for the self-appointed pink master race that paradoxically needs them to define itself.

The "good" pinks soothe their guilty consciences with inane rationalizations of this irrational fear, ignoring its roots and its disreputable manifestations in all the ways that we have mentioned, ignoring also its *de facto* immoral character, but rather questioning its *de jure* violation of the homan rights of those who are subjected to global racist discrimination. They pat themselves on their backs for having taken a stand for equal rights and against injustice, even if nothing constructive or remedial results from that stand, because they know that they dare not betray the pink cause for which all of them live by advocating a change to the status quo. So they end up meting out the same undignified treatment to their brown victims, but they exonerate themselves by blaming their actions on the system that imposes more rigorous demands on browns for any kind of recognition e.g., qualification for homane treatment, than it does on pinks. They claim to be powerless to change the system; and that is where it ends for them, because they have no idea of what it is to live with daily derogation, insults, and maliciously imposed hardships. Their favourite self-exonerating ruse is to proclaim that they have brown friends, who are even privileged to use their pink toilets (asinine); so they know (indeed, they do) and decry the humiliation that browns endure. Regrettably, sympathy doesn't make their friends pinks, only déclassé browns with choice excrement. Looking at their deprived lives from afar, but not living any of their experiences, these pinks urge browns to endure the hardships imposed on them by pink selfishness with patience, pointing to the limited brown participation that exists in some less consequential pink activities, if only to make them believe that they count like everyone else in their pink ranks. The strategy often succeeds in appeasing some browns who fail to recognize this hijack, and it also buys time and peace of mind for both the "good" and the mean-spirited pinks, allowing them scope to clamp down in other areas of consequence that they wish to reserve solely for themselves.

We see, therefore, that while life is relatively easy for pinks who only have to dish out dirt customarily and without effort, it is always difficult for browns who have to swallow the goo or wallow in it, willy-nilly. They depend on the pink architects of their misery to release them from it, because they have been rendered helpless by the restrictions imposed on them by these same brutes who have left them with no route of escape on their own. They have locked them into slavery and thrown the key away, because they fear to unleash the latent capabilities of their victims, if they should by chance grant them equal opportunities and a level playing field in all avenues of life. And so they play the hypocrisy game all the time by opening up part of the field, but ensuring that browns don't meet the requisite standards for admission into those fields, especially the economic ones where academic and technical qualifications are useless if they cannot facilitate entrance into the economic domain. Ask the PhDs and the MDs who are driving taxis, washing dishes, and doing other menial jobs. If any brown is lucky to get the job for which she has been trained, she can forget promotion, because in almost all pink establishments that sacred privilege is reserved for pinks only.

It is no wonder that many browns succumb to the pessimism and existential nihilism described by one author as "a pervasive sense of utter meaninglessness, dependency, self-loathing and impotence . . . a life without hope that constitutes a severe threat to [their] survival"[1], an existential anguish resulting in different forms of aberrant behaviour imposed on them by the entire machinery of pink oppression. When their lives acquire these absurd dimensions that are occasioned by the daily travail of their very existence, and when quality and quantity ebb from those lives, they clamour in vain to those who brought them the salvation that comes wrapped in their holy books, only to find that they have been presented with Trojan horses. Even those misguided ones who thought that they had arrived in the ranks of the few pinks who have accepted them for conforming with the stringent, inflated standards and requirements demanded of them (like denouncing their own culture), but not of pinks (they never have to denounce their culture; they force it on everyone), discover to their utter dismay that the rest of the pinks into whose ranks they think that they have been genuinely assimilated still regard them as inferior to them, and they obligingly honour them with the disdainful deference that is commensurate with their inferior brown status.

As we have already noted above, the society of twin world is plagued by problems with oppression of the have-nots by the haves and by other cliques that have installed themselves as the sovereign lords of the people, sucking their wealth as leeches suck blood from their hosts, and elevating themselves far above the people that they regard as commoners with whom they cannot mix. These homans are so misguided as to think that they have special carcasses that can't be touched by "commoners", when they are mere flesh, bones, and red blood (blue blood lacks enough oxygen to sustain the lives of those who claim to have it, and would therefore impair their ability to live off the rest of the people like the bloodsucking leeches referred to above). Blue-blooded persons, so called, have been smart enough to set themselves apart as kings, queens, lords, and masters, and have exempted themselves from earning a living by the sweat of their brows like everyone else who didn't have the wile to declare himself a sovereign. To see them carrying themselves around with pomp and airs of superiority, when they are not stooping to steal benefits due to their poorer subjects, is as sickening as it is to watch those who have been elected to serve the people passing themselves off as their lords and masters who must be obeyed without question, even when they are lying to them. Pomp and lying seem to be the essential attributes of those who have positioned themselves to steal from others in all sectors of twin world, and anyone who questions the *ultra vires* status of either group or the inhomanity of them and their friends already stands accused and convicted of lack of patriotism or of treason.

The tradition of lying and torturing to have their way is not new to the modern pinks of twin world; it dates back several centuries. Weaker tribes of indigenous peoples were always accosted by strangers who came into their midst to steal all their possessions in the guise of civilizing them, as if the aboriginals had invited them or hinted that they were not happy with their own civilizations and desired the depraved type of civilization that the strangers were hell-bent to impose on them. Needless to say, they were then, and still are, always hiding their ulterior motives and vested interests when they claim honourable intentions or benevolence, a virtue that is as far from their scheming minds as the sun is from Neptune or Uranus. That this is always the case is borne out by their unceasing efforts to portray their honourable role in shaping the happy destiny of their victims in the face of glaring historical evidence to the contrary. Their trail is littered with the death, plunder, destruction, and inhomanity that reflect their true nature and their unceasing attempts to erase any remnants of the national pride of those whom they degraded and slaughtered while they stole their lives and lands. Conquerors or thieves, or whatever these pink invaders are called, always alter the history of the valorous struggles of indigenous peoples against conquest and humiliation to portray themselves as benefactors and saviours to whom the people should be eternally indebted for saving them from themselves, while branding their resisters as murderers.

They always depict their victims as savages and cowards who launched barbarous attacks against them on their property, the property on which they found browns living since the beginning of time and out of which they have expelled them with treachery, brutality, and murder by the millions. They put themselves up as the good guys who are only defending their rights to that property and trying to bring civilization and freedom to a free people, until they enslave them. They claim to be bringing democracy to a people who have lived by consensus of opinion for centuries and who have not ridden roughshod over the will of their minorities or allowed the few to take advantage of the majority by cunning, cruelty, and lying; who have not suppressed freedom of speech and action or promoted inequality among citizens with marginalization of a majority of them for irrelevant reasons of skin colour and religion. The broken promises of peaceful coexistence and the dishonoured contracts into which they entered for the lands that they stole from the aboriginals stand out as incontrovertible proof of the insincerity of their proclamations of the equality of all persons that they profess, and as a glaring indictment of their pathetic unreliability. Their principle of equality applies only among themselves and does not embrace those from whom they steal to hoard possessions, while leaving with nothing their victims who are accustomed to distributing wealth and possessions among all citizens to ensure the survival of everyone in the tribe. These guys practice a selfish, vicious, bloodthirsty, hoard-all type of capitalism; the virtues of communalism and compassion are alien to them.

They have been known to destroy property and produce that they cannot unfairly and forcibly appropriate, rather than leave it for the benefit of those that they came to civilize with their uncivil manners, Krustanize with their vile unKrustan behaviour, and liberate (from what?) with their cruel enslaving actions. Wherever they have been, they have left an infamous trail of devastation behind, although they will deny it as vehemently as they deny their racism, but their victims know that it is true, because they have lived and are still living with those acts of pillage and naked discrimination. Anyone who rightly accuses them of the racism that they vocalize and practice becomes the object of their extreme wrath, and if she is one of their tribe, they will even ostracize her for telling the truth. Only lies that breed evil are acceptable in their world. As we have already noted, when it suits their selfish interests, they pretend annoyance at some of their tribe in other parts of twin world who engage in their kind of behaviour, and they employ the shady but highly transparent ploy of berating them as the best way of diverting attention from their misdeeds and directing public attention to someone else who is behaving in the same obnoxious fashion as they are doing. When foreign dictators are killing their citizens for demanding their rights, these cats are the first to play holier-than-thou saviours while they are assaulting their own citizens for exercising their rights of assembly.

They mouth ostensibly sincere apologies for all categories of the inhomane treatment and abuse that they meted out to browns in the not so remote past, but they do nothing about the inhomanities, injustices, and genocides that they are still perpetrating on them today. Phantom commissions to address old issues of only emotional exploitation, which provide a platform for the aggrieved to vent their emotions, are just that. They are meant to appease the aggrieved and to keep their mouths shut for ever while the business of pink supremacy and brown exploitation and dehomanization carries on as usual. After all, some truths and untruths have been vented by the small-fry operators without exacting any confessions, apologies, or redress from the big-time directors in the capital cities of twin world, socio-economic oppression continues unabated, and a bogus form of reconciliation has been imposed. Pinks have hoodwinked browns into pardoning their misdeeds and saving their skins from the same kinds of abuses that they inflicted on them, and browns have allowed them to continue to heap evil on them in more subtle ways, while they fondle and pre-occupy themselves with the toys of political freedom that these scalawags have allowed them to play with as they carry out their long-term program of pink domination. Browns can forget their dream of the abandonment of pink supremacy as a philosophy of life, or of equality of relationships as a way of life; that can and will never happen, because the survival of the pink tribe depends on its persistence. They always have to rule on what is best for themselves and what is "plenty good" for their browns inferiors. (See page 138: "plenty good for an Indian.")

It is not surprising, therefore, that when the people who have been deceived complain about how they are being treated, pink governments callously wave them off with announcements that they are still working to resolve their cases, cases at which they have been working for centuries. The best they can promise is that they need another century to address the problems adequately so that they can *begin* to *start* to *commence* (gibberish) to find a devious way to appease the claimants. If that is not a cheap way of stalling the issues, what is? It is quite obvious, even to a child, that when anyone engages in such idiotic talk he has no intention of settling any issue, especially with the dismal track record that these frauds have established over the centuries. Their insincerity and chicanery are as legendary as their lack of respect for the personhood of others.

In sheer desperation, the dispossessed resort to physical but non-violent means of protesting their unfair treatment by these vultures, but they are met with violence and imprisonment under laws that are fashioned to keep them in check, so that they are not able to bring their grievances to attention. And then, to crown the insult, ignorant pink citizens who are squatting on land that does not belong to them, but to which they claim to have title, turn against the rightful owners of the land, demanding their eviction and incarceration under pink laws for disrupting their comfort and free movement, as if browns have had comfort in all the centuries of deprivation and dispossession to which they have been subjected. But what do they care about the comfort or rights of savages, as long as they are comfortable and are protected by their pink laws that victimize the rightful owners of the land on which they are squatting. The ignorant, arrogant fools have not bothered to acquaint themselves with the sordid history of how their forebears acquired those lands underhandedly and unjustly from their owners; they only know that they are entitled by their unjust pink laws to those properties.

Regrettably, this despicable behaviour is not limited to one isolated section of twin world, leaving the rest unblemished; it prevails wherever the presence of the usurpers has cursed the people's lives, infecting even the circles in which clear thinking should prevail. The result is willful blindness to the history of oppression and its effects on the thinking and actions of brown populations and students, which results in what pretends to be genuine pink criticism of their demands appearing as racist ranting that misses its point. One observation relevant to this attitude in twin world has come from a writer from our world who has contrasted the "clearly silly and outrageous" demands of "Negro" students with "the disinterested and *usually highly moral* claims of the *white* rebels"[2] (my italics). Does this imply that the claims of "Negro" students are always base and immoral, perhaps even amoral, other than also being silly and outrageous? Is this the language of rationality or of racism? Even after applying the principle of charity, we are still left with concerns about the implications of such statements whose authors claim that they are not racist, because they are not racist persons and cannot, therefore, utter racist statements. But could they be blinded to the facts by a lack of objectivity caused by being an integral part of their racist community and thus believing their words and actions to be the norm that should be accepted without question, like the right that they claim to land that they have misappropriated?

Indeed, their blindness is ubiquitous. When the people who have been deprived of their rights try to repossess their stolen lands, the outcries of the land thieves, who are claiming infringement of their rights to stolen property on which they are squatters, proclaim how hard they have worked on the lands of which these savages are now trying to un-democratically dispossess them; forgetting that they undemocratically forced the people from their lands and killed them brutally in the process of stealing them. These uncivilized regimes of indigenous peoples have no sense of fairness, they cry. Fairness? Where was it when they and their children continued to live off the fat of the land while its rightful owners and their children were starving to death, because they had to toil on "their" land while they (usurpers) were bowling or engaging in other trivialities of life? Where was it when they failed to leave "enough and as good" for others, appropriating >87% of the land that proved to be fertile and leaving the arid <13% for brown squatting, until they discovered minerals on it, at which point they promptly robbed them of it too, summarily bull-dozing their modest dwellings and huddling them in tents? If there has to be fairness, let it be fairness for all, not only for the select few who belong to chosen tribes. Every homan being desires and deserves respect, fairness, and justice, by virtue of her homanity, regardless of the colour of her skin. These natural virtues are colour-blind, and they should not be denied to some persons, without moral justification, for the same foolish reason that they are made accessible to and are enjoyable by others, viz., skin colour.

Since moral codes in twin world are not different from those in our world, their utilitarian principle requires that those who claim to have the superior morality that is lacking in others do their utmost to promote the greatest happiness of all without sacrificing the good of some persons for the good of others. They should eliminate suffering among peoples of all creeds, colours, and tribes, respect their basic homan rights, and let them live their lives without hindrance from anyone. However, the moral history of colonization and occupation in twin world is one of ruthless exploitation, oppression, inequity, plunder, and murder to maintain the superiority of the few over the many and erect a monument to immorality. When the land thieves have been forced by circumstances to give up their control of those lands, they have left behind desolation, poverty, and death. But they still have the audacity to return under the cloak of their religion to try to tell the people how to deal with social realities that they have accepted, inciting them to harm the persons implicated in those realities, instead of helping them to cope. Pink missionaries preach their distorted values to Afibikans, urging them to kill gay persons in their country, because where they live, they have vilified but not been able to strangle this same class of persons; their state laws will not allow them that liberty; so the best way they have to gratify their hypocritical egos is to impose their will on browns. If the tables were turned, would they allow browns to tell them how to be inhomane to their gay communities by killing them or by any other means? Of course, not; they are only happy as long as they can still give them orders, sow dissension among them, and diminish their numbers and the threat that they pose to pink supremacy.

On the other hand, when the same persons that they dispossessed want to come to the prosperous lands of their heretofore enslavers to seek work so that they can earn a pittance to help them survive the ravages of hunger and other ills legated by those who are now living off the spoils that they looted from their colonies, they are shunned and declared undesirables who are barred from entering their lands—they threaten our tribal and *democratic* character. These legendary, illegal immigrants into brown lands now pass laws to outlaw them, and politicians gain popularity based on their resolve to keep this vermin out of their sacred countries and to discriminate against those who have already entered, in order to force them out. In the meantime, in those countries where they have struck deep roots, new foreigners who have come to join the descendants of the original colonialists display their arrogance and audacity by asking third and fourth generation brown citizens of their host countries where they came from and when they arrived in "our country", simply because they have a different complexion from them. They know that they have more clout than the aboriginals and the fourth generation brown citizens merely by virtue of their lighter skin hue, which is a passport to entitlement in what they pontifically call their country.

A brown friend told his brown friend how one of these arrogant pink immigrants asked him, "how du ju laek ze weazer in auver kontry?" to which he replied, "I was not aware that I am in

Bavinia (a region in Eubopa from which this self-assured fool had recently emigrated), I thought I was in Konato" (a state in Noambika where they are both immigrants). As this friend so curtly concluded, "He promptly shut up, because he realized that I could pinpoint the specific area in his country of origin from which he came." He quite literally retreated from his attempt to assert his pink superiority with his tail between his legs, realizing that he had been stripped of his superiority complex and exposed for the fraud that he is, claiming ownership of a country in which he was an obvious recent arrival who was taking advantage of the tradition of his kind to place themselves in authority over browns who are only theoretically supposed to share the same rights with him. A standpat pink twaddler immigrant also ironically chided a pink fellow immigrant who was protesting infringement of brown rights, expressing disgust at the admission of people like her into "our country".

Amidst of this gloomy atmosphere of crass domination, there are the select few of the ruling class who have genuine homanistic leanings that prompt them to recognize that they are called upon to relieve the many areas of suffering in their world that are caused by the arrogance, lack of compassion, and greed of their kind, and they should be duly acknowledged and respected for their homanity and forthrightness. They realize that "no man is an island" unto himself, that no one is completely insulated from the "slings and arrows of outrageous fortune", and that solutions of brown social burdens require empathy with those who are facing problems that have been cast upon them by their pink brothers, remembering also that what goes around comes around. They spare no effort to uplift others by showing concern and care, and by promoting their well-being out of respect for their feelings, homan dignity, and aspirations, which are no different from their own and from those of everyone else who is privileged to live in twin world. They have learnt to exercise respect for the autonomy of underprivileged persons in a dignified way, recognizing that no one has the right to place impediments in the way of any who would avail themselves of the natural and man-made benefits that their world has to offer, and that all persons are entitled to an equal share of the fruits of twin world. As Jean Jacques Rousseau said, "The fruits of the earth belong to us all, and the earth itself to nobody. . . . [Therefore] it is plainly contrary to the law of nature that the privileged few should gorge themselves with superfluities, while the starving multitude (sic) are in want of the bare necessities of life."[3]

The fact that certain well positioned sections of the population can be credited with being responsible for generating some of the benefits that are available to all the citizenry does not disqualify others from sharing those benefits, because of their politics, creed, race, colour, etc. This interdependency does, but should not, expose some to victimization by others who flout their entitlement by virtue of being part of the ruling clique, or by simply being members of the pink herd. None should be sacrificed for the good of others in a world of justice and fairness, where everyone's right to life should be respected and promoted, besides allowing each one to decide alone what to do with her life. Other persons may advise or help, but they may not coerce or impose their will as pinks are accustomed to doing with browns, individually and collectively.

One can virtually hear them gloating about their one-upmanship over browns: our policies also make it difficult, if not impossible for you to afford the cost of medical services, a decent, nourishing meal, and even the cost of water, which nature provides abundantly, but for which we are making you pay through your noses; and soon we will be making you pay for the air that you breathe, which we also own, because we have appropriated space and the air that fills it for our missiles. Then you will all succumb to starvation, ignorance, and disease, which will be good riddance, although we still need you to perform the menial tasks that are below our dignity to perform. Yes, we fly first class to hold twin world summits about your poverty and hunger where we gorge ourselves lavishly on everything edible, and where we enjoy billion dullam security to protect us from louts like you. We even attend those summits under the inebriating influence of the expensive drinks that we imbibe to help cloud our minds to your reality, and where we display our dismal ignorance of what we are about by reading from inappropriate scripts, because we don't speak from the heart; we only rattle off the lies that have been written for us to read like automatons. If you protest at these elite gatherings, we have our world's brutal police goons assault, maim, and detain you arbitrarily and indiscriminately just to teach you a lesson not to question your inhomane, larcenist masters, thanks to the unfair taxes that we have imposed on you while we and our corporate friends enjoy a ride on your backs. It is sadly true, as one highly religious chiseler said, that "the poor (the undesirable desirables) will always be with us" to walk on and to sustain our economies.

Of course, once browns are in the these pits of misery where they eke out a mere existence, their aspirations fade, their purpose in life evaporates, and they no longer care about their limited standards of erudition that frustrate every spark of inventiveness or desire for discovery, which their counterparts who live in surroundings that promote these values enjoy, and then it appears as if they are not cognitively capable of ameliorating their doleful situation or lifting themselves out of it. Their exploiters then dare to label them as lazy savages who are unfit to mingle with them and deserve to be kept far enough away, so that they do not taint the purity of the pink tribe.

Nevertheless, these conditions of oppression and privation have not dulled the inventive minds of browns who surprised their oppressors with inventions like those of some of the underprivileged persons of our world who have left their mark in it with their inventions, proving the oppressors to be contemptible liars. To quote just a few: George W. Carver who invented many uses for the peanut; Percy L. Julian who first synthesized cortisone; Lewis H. Latimer who invented the carbon filament for electric lights; Granville T. Woods who invented the first telegraph that facilitated communication between moving trains and train stations; Garrett A. Morgan who invented the gas mask and the traffic signal with automated "stop" and "go" signals; Patricia Bath who invented the Laserphaco Probe for the treatment of cataracts; Siyabulela L. Xuza, a youngster who recently had a planet (Siyaxuza) named after him, developed cheap, safe, efficient rocket fuel; William Kamkwamba, another youngster, defied starvation crises to provide his doomed village with electricity and running water by crafting a windmill out of scrap materials; and many others listed in "Black Inventors A-Z". Pinks of twin world can try their utmost to deny or try to erase the achievements of browns, but they will persist through time like those of the "blacks" of our world that cannot be denied or erased. Those who do not want to credit them with intellectual ability that is second to none may successfully suppress them, in the same way that they have suppressed their history and replaced it with their scurvy lies, meant to discredit browns while placing pinks in a better light from where they can assert their contrived superiority, but they will be crushed by the truth before they can smother it.

In our own world a "black" presented an MA dissertation on the archived history of the struggles of his people against the usurpation of their land by settlers, but it was rejected by a "white" university for its forthrightness in representing the uncomfortable truth about the initial contact between the two groups as the latter began to spread their tentacles in the new land that they had "discovered" together with its inhabitants who were counted with their livestock (which they brought with them or most likely found there). The university told him to alter the facts to conform to the distortion and fiction that was being spun about how the settlers discovered uninhabited but populated land, and how they met with these marauding hordes of blacks (blacks maraud; settlers explore and discover) who were migrating from somewhere in the north in search of places where they could settle; all lies that do not explain how it is that skulls of the precursors of modern man found in that country predate the arrival of colonialists by centuries. The fiction served to justify their mendacious claim to what they called their country, in the same way that others in twin world recite the self-serving lie that "their country" is being taken over by foreigners that they have branded as undesirables, conveniently forgetting that their forebears slaughtered millions of the original owners of what they now call "their country". Some of them still have the nerve to tell so-called visible minorities to go back where they came from, when they should be leading the way by going back to where they came from. Needless to say, he would not agree to that blackmail and sell-out of his people's history, and he never got that degree. Is he the only one who has suffered humiliation and denial of recognition of his intellectual prowess at the hands of Krustans and their equivalents? Not by any means. The history of browns everywhere is replete with this kind of outrage.

And so the lies, repression, exploitation, dehomanization, and oxymoronic obscenity of luxurious living in the midst of poverty, misery, starvation, and death all continue to thrive in the same crucible of time by dint of the discrimination that has kept browns in the gutter, and the greed that has dispossessed them of even the little that they have managed to rake together for their survival. Will this evil situation outlive time? Its deluded architects think so, simply because they have pulled it off thus far; but the brown tribes of twin-earth will not be pummelled into pessimism by the adverse trend of past and present events in their lives, however much their oppressors are trying to keep them down with the aid of dictators from among their own people. The silver lining to this dark cloud of pink oppression and exploitation that has been hanging over twin world and its browns for centuries is spreading, the cloud is receding, and as sure as day succeeds night, a new era of buoyant radiance has dawned in Afibika and other brown territories, thanks to their undaunted youth. Salvation is no longer a forlorn dream, but an imminent reality that is sending shivers down the spines of the pink oppressors of twin world; hence their clandestine incitement of clashes and civil war among the people, and their utilization of the principles of initiatives like Global 2000 and NSSM from our world detailed on pages 198-199.

# Chapter 11
# Governmental inhomanity

Amidst this brown hope for future bliss, the forces of pink evil continue to inject despair and suffering: life expectancy among browns in twin world remains deplorably low; many children do not survive beyond five years of age or develop normally physically and cognitively, if they are lucky to survive beyond that age (a result of the oppressor's design to decimate and limit the size of brown populations); the well-off enjoy health care benefits while the poor succumb to disease and injury, because they can't afford health care; the fat cats who benefit from the same "socialized" health care that they are denigrating, and for which the poor from whom they wish to keep it are paying, misuse some of their ignorant, racist, pink supporters to stridently oppose any plans to extend that health care to the poor, the majority of whom are browns; the small section of the population, the elite, who are very rich become even super rich, because they steal the hard earned savings and investments of the better off among the poor that were acquired by sheer sacrifice; democratically elected governments that promote the welfare of the people are sabotaged by governments of rich countries that would rather see their dictator friends in power in those countries for ease of regional exploitation of oil, diamonds, land, etc.; state organized, directed, and operated hit squads with fancy names systematically liquidate non-compliant leaders of other countries to facilitate the spread of colonial empires of the bully states and to help them acquire regional control and free access to their resources.

This litany of misdeeds does not augur well for hope in a future world of homan homanity, as the evil monsters of twin world are seen to engineer and precipitate what they style shock and awe situations resulting in chaos and confusion during which they attack other states and try to steal their possessions. Of course, their biased news media help them to spread the news of the doom and gloom that has befallen their victim states that only they can dispel. They also wait for natural tragedies like ravaging hurricanes to quickly move in and implement their selfish programs of dispossession, domination, and dehomanization, taking advantage of the state of disarray and fear among the citizens to implement their ravenous new world order of larceny. Heartless governments that should be helping brown tax payers overcome these tragic circumstances are the very ones who are guilty of turning their backs on them, leaving them at the mercy of their mercenary accomplices.

In other situations, when they pretend to be protecting citizens from outside dangers, they are really creating opportunities for their corporate friends to come in and garner huge profits from cleaning up the mess that they have disrespectfully created in the process of destroying other people's property, or else they are gearing up to entrench themselves and continue to siphon the wealth of their victims *ad infinitum*. Clearly, pink governments are determined not to let that silver lining spread any farther than it has gone, and there is not a shimmer of hope that they ever intend to relent from their inhomane, exploitative behaviour; their evil ways appear to be fixed for all time, never to yield place to homane ways. John Milton likely had their kind in mind when he wrote these words:

> To do aught good never will be our task,
> But ever to do ill our sole delight.[1]

These bullies have perpetrated atrocities on browns, and they have intimidated weaker nations and assaulted them without cause. They boast about their incomparable might that they think gives them the right to bully and dispossess others, and some of their elite religious men still have the temerity to use their holy bubels to justify aggression of weaker tribes and to add their unholy "holy blessing" to the inhomane abuses meted out to them by their pink tribe: "We have the ability to take him out, and I think the time has come that we exercise that ability"[2] — with the help of covert operatives. And this is the same "holy man" who said of another religion, "It's clear from the teachings of . . . and also from the history of . . . that it's anything but peaceful"[3] — as peaceful as the murderous history of his religion that he is perpetuating? They have huddled browns in camps where they can be controlled and exterminated with ease if they want to exercise their democratic right to choose a government of their liking. When they have resisted brute pressure from these inhomane fiends who are urging them to defy their own government that they have freely chosen, because the pink clique does not approve of its personnel and its philosophy of life, which does not kowtow to pink stipulations, they have inhomanely blockaded them and systematically starved them to death, brutally ended their lives with virtually heartless and cold-blooded gangland style executions, destroyed their habitations, and attacked anyone who has dared to bring them homanitarian aid. They've also seized any weapons of self defence that sympathizers have sent them, while they freely receive sophisticated weapons of offence from their cheer-leaders for brutally demolishing their victims. Meanwhile, the rest of twin world unctuously mouths disapproval but does nothing to stop the carnage or punish the perpetrators, as they are so quick to do with regimes that are not part of the agenda of pink herrenvolkism.

That is the price people pay for assuming that gangsters have the same kind of integrity as they have, and not leaving any room for the evil that lurks in their perverted minds. In other contexts, they promise the poor that they will reap abundant harvests from the wealth that accrues to their rich friends (who earn 158 times what the best paid of them earn) on their backs, if they wait long enough for it to trickle down to them. Meanwhile, these people are sliding further down the ladder of poverty into utter deprivation, starvation, and death, while their exploiters are throwing away food to keep it from finding its way into their hungry stomachs and from glutting the market and cutting into their profits by forcing down the prices of produce and other commodities. Alternatively, they discard some of the food (vegetables and fruit), not for its lack of nutritive value, but because its warped shape has blighted its aesthetic value for adorning their tables. The result of these selfish actions is that the prices of these commodities remain high and out of the reach of the poor, thus propelling the spiral of succumbing to hunger and poverty further down to an assured lethal level. But that is not the end of the inhumanity of some twin world governments and their friends; it follows browns everywhere in twin world.

If a brown person happens to be jailed in a foreign country on questionable charges and with their assistance and connivance, they will malevolently let her languish there without trying to intervene on her behalf, all the time lying to the citizenry about their efforts to bring her back home when they are instead helping to fan the flames that are consuming her. Perhaps they are hoping that if she dies in captivity, away from her children while they have their own children with them, there will be one less brown to tolerate in their midst. It is no wonder that their jails are filled with many more brown men, women, and children than pinks who have been implicated in crimes that they didn't commit. Some on death row have been tarred with undeserved guilt just because a pink woman claimed that she had been assaulted by an imaginary brown man or that a man of the same description had abducted her children that she disposed of by drowning, etc. Many browns are guilty of petty crimes triggered by the dispossessing system of pink supremacy that has reduced them to a level worse than that of their own pets. Nevertheless, all of them are subjected to one form or another of oppression, humiliation, and dehomanization, regardless of why they have been jailed, and their victimization is misused to provide statistics about brown crime rates that exceed pink rates by far — a self-fulfilling prophecy.

The extent and magnitude of the dehumanizing tortures carried out by these pink governments and their proxies in their known and secret prisons further expose the degree of depravity of these so-called leaders of the people who derive their happiness solely from perpetrating evil and misdirecting the lives of others, thwarting their desires for self-identity and self-expression, stunting their potential for self-development, denuding their self-pride, and depriving their lives of relevance and meaning. If that were not the case, they would spend more tax dullams on education and training to mould these same persons into productive citizens, instead of building more and more hell holes in which to incarcerate them and subject them to a kind of life that is incompatible with the dignity of their personhood and homanity. To these fiends, the immense cost of erecting and operating these pits of misery to ensure their security by stealing the liberty of others, instead of financing educational institutions that will help to mold their characters and turn them into useful citizens, is never a source of embarrassment or shame, as long as it fits in with their perverse agenda of constraining and dehomanizing browns, as the statistics of our world have clearly demonstrated. Perhaps that is why they are so determined to distort these statistics to hide the truth from which they are running away, which is to facilitate the confinement of more victims to fill the contemplated new prisons of their liberal police states by lowering the threshold for mandatory jail sentences with new laws and old ones with an extended scope that will haul in many more unwary brown victims.

In this jungle of blatant inhomanity toward browns, some of the pertinent contextual questions to ask are the following: if a pink is jailed in a foreign country after being convicted of a crime in the criminal courts of that state, will they bend over backwards, send high level representatives on her behalf, pay her fine, and charter a private plane to bring her home to the country that they now call their own, after displacing the rightful owners of the land, or will they let her also languish in her misery while they are dragging their feet? Would they justify their colour-tinted favouritism by claiming that they are saving her from a corrupt judicial system, a kind of system in which they have participated in another context, one that is perhaps as corrupt as that in which a brown was left to languish, and one which directly owes its corruption to them as erstwhile colonialists? How adamant are they in their determination to let foreign systems of justice take care of their pink victims their way (with their connivance and cheer-leading) as they have been when browns are the victims who are subjected to unjust justice that violates their rights at every turn? They might claim that they treat both alike, since their systems of justice are colour-blind; but that answer has a nauseating stench of mendacity, and they know it.

If browns could seriously evaluate all the adverse situations that they encounter in their lives, those that arise spontaneously as well as those that are contrived and imposed on them by scheming pinks, and if they could unite in rejecting their dehomanization without reservation, they would rise up against this abuse and humiliation that they are forced to endure and elect to die once, rather than a thousand times, like Shakespearean cowards, as they are now doing. But they are not cowards; they have been effectively emasculated and paralyzed by the machinations and brute force of suppression wielded by their oppressors and dispossessors. Besides being gullible and devoid of foresight and planning skills in some cases, they are also easy victims of bribery who salivate profusely at the sight of the bubelical thirty pieces of bloodstained silver for which they will betray their tribe in other cases; hence the ease with which the oppressor can exploit their greed to drive wedges among the rest of people for the achievement of his nefarious goals.

In addition, their ingrained dependency on favours from pinks for survival has conditioned them to wait for orders to act, instead of initiating actions that will cater to their needs. Such has been the fate of newly minted, brown democratic states where pinks outwitted brown negotiators for peaceful transfer of power by allowing them to collect taxes from the people while they held on to the economic power that should also have come under their control. Instead they end up as just that: tax collectors who are paying inflated pensions to retired pink oppressors who are now their overpaid consultants. They have become victims of an oxymoronic situation with all the external dressings of political freedom, but an internal, unpalatable reality of economic serfdom, thanks to their economists and leaders who collaborated in strict secrecy with the oppressor. The result is that the people are left carrying an even bigger burden than they bore during the dim years of pink political and economic oppression, enough to sour the sweet taste of their political freedom. Debt and trade pacts inherited from past oppressors, pauperizing structural adjustment programs that consume huge chunks of gross domestic product, and the greed of lenders have placed the realization of their dreams of land reallocation, job creation, housing, and provision of the most basic essentials of living beyond reach for now. Also, their subservience and often misplaced eagerness to oblige have forced them to readily accept positions of make-believe authority that these rascals thrust on them for the sake of covering up their tracks and shifting onto them the blame for their heinous deeds against their own people. They have been turned into tools of oppression of their own people by their common oppressor, zealously carrying out the diabolic task assigned to them to maim and kill them for cheap favours. (See page 162).

Governmental inhomanity does not only confine itself to making browns miserable. It extends its tentacles to constrict the liberty of many other citizens who pose a threat to the selfish aspirations of the power hungry "leaders". In some jurisdictions, if they temporarily respond to the pricks of their absent consciences by feigning a feeling of concern for their victims, or if events force them into untenable situations where they do not, as usual, favour the direction that some of the thinking people in their tribe would have them follow, they always employ the stunt of playing for time while weaving their spiders' webs by appointing commissions of their friends and cronies to study and re-study the problem at hand *ad infinitum*; or else they shamelessly use military men and women as shields by claiming that their critics are attacking these brave souls whose ranks they shunned to save their own lives, abusing the people's sympathy for them; or else they hide under the skirts of the more authoritative and suspend the functions of legislative bodies to allow themselves time to scheme ways out of the dilemmas that they have created, and to safeguard their positions of power. This way, they believe that they can appease those who disapprove of their self-serving actions without providing an honest solution to the original problem; and they often get away with murder, because the electorate is a bunch of dolts. They are so stupid that these power hungry buffoons can disdainfully spurn their demands for accountability in the positions to which they have elected them to carry out their wishes for the running of their state by claiming to be protecting national security when they hide information from them, and they readily believe them and allow them to continue to railroad them like little dictators who rule as they please and are ready to vilify and crush anyone who dares to question their misdeeds with tweets. Their packs of ferocious pit bulls are always waiting to be unleashed to pounce upon and destroy the critics of their autocracy, or they personally spend their days in office reviling other persons to direct attention away from, and to cover, their ignominious tracks.

The pity is that when honest whistle-blowers expose these frauds, brainwashed citizens believe the frauds and disbelieve the whistle-blowers. They swallow the lies of government and its attack dogs, thus leaving every thinking person to wonder whether they have brains or amorphous protoplasm left in their skulls after their brain-washing. The whistle-blower has put her job on the line for truth, while the politician is covering his butt and protecting his milk cow with lies and malicious attacks on her, and the duped citizens still don't get it. They should know, if they have any intelligence to learn from past experience, that asking for the truth from these people about most matters that affect the citizens is like trying to pull teeth from a ferocious tiger that will not let one approach it until it has been tranquilized. Most of the time, if they can be tranquilized and dissuaded from spitting the venom for which they are noted, they will part with a fraction of the truth clothed in tons of distorting verbiage, but never with the whole truth unadulterated. What they can do with ease is vilify and demonize those who oppose their ruinous policies with skills that far outstrip their meagre governing skills. Even that (applying the phrase "governing skills" to them) is outstretching its meaning to accommodate this bunch of inept opportunists in their undeserved positions of leadership, if the meaning of this word can also be stretched to include these creatures and the incompetent, corrupt rabble of surrounding cronies that is serving their selfish interests. As noted, their attack dogs are always poised to intimidate critics and to heap excrement on them, with the result that citizens are fearful of saying anything that might even smack of criticism, because these dogs will spare no effort to destroy their careers wherever they may be working hard to shape them. No shenanigan is too dirty for them. Where are they to be found? They constitute the despicable governments of the day in twin world that spend more time assassinating other people's characters with their lies and vitriol than taking care of the affairs of their states.

Their style of government is also dominated by extreme secrecy; no one outside their internal circle should know what they are planning to do to the people, rather than for the people, although they pretend that all their plans are for the good of the people and not for their own selfish goals, until these plans threaten their quest for votes, and then they expeditiously jettison them. Their stock argument to dissemble their intentions is that the whole truth cannot be known before the task about which it is being sought has been completed, as there are always aspects of the task about which speculation is bound to err, producing a kind of chaos effect where outcomes cannot always be predicted accurately from given causes, because many unaccounted for situations will necessarily distort the course of events to yield a different result from one that is intended and anticipated, thus creating the mistaken impression that these geniuses failed to paint the correct picture in the beginning. No one is so stupid as to think that what anyone intends is what will transpire; but politicians probably know better than thinking people that the electorate does not think or ask searching questions; and that is why they can get away with lying to them with impunity.

It is equally distressing to see how when difficult decisions have to be made on disconcerting problems and sensitive issues that will affect the more privileged citizens as adversely as they will the underprivileged, but are to the advantage of this breed, they will present the people with Hobson's choices, which compel them to make unpalatable decisions to strangle themselves while they sit back, pretending that the powerless people have exercised their power and free choice as to how they should be ruled. This way they escape blame for any undesirable consequences that are certain to result from the implementation of those covertly coerced, selfish decisions. If citizens ask them the most innocent questions about how their taxes will be used, their duplicitous reply is: "trust us". Now, who can implicitly trust persons who will not give prior accounting of how they will use tax money? They have used it to buy the votes of foolish citizens who have fallen for their ruses and lack of accountability over the years; the same citizens whose reply to this insult is a re-affirmation of their confidence in these arrogant louts who are not accountable to anyone, even though they are holding positions as elected representatives of the people to whom they are accountable. They have elevated themselves to the status of kings whose prerogative is to suppress any demands for accountability and transparency and to react to deserved criticism with a more vigorous wielding of the stick of demonization, vilification, and victimization.

So, if they should ever condescend to answering questions about what their wild warmongering escapades will cost the nation, for instance, they hide behind their stock argument and distort the real estimated cost by downplaying the numbers to escape censure for their senseless dissipation of public funds in the counter-productive slaughter of other homan beings, a perversion that they seem to relish, because it keeps them in power as they claim to be protecting the citizens from foreign onslaught with these needless murderous escapades. They also lie shamelessly about matters that they have allowed to slide beyond their control, such as budget deficits that have been imposed on the citizens by the collapse of global financial markets, because they want to create the false impression that they are well in control of economic situations and do not need to be replaced for all their glaring failures. Nothing will stop them from resorting to outright lying and demagoguery to entrench their positions, knowing that their unthinking racist supporters will always prop them up, as long as they keep brandishing the big lie of the bogeymen of brown terror in their faces. They have succeeded in commandeering the blind trust of their pliable supporters with two slogans: "trust us", "only we can protect you from bogeymen".

Creating crises in security, as they have done in education and in other areas, seems to be their specialty. They can pull off these stunts with ease, because their subjects have been brainwashed into a submissive war mentality in which they will allow their rulers to abuse them for the fictitious protection that they seek from them. For instance, they tolerate and permit eavesdropping on their telephone conversations, interception of their other means of communication, and monitoring of their reading materials on the orders of dolts who don't read, because they've been scared into docility by the dangling of brown bogeymen before their eyes as part of the grand plan to take control and foster the new world order of selective pink supremacy. In the meantime, the people will wait until the cows come home for the restoration of their hijacked liberties, not realizing that they have lost them for ever. They also believe that everything about war is ennobling and glorious for their country and themselves, and they are prepared to sacrifice the lives of their children for the certain victory that they've been told can never elude them, until they suffer the bitter humiliation of defeat. Is there such a lack of noble pursuits that wars and murders should be elevated to such a lofty status in the lives of nations, or is this an index of the gutter in which the leaders exist and out of which they are incapable of extricating themselves, because it is the only level of operation that is consistent with their moral and cognitive abilities? Or is it a way of diverting attention from the immensity of the problems that they have brought upon themselves and upon the people. It is mentally and morally taxing and exhausting to try to envisage persons who can devote their lives to killing others wantonly, because the excuses they give for their murderous pursuits are senseless. But sense was never a prerequisite for leadership or for disposing of cheap brown and other lives, anyway.

When citizens have serious concerns about brown affairs, the environment, health care, the economy, their self-serving wars, etc., that they wish to discuss with these types, they are never given the opportunity, the stock answer being that the "boss" and his cronies are busy. If journalists happen to catch up with them by waylaying them, they just brush them aside, or else they answer irrelevantly and just keep walking to disappear behind well guarded doors. Most of the time journalists (who cannot always be trusted, because they are often guilty of assaulting the truth by reporting slanted "facts" in favour of the ideology of their particular puppet news media) cannot get near to them; their chaperons make quite sure that they whisk them away to avoid interviews, because some of them are so unintelligent that the illogical statements they utter and the answers that they give to questions would make even a little child ashamed of displaying such ignorance; so they have to be shielded from exposing their ignorance and shallowness notwithstanding their glamor and populism. And these are the nitwits who are ruling or are being groomed to rule the rest of the citizens who are not all chumps — what a crying shame.

This usurpation of democracy and its concentration in the hands of cliques, who are selfishly serving the interests of corporations in preparation for their retirement into those corporations, to the exclusion of the so-called elected representatives of the people never seems to perturb many of the citizens. They are happy as long as they can watch their trifling shows on television, attend their ball games, and purchase their boxes of beer, etc. Thoughtful discussion of the greatest scourge of democracy in the form of one person being allowed to dictate to the rest of the citizens how they will live and die, as if democracies have now become dictatorships, is not a part of their intellectual repertoire. They are content to remain in their torpid state of mind while they allow one person, the egotistic oracle who thinks he knows it all and can provide caddish solutions to all questions (aided and abetted by his cronies), to trample over millions of them with impunity, claiming that their votes gave him the mandate to run roughshod over them; and that includes some of the best brains in the tribe who are purportedly serving as the people's representatives, but are no better than stooges and lapdogs vying for favours. Little wonder that all these "democratic" dictators subvert the constitutions of their states and place themselves above their laws with impunity; and still no one's stomach churns at their nerve and arrogance, or at their litany of blatant lies to justify their egregious hijacking of the people's nominal freedom of self-determination by hiding behind transparent tricks like not wanting to jeopardize national security.

When they want to look cute at the expense of brown states, however, they borrow tripe from our world, like that which says, "the whole nature of Africa is such that there can be no such thing as a constitution"[4]; and yet they flout their constitutions and encourage their conservative judges to let politics colour their interpretations of their laws. They, not browns, are guilty of suppressing government "by free rational laws. . . . [where] even the family ethos is lacking in strength."[5], as in some advanced states of twin world where families are so unstable and disintegrate regularly because their members are always at war with one another owing to their lack of the cohesion that is characteristic of brown families that are governed by *Ubuntu*; In their civilised governments the executive branch and the oligarchs who control them have usurped the powers and responsibilities of the legislature and subverted them by substituting fear-instilling codes that they manipulate at will to subdue the docile masses of citizens, so that they can secure their positions and wage iniquitous, life-squandering wars that "respect nothing and destroy everything"[6] without hindrance.

These usurpers of twin world act as if they can provide answers to all questions and solutions to all problems; and everyone seems to believe their lies without question, including the news media that they use to create confusion, the intelligentsia, and the poor people who are the worst affected victims of this rape of democracy by economic greed; and yet they all should know that the yarns spun by these usurpers are unadulterated lies euphemistically called bad intelligence. Are they all too scared to protest? Their corruption and filching are also enough to prompt some people to say that if they saw someone robbing a bank they would not turn him in, because everyone robs everyone else, especially the rich and powerful who rob the rest of the people who are poor and powerless. And so it appears that the only fitting answer to the question whether there is likely to be a faint ray of hope for a better future in this murk of present-day corruption, theft, lies, and mismanagement is that the future of twin world is still really bleak.

Nevertheless, the people of twin world continue to live with the hope that nothing of that sort goes on for ever, that one day this corrupt system will disintegrate, and the mighty will fall even as they are now beginning to fall in private and public life as the economic structures that they have built to suck money out of the rest of the people have begun to tumble and crumble. The sad corollary to this selfishness is that the lives of the people are also crumbling; people are dying all around these fat cows, but the majority of them remain oblivious to the misery that surrounds them and their families, because browns are predominantly affected. The millions who die from diseases like those in our world (malaria, AIDS, sleeping sickness, diarrhea, and tuberculosis) are only an addition to the other millions who die and suffer displacement as a result of the callous, self-aggrandizing, and greed-inspired military escapades of these fat cows and their government proxies. To their way of thinking, none of these lowly lives deserves a second thought; they are all expendable in the quest for glory, supremacy, and possessions of all categories: slaves, territory, oil, diamonds, etc. In our own world, after over 300,000 people perished in a few hours from poisoning by a gas leak from a chemical factory and each family was compensated with $550 for the life of its bread-winner, a spokesperson for the company that bought the responsible company is reported to have remarked that the amount was "plenty good for an Indian". No comment required; the contemptuous statement, which is also representative of pink sentiments about the worth of brown lives, speaks for itself. The pity is that this ignominious superciliousness is universal.

The sorry state of the masses of people that results from the attitudes and actions of those with privilege and clout stands as a monument to the inhomanity of homanity as we understand it, although it seems to elude the bright minds of twin world; they remain unperturbed in their state of torpor. The oxymoron "homan inhomanity" with its culture of entitlement that is exercised by the selfish few, in and outside of government, and from which the rest of homanity should continue to struggle to emancipate itself, contrasts starkly with known homanistic values. Homanism as a philosophical outlook believes in a commitment to the basic values of respect for homan freedom, autonomy, rights, and dignity; freedom of thought and expression; freedom of religious and non-religious choices in life, which entails freedom in choice of life-style; and freedom from the kind of political, social, racial, and economic exploitative oppression that has been the way of life in all of twin world.

These rights and values that people should be enjoying, have been withheld from them by rulers who don't want to acknowledge their obligation to accord respect to their holders by not violating them at will but protecting them against violation by government and by all sectors of the community, as long as their holders have not done anything to abrogate them. But the rulers cannot seem to get that fact through their thick skulls; they want to decide who lives and who dies, how they live and how they die. They cannot understand that these rights might not positively compel them to go out of their way to perform certain functions for the benefit of their holders, but they certainly should protect them from interference by them and by other persons in what is popularly termed the negative rights sense of not thwarting anyone's desire and effort to live her life rationally in the way that she pleases, as long as her way does not encroach on the next person's right to live her life her rational way or cause her any harm. They also compel those who claim to be governing on behalf of their holders to ensure that the minimum essentials of life are accorded to them for their sustenance and flourishing, regardless of tribal nonage.

Nowhere in twin world are people being given the opportunity by their selfish rulers to think for themselves how they will live their lives and decide their own fate. Instead, they have courses of action and solutions to their problems dictated to them by those in authority and they are denied the liberty of taking advantage of the opportunities that their franchise has earned them by the iniquitous structure of their society that rightly maintains high standards but does not provide all citizens with the means of qualifying to meet those high standards. Even if they were to exercise their franchise fully and effectively, they would still have to beat the constricting economic burdens that have been imposed on them; so what is the use of that franchise to a perpetually hungry man or woman? It is not edible and does not put food on the table. They would rather have food and trade away that franchise for the chance to stay alive and keep their children healthy and alive, in the same way that the rich politicians are doing that and more for their precious children. These rich cats look at them with disdain and can literally be heard saying to them: what use is your franchise when we dictate the policies that keep you in the gutter so that you can't afford to send your children to college or university to come and compete with us and even beat us in the competition. Already, we are denying them the full day care that we give our own children, to ensure that they are left behind and hampered from catching up with our children.

Denial of opportunity for acquiring a sound education amounts to denial of opportunity for advancement, which in turn qualifies the victim for subordinate status where she is powerless to ameliorate her craftily contrived circumstances of socio-economic privation. Meanwhile, pinks who can't wield economic power try their utmost (and often succeed) to secure a niche for themselves in the corridors of political power where they can control the rest of the people and use them to feather their nests and further their selfish ends, in keeping with their contribution to the promotion of the new world order. Once in those positions of power, they do not hesitate to use their clout to pigheadedly and maliciously obstruct progress in the affairs of the state to spite brown authority and to promote their political careers, and they have no qualms about lying to the people to achieve these ends. Their fortunes in the next election become the centre of all their activities, and they are willing to sacrifice the welfare of the entire country and the future of its citizens to their evil motives and their jockeying for re-election; hence the power games that they play in place of executing their political obligation and responsibility to the people who were duped into electing them, believing that they could entrust them with their present and future welfare. But, of course, the people choose not to be aware of being manipulated by these egotists who are now both drivers and elite passengers in their new gravy train.

Even the economically secure ones are not satisfied with the immense power that their wealth gives them over the rest of the people; they also strive for political power to enhance their control of the citizenry, regardless of whether they belong to the brown or the pink tribe, while they are in turn being used by others to further the goal of the new world order of dog eat dog. They want to dominate everyone to feel big and important, but also to use them as their security blankets against being eaten by the other dogs. Of note are the gratis (tax-free) sums of money that they receive; the generous salaries to match and encourage their often contrary and puerile behaviour in the legislatures; their irresponsible absenteeism from the legislative chambers; the corruption by which they acquire and squander large sums of public funds, which they would not do with their own money; the hefty handshakes that they receive when they are fired from the jobs that they have messed up, after which they shamelessly sue for more money; the secure pensions that they receive at the end of their unproductive careers that far exceed the annual incomes of some of the most hardworking folk; and the outrageous bonuses that some of them take away from the faltering and the failing business enterprises over which they have presided (rewards for pilfering from state coffers) while ruining the futures of their investors. There is no end to this legalized theft and corruption.

Meanwhile, their reckless styles of government continue to dig enormous economic hell-holes into which many have fallen and all may soon fall, during which time they and their rich friends will be bilking the rest of the people for all they are worth and leaving them to wallow in the mess that they have created, as some of them are already doing. They mess up, and then they retire to their ranches and to directorships of financial concerns to which they misdirected billions of tax payers' dullams while they were in government, waging unnecessarily destructive inhomane wars for the very purpose of benefiting themselves and their friends from repairing the needless carnage that they were causing. Now they continue to draw disproportionately large salaries, leaving the people that they have screwed up high and dry, but still daring to shamelessly justify their devious ways in the vain hope of succeeding at the herculean task of cleansing their filth and polishing their lustreless legacies.

But not all filth is amenable to cleaning up; some filth just resists cleansing, no matter how hard one tries. So, no matter how much the architects of this filth may try to cleanse themselves by pushing the blame for their dirty deeds onto others, like the proverbial terrorists that they blame for making them take the liberties that they are taking with the citizens' misplaced trust in them, or the brown or liberal administration that has inherited their mess, the muck still sticks to them like crazy glue, and they are known by it. Investing them with undeserved, ponderous academic garb or citations will not erase their evil deeds; it will continue to live long after they have gone, and they will for ever remain the villains of society. For some of them, it is true that you can try to lift them out of the gutter but fail miserably, or else succeed in lifting them out, but still fail to take the gutter out of them. They remain, deservingly or otherwise, the toxic and vulgar specimens of humanity with which twin world is cursed to contend for as long as it cannot disgorge them.

In so-called democratic twin world states, citizens always get the leaders and government that they voted for, which is the one they fully deserve, the ones they later call "traitors". So they have no one but themselves to blame when they are hijacked by an ignorant, reckless, highly unstable, and narcissistic con man who flounders hopelessly, because he has not the slightest clue about his responsibilities except that they comprise nepotism, racist rants, and licence to enrich himself, his family, and his absurdly extravagant friends, all of whom have no respect for public funds that they thoughtlessly dissipate on trivialities and unnecessary expenditures at the expense of the welfare of the people that they have been called upon to serve. Unfortunately, they have a following of bigots who are ready to swallow anything that they tell them and who will give them full licence to persecute children with the full knowledge that they are ruining them psychologically for the rest of their lives — another way of eliminating vermin. They are not ashamed to claim their barbarous and heinous authority to abuse children from their gudd in their appeal to this world's scriptures:

> Let everyone be subject to the governing authorities, for there is no authority except that which God has established. The authorities that exist have been established by God. Consequently, whoever rebels against the authority is rebelling against what God has instituted, and those who do so will bring judgment on themselves.... rulers do not bear the sword for no reason. They are ... agents of wrath[6]

# Chapter 12
# Governmental Terror

With such mean characters on the loose, it isn't surprising that terrorist pink states of twin world accuse brown states of terrorism. Equally unsurprising is that privileged pink citizens of these racist governments, who are also wrestling with denial of their racism, accuse underprivileged brown citizens of playing the race card when they object to the racist discrimination that they impose on them; both blaming the victim, as usual. In another context, they protest loudly when repressive state laws that have been framed vaguely, but meant to trip up only the brown citizen, now catch up with them in a case of racists crying foul for being hoist by their own petard in states that cater only to their needs. Furthermore, in what they style reverse discrimination, they gripe about affirmative action programs that preferentially admit browns into programs from which they would otherwise be excluded on a racist basis or for ineptness. But they forget that even the highly capable ones are excluded from these programs on the racist basis of skin colour, regardless of their achievements and qualifications. They want to hide from their habit of racist exclusion by claiming that every case belongs in the category of exclusion based on ineptness, when they know very well that their criterion of exclusion and scandalous discriminatory practices is skin colour. They also forget the monopoly that they still enjoy in jobs from which browns were priorly bluntly excluded and are now systematically excluded for lack of experience relative to their adopted countries, e.g., Konatian experience.

They further want to pretend that the best suited persons for every respectable and high profile job come only from their tribe, and they want to attribute blame for the marginalization of browns to circumstances other than racism, like their lack of initiative, which, unfortunately, results from eking out an existence in a deprived environment that has been thus contrived for them by the same oppressors and the forces of their marketplace. They pretend to grant them equal trading rights while exposing them to exploitation via their craftily constructed markets where they cannot find their way and are forced to seek advice from the very same people who designed and created these markets with the intention of using them to shut them out while exploiting them by using underhanded, dirty tricks styled global "apartheid". Thus, they end up losing most or all of what they had invested in the markets, as expected. In that marketplace the deprived do not pay less for a loaf of bread than the oppressor who lives off the fat of the land that he has stolen from them, and they are also taxed doubly by having to pay tax on the articles that they purchase, after they have paid unfair income tax from which the rich get exemptions that they cannot claim.

In more recent times, some of twin world's intelligentsia have conveyed equally depraved sentiments and convictions in words that we have seen used in our own world by persons who did not have the interests of others at heart, and, in fact, devoted significant parts of their lives to making the lives of others hell on earth. Perhaps that is why their governments have departments of "brown affairs", (but never of "pink affairs") that are ostensibly designed to cater benevolently to brown needs and welfare by underfunding their social, educational, health, and other services to thwart and stunt their development and keep them perpetually subjugated. In those departments pinks alone decide on how browns will live. Their input is not invited or encouraged, because arrogant pinks claim to know best what is best for them. The brazen-faced talk in which they have engaged in different regions of twin world where the tenor of their vitriol is notably consistent, reflecting a global unity of purpose, viz., pink supremacy through brown suppression, has left no doubt about this hatred-driven knowledge and their evil intentions.

The following borrowed words bear witness to these hateful attitudes that determine how pinks intend to live with browns: "There is a need now for strong and brutal reaction. . . . We need to harm them without mercy, women and children included."[1] So they use assassination, targeted terror, intimidation, land confiscation, cutting of all social services, and strangulation of the economy of their victims to expel them and take their places. "Every attack has to end with occupation, destruction and expulsion."[2] After all, as they said, "Is it not time to get rid of them? Why should we continue to keep these thorns in our flesh?"[3] Elsewhere they said, "When I have control over Native education, I will reform it so Natives will be taught from childhood that equality with Europeans is not for them."[4] "There is no place for him [the "Native"] in the European community above the level of certain forms of labour. . . . Until now he has been . . . misled . . . by showing him the green pastures of European society in which he was not allowed to graze"[5]. These are all chilling words that could have been uttered by the phantasm that they call the devil. But they are also brazen-faced expressions of unjustified intent to dehomanize, enslave, and murder another homan being without compunction. They reflect an odious display of arrogance that is at variance with the religious morality professed by both the morally bankrupt embracers of these sentiments and all their co-conspirators against the browns of twin world, and they inspire the compositions of the same kinds of scenarios portrayed in the supposedly fictional protocol mentioned on page 30, reference[1]:

> We have got our hands into the administration of the law, into the conduct of elections, into the press, into liberty of the person, BUT PRINCIPALLY INTO EDUCATION AND TRAINING AS BEING THE CORNERSTONES OF A FREE EXISTENCE. WE HAVE FOOLED, BEMUSED AND CORRUPTED THE YOUTH OF THE 'GOYIM' BY REARING THEM IN PRINCIPLES AND THEORIES WHICH ARE KNOWN TO US TO BE FALSE . . .[6]

The same persons are reported to have said that to control a people, one must control their education; hence quotes [4 & 5] above.

The rapscallions who employ this overt racist language are, however, less sophisticated than their smooth-talking brothers who use cryptography to achieve the same ends; e.g. denying browns job opportunities by telling them that they lack job experience relevant to their adopted country; streamlining their children in high school away from academics to the trades, as is the case in our world, as reported by Megan Ogilvie: "...was told by his high school guidance counsellor to consider being a tradesman . . . A profession really wasn't expected of him."[7] Meanwhile, they are encouraging and preparing their privileged pink class-mates for university in the same professions where browns will serve under their authority as their perpetual subordinates; discriminating against stellar brown students by rejecting their university admission applications, while preferentially admitting mediocre pink students; and using many other ploys to perpetuate global pink supremacy over browns educationally, politically, economically, and socially, strictly on the illogical and idiotic basis of skin colour. The adverse social results of this evil agenda have been immense, and its long lasting and devastating effects will continue to haunt, gnaw into, and fragment the integrity of brown society for decades to come before they can be fully reversed. The same results follow the pink bombing of their schools and other centres of brown learning for the express purpose of trying to thwart their intellectual development and free thinking.

The deeds of evil minds leave long-lasting scars behind, and as one brown remarked after observing and studying the inhomane ways of these people to control brown destiny, "When you control a man's thinking you do not have to worry about his actions. . . He will find his place and will stay in it."[8] That is exactly the intent of pink supremacy policies: to conquer, control, and enslave by brainwashing people into perpetual subjugation as noted here:

> The Black Slave, after receiving this indoctrination, shall carry on and will become self-refueling and self-generating for hundreds of years, maybe thousands. Don't forget you must pitch the old black versus the young black and the young black male against the old black male. You must use the dark skin slave vs. the light skin slave and the light skin slaves vs. the dark skin slaves. You must also have your *white* (my italics) servants and overseers distrust all blacks, but it is necessary that your slaves trust and depend on us. They must love, respect and trust only us. Gentlemen, these Kits are keys to control, use them. Have your wives and children use them, never miss an opportunity.[9]

This blatantly expressed attitude of dividing browns and then exploiting divisions among them to perpetuate their enslavement is the same one that was expressed by the same Hagala that we met before. He boldly said that slavery is the only connection that exists between browns and their pink masters; to which another pink added that there is no place for them in their select society above the level of certain forms of labour for which his educational policy would befit them. All of them operate with the same mind-set: to enslave browns permanently. Regardless of any controversy about the authenticity of the Lynch sentiments quoted above, the fact of the matter is that they convey the character of the entire racial system, that stifling cesspool of racist subterfuge begotten of evil, scheming minds, founded and constructed within a social framework whose single intent is the maintenance of pink supremacy with its evil trade marks of injustice, dispossession, and inhomanity directed solely against browns. Underlying this vile attitude is the constant fear that browns might one day rise up and break the shackles of their mental and physical oppression, thereby scuttling the best laid schemes of psychological subjugation on which the political, socio-cultural, and economic success of pink domination depends.

These pink fiends have been known to lift browns words aimed at their racism out of their context and distort their meaning to incite the hatred that their gullible ilk harbours for browns, to take aim at those of them who hold the highest offices in their states, and to discredit brown representative organizations by smearing them with false accusations of racism to disguise their own racism. They have used the same tactic to justify the withdrawal of funding for brown concerns that educate and mobilize them to exercise their moral and constitutional rights of voting, etc. When they have been exposed for the lowborn maggots that they are, they have again turned around and accused their accusers of racism to conceal their heinous intent of always furthering the agenda of pink supremacy. The absurdity of the system, upheld by government, reveals itself on many fronts, such as when pinks who have strange sounding names accuse browns of being unpatriotic when they pronounce their own names as they should be pronounced and not as the pinks would like to pronounce them, or when a child who looks brown is born to pink parents and becomes an outcast in her pink society, in spite of her parents' assurances and protestations that she is their indisputable pink progeny, confirmed by genetic studies. It seems that nature has no business permitting atavisms in pink lineages without exposing them to the wrath of their brothers who deny the full personhood of anyone who is not of their skin colour, regardless of her pink family origins. This stupid mentality drives a wedge between parents and their child, resulting in their ultimate estrangement from one another. One would think that after having confronted the truth about a system in which they were steeped, but whose effects were so distant from them that they did not feel them, the parents who are caught in this idiocy would, after being thus humiliated, realize the folly of their racism and abandon it. But they still firmly believe in and defend it; perhaps because it is their ticket to a better socio-economic life and a blanket of security against being overtaken by barely surviving browns in their struggle to maintain their contrived position of superiority.

Some homans, particularly those who live in better conditions than the rest of the twin-worlders, do not like to see their prerogative to wealth and comfort infringed upon by efforts to extend public assistance to these poor homans who exist on the barest minimum of essentials in an economy created and derailed by them. They even begrudge them the aid that they are receiving from those who feel for them in their suffering. As we have seen, they even deny them health care, because they will have to pay higher taxes to meet the increased costs involved in extending health care to them. They prefer that those who do not have the means to pay for their health care should be left to die, because their lives are cheap, anyway. Regrettably, this contemptible attitude is also found in some pink physicians, the very select group of persons whose oath of service demands that they save lives of all tribes where it is possible, homane, and reasonable.

The filthy rich who are gouging browns in health insurance premiums and in other commodities will not admit that they too are responsible for forcing them into that hopeless situation where they do not have a choice; their only painful choice is death. They will also not acknowledge the plain truth that the sorry plight in which the rest of the people find themselves is a product of the trickle down, egocentric fiscal policies of the governments that they control. and that do nothing to cater to the welfare of the rest of the citizens but are geared only to the prosperity of their corporate friends who are already enjoying the rich benefits that come with the tax cuts that they have bestowed on them in return for bolstering them financially in their positions of power, from where they can crush opposition to their authority to dispossess all the people, especially browns.

Undergirding some of the arrogance that prompts these people to think that they are Gudd's gift to their world is their twin world analogue of the Doctrine of Manifest Destiny, copied from our world, which is a self-generated but allegedly also Gudd-given right to expand territory that they originally took unjustly from its owners, driven as they were by the greed and selfishness that impelled them to seek and acquire it exclusively for themselves and their children. In following the terms of this doctrine, they continue to dispossess and decimate those who originally occupied the land that they stole, and to justify the theft by their own terms of the right to possession of that land. They claim to have "mixed [their] labour with [it] . . . joined it to something that is [their] own, and thereby [made] it [their] property".[10] They also claim that the rightful owners have lost their possession rights of it by living on it without developing it fully, but rather mainly rearing livestock, which predisposes them to a nomadic lifestyle that is inconsistent with permanent settlement, thus justifying the impunity with which they confiscate that land. As usual, they disregard the proviso that there be "enough, and as good, left in common for others"[11]. Hence their inhomane appropriation of 83% of the best lands for their small population and allotment of only 17% of arid land to the brown population, which is four times the size of their population. Did their bubel tell them that that is the Krustan thing to do?

However, in their attempt to appear homane, these inhomane pink brutes have offered some of the browns with lighter skin complexions the privilege of assimilation into their way of life, on condition that they agree to be bludgeoned out of their languages, cultures, and traditions and assume the inferior status that has been set aside for them by their superiors to make life easier when they are dealing with them at close quarters from their vantage position of superiority, unlike the rest of the browns who are kept at or beyond arm's length. Assimilation in this sense is not, however, becoming one with the master, but being allowed to be close enough to him so that he can be aped well enough to keep him happy and comfortable in the subservient company of his inferior, without the fear that she will want to be on par with him, except when he frequently ventures into her chamber to place himself literally on horizontal par with her. It seems that boundless, but selectively vulnerable, pink conceit and hypocrisy can be easily debunked in the appropriate circumstances; but these occasions are so unorthodox that they are not permitted to see the light of day, except when they eventuate in hybrid progeny, and so they fail to leave any alerting impression of his hypocrisy on the mind of the domineering party. He looks upon them as one more area in which he can assert his superiority to get what he wants when he wants it (See reference [4], page 80), and also as his breeding ground for needed slaves. This is the hypocrite whose equivalent of the Immorality Amendment Act, 1950 of South Africa under the rule of the apostles of apartheid oxymoronically prohibits him from engaging in intimate relationships with inferior brown breeds.

Besides fulfilling their allegiance to their herrenvolk ideology, which believes and is possessed by the warped idea that the lives of other people are cheap and only their own lives matter, these miserable creatures are under the control of big business, which also controls their governments, compelling them to commit themselves to wage wars and to support the vast industries that are required to produce and replenish all kinds of war machinery at astronomical cost to the state and unmatched profits to the war industry and its operators. Similar benefits accrue to reconstruction gangs (some with dismal track records, and others producing the destructive war machinery, but both with close connections in high places) that move in, like vultures descending on a carcass, to monopolize government contracts for rebuilding infrastructure that the same government demolished deliberately to create obscenely lucrative jobs for their friends. They shun the available skills of the locals that they have relegated to the poor house in a calculated move of indirect genocide, while they plead shortage of funds for public services at home for which they are responsible, and for which they tax the citizens to death. Lately, these vultures have drawn up lists of states that are the potential victims of this kind of banditry, so that when their bully friends attack and destroy, they can be ready to walk in, rebuild, and reap their enormous profits at the expense of the unwary, trusting taxpayer who just keeps on shelling out money, but not exacting and receiving credible accounting for it. It's time to wake up, tax payers of twin world!

Throughout twin world privileged pinks and their racist governments have no qualms about telling people who have been victimized by oppression that they should take the chips off (not off of!) their shoulders, look ahead, and let bygones be bygones, forget their persecution, forgo their stolen lands, and continue to enjoy life in poverty and misery. But some others of their type who have also been victims of oppression and murder in the past are allowed, nay, encouraged to intrude upon the lives of the rest of the citizens by constantly reminding them of their suffering, even *ad nauseam*, and commemorating it with statewide monuments and irksome annual ceremonies, while they are inflicting unrestrained suffering and murder on defenceless others under the guise of self-defence; for what? For their blatant hypocrisy, sheer arrogance, unadulterated duplicity, or just as another scurvy attempt at masking their racist inhumanity? How does anyone go out of his way to attack another person in his home for no reason other than that he wants to steal his land, and then claim self-defence when the other person repels him forcefully? Such absurdities are the illogical concomitants of pink supremacy, which commands that its victims yield to its wishes and demands without question. Racist governments encourage these butchers to exploit all citizens by unfairly defending them against criticism by their own citizens who advocate regard for the substantive and procedural rights of those oppressed by this cabal of thieves.

This bizarre situation is a commonplace in twin world. The logic behind it is even more bizarre. Its architects shamelessly fabricate breath-taking narratives of scenarios equivalent to Armageddon, where everything happens exactly as laid down in their script, except that it never really happens. Their citizens are forced to ride on a roller-coaster whose track is studded with grim signs warning of danger, less danger, and more danger, but never extreme danger or no danger. They are thus kept in a steady, unbalanced state of fear, enough to jar them out of the complacency of their relaxed lives, and yet insufficient to thrust them into mental paralysis; and there they are left dangling in confusion and bewilderment, ready to commit themselves to the servility planned for them by their scheming rulers. In this kind of atmosphere, simple colour-coding assumes a supernatural hyper-reality, an unrelenting, dominating part of daily living, a determinant of what life means in the domain of fear that has been constructed by the operators of the code. Who ever thought that juggling simple colours could have such an enslaving effect on people's minds and behaviour for the rest of their lives? Yes; they have been turned into psychotics who run for shelter from phantoms even in the absence of the colours. The myth of the colours is firmly etched in their minds. Other manipulators and cabalists have invented threats from phantom foreign fighter jets to justify diverting billions of dullams from social and other programs needed to help citizens in need (for whom they don't care a hoot) to needless war toys whose escalating cost is their secret. They want to look like tough guys.

To date, myth rules every circumstance of pink lives; they live it and they identify with it to the exclusion of all reason at a cost, still allowing it and its architects to command total authority over them and to shape all their tomorrows of every day. They are wedded and welded to the mantra of the myth that they chant every hour of the day, believing that it can't be questioned or analyzed for irrationality and sheer lack of truth, and they remain mesmerized by the promise of the comfort that comes with first trusting in it and then living by it. Figment and myth have become realities for them as they allow their rulers the unopposed liberty of fabricating evidence to justify assaults best styled as ethnic cleansing to purge themselves of the problem posed by the mere existence near them of other people. Their intolerance to tribal and religious differences blinds them to the fact that all of their different religions have been manufactured and tailored to suit their respective cultures, and there is nothing sacred or superior about their own religion, culture, and tribe. Contrariwise, there is everything repugnant about their lust for and worship of money, power, and herrenvolk-tainted domination, and about their readiness to sacrifice other homan lives for these vices.

Not surprisingly, this attitude pervades most members of the ruling tribes of twin world, affecting even those selfish ones who should know better, after they were shielded from annihilation by altruistic sympathizers of other tribes who created a home state for them by dispossessing browns. But they are, instead, the persecutors of browns from whose ranks they have recently emerged to dictate to their benefactors policy on matters that cater to the establishment and continuing maintenance of their own regional supremacy. That is a pity: that the only persons who can emancipate the oppressed from their plight have forsaken them to pander to the wishes of heartless self-aggrandizing butchers who are a part of the burden borne by the persecuted who live in proximity with them. It is heart-rending to hear them blaming the victims of discrimination and calculated extermination (I use the word "extermination" advisedly, because the weaker and poorer people are looked upon by their persecutors as vermin that "infests" twin world countries that they stole from the natives and now call their own), instead of using their power and influence to right this and other colossal wrongs that are being perpetrated by inhomane homan beings on other (powerless) homan beings. This way, they would be placing the blame where it rightfully belongs, instead of playing political games with the lives of victims of decimation and becoming rubber stamps and tools for the selfish agendas of zealots and pressure groups. Politics is indeed a dirty game that robs even the most principled persons of their consciences and moral duty to the underdog and victim of the discrimination that these specious do-gooders do not cease to decry in their passionate pronouncements about respect for the dignity of all persons, regardless of colour or creed, and yet do little or nothing to uphold when the dignity of browns has to be respected.

The same kind of blaming game is played in trying to scuttle the efforts of victimized brown states from acquiring the capability of modernizing their sources of energy by inventing transparently fatuous reasons why such a venture would pose a threat to the peace of twin world. The threat may be true, but look at who is engineering the frenzy. The same supremacist states that enjoyed the unfettered ability to develop and relish the convenience and comfort of the same technology but have gone even further to extend the uses of that technology for the control of every other state around or far removed from them, to the detriment of the inhabitants of those states. We do not have to go too far back in the history of twin world to find evidence of the evil that lurks in their power to inhomanely roast alive, vaporize, and brutally and permanently maim the citizens of weak, "inferior" states. However, like all bullies, they are not so foolish as to attack or provoke those who can respond in kind to their provocation or assault. They only threaten them with loud barks unaccompanied by the daring assaults that they have launched on defenceless states. International bullies know not to try their luck on their technological equals, but they remain dogs in the manger who will not share their bone; and they go one step further by ensuring that the other dogs don't acquire their own bones and thereby neutralize their coveted monopoly on all available bones.

These same supremacist states have consistently and arrogantly ignored countless admonitions from the rest of twin world about their hubristic, reckless, belligerent, and lethal behaviour toward their defenceless neighbours. While their duplicitous sponsors display their hypocrisy and shameless posturing by pretending to admonish them, they have cried wolf for the selfish reason of trying to shore up one-upmanship over those that they want to dominate and exterminate, using cheap shots and big lies as a pretext for attacking and wrecking the habitats of weaker nations that do not boast the prodigiously destructive capability possessed by these real disruptors of the peace of twin world and killers of its citizens. They have used the same self-serving reasons, wrapped in the noble garb of saving their world from the devastation that is lurking in the phantoms that they have conveniently created to justify all their heinous deeds. They have learnt their lesson to skilfully tell only big lies that the ignorant masses will swallow readily and to tell them frequently enough until they and the citizens believe them, and also to paint the dark horrors of hell with the glittering colours of paradise to give their heinous deeds a virtuous appearance.

Governmental inhumanity is further manifested in how the lives and sheer homan dignity of the poorer sections of the population never seem to have a voice or to matter to their elected rulers who always have an ear for the rich and work for their interests at great cost to the interests of the rest of the insignificant citizens who have been stripped of their entitlements to common decency and fair play; hence the obscene tax cuts for their rich friends and sustainers. It is also clear that twin world, with its culture of duplicity, stands in stark contrast against the enviable background of desirable behaviour exhibited in our world, as evidenced by their shameless politicizing and doctoring of scientific data relating to the hazards of their variety of global warming, a practice that has no place in any decent, self-respecting community of rational persons who should be aware of the dangers that lurk in exposing citizens to such climatic conditions. Their pseudo-scientists will never publicly admit to their lack of relevant research and to being funded by the polluting industries that pen government environmental policies, and for whom the same government spreads baneful misinformation about the sun being responsible for all the effects of global warming and destabilization of the balance of nature, not their industries. Who will believe that the sustainer of life (the sun) is its wrecker? Perhaps they will see the light of day (from the same sun that they are maligning) when they and some of their families fall victim to the ills of the global warming that is being aggravated by their sponsors. But my guess is that they will be told to rationalize that misfortune by conjuring up more reasons why the sun should be blamed and banished for their plight; and being the immoral and spineless creatures that they are, they will gladly continue to sacrifice their families and other people for thirty more pieces of silver even as they are taking their last gasp of polluted air.

This dim-witted, greedy, and egocentric scum of twin world engages in machinations to suppress glaringly evident objective and well researched facts that don't favour their abuse of the lives of ordinary citizens and their environment to enrich themselves, their friends, and their minions by denying the science behind global warming and the accelerating effects of their money-making oil and coal industries from which government draws its personnel and to which they retire after carrying out its mandate during their terms in office. In their self-indulgence, they do not have time to give thought to others around them who are suffering the lethal effects of their habit of grabbing everything for themselves, or to those who will succeed them to inherit the desolation that they are leaving behind. If they are bent on killing themselves for money, let them do so without implicating other people who still value their lives more than money; and let's see how long they will live to enjoy that money.

They are so committed to their quest for money that they will maim or kill anyone who tries to direct attention away from their lies to the truth, if they cannot intimidate or muzzle her, or even elbow her out of her job. They think that public servants (scientists etc.) work for them and not for the people. Their lives typify the sad oxymoron of living (their lives) by killing (others) and building (their ill-gotten fortunes) by destroying (the lives of others and the sources of their livelihood for generations to come). In short, they are defying logic by acting illogically. But that should not surprise us, because that is how they operate. We should, however, guard against labeling such behaviour as worse than animal behaviour, because animals behave far more homanely and logically than many homan beings, and to call callous homan behaviour animal behaviour is to insult the animals. But what has now become more scary is that a stupid, gullible, and self-satisfied section of the public is being taken in by this foolishness and displaying their inability to think for themselves in the face of a host of scientific facts versus the cheap commercial propaganda that they are being fed by these liars who know the facts but are suppressing them for financial gain.

The terror that emanates from governmental circles is always more destructive than that perpetrated by individuals or groups, because, while there may still be ultimate (although biased) recourse against the latter, this final court of appeal is already closed to the victim of the former. Hence the significance of situations that exist in pink states of twin world which are revealed in the telling anecdotes from some of the oppressive racist regimes of our world: in one case, their law allowed for the granting of citizenship to *white* immigrants only, on the assumption that only Caucasians are considered *white*. A Caucasian of dark complexion was, however, denied citizenship on the basis of his skin colour, even though he was *white*. So how is this situation to be explained? It can only make sense if *white* is sometimes not-*white*, or, as the wise men of our time have said, truth is not truth (A is not-A) = nonsense. Is the ridiculousness of racist logic beginning to consume it? In another part of our world a government report stated that during a certain period no blacks became white, while three Chinese did, and in the same period no whites became blacks. People have now become chameleons that change colour to fit in with the racial environment that can bring them benefits. Today the same people who were striving to be white have won the right to be classified as black, which happens to be the side on which the bread is now buttered, lending further support to the ridiculous unreality of race and its expedient utilization for personal gain. This arbitrary, asinine classification of the population is the progeny of the evil design meant to divide and rule the people by stratifying them according to their proximity in skin colour to the presumed resplendent norm, which is White. Orientals (honorary whites) are next inline after Chinese, but still a fair distance above Blacks (everyone's doormat), from whom they are separated (in descending order) by Coloureds (hybrid generation of whites with blacks and all the other races) and east Indians. What is wrong with people just being people?

In their attempt to mimic the model of this world, the misguided people of twin world realized that every group thinks and acts as if it is better than the ones below it on this stratification scale, and all the whilom outcasts of their pink world have competed successfully for inclusion in pink ranks by vilifying and oppressing browns, like some in our world who have erected "apartheid" or "apart hate" walls that separate them from browns. Peace bridges are not in their vocabulary. Other pinks enforced separate habitats, schools, and socio-cultural activities on browns, based on their minor tribal affiliations, to ensure that they live in an atmosphere of antagonism that will in turn prevent them from engaging in any possible joint action to relieve themselves of their burden of pink oppression. Needless to say, pinks initiated and still continue to foment ongoing strife among the different tribal groups and then sit back and condemn what they call brown on brown violence. When warring factions of the same tribe bury their hatchet and unite, pinks urge one side to tear up their détente, because it defeats their ploy of divide and rule. If they clamour for the statehood of which they were stripped by cold-blooded murder, their oppressors and dispossessors have the audacity to say that they will not allow their state to have an army, while their own army continues to terrorize and murder the citizens of their victim tribe to avenge their reciprocal acts of terror. They have clearly become totally intoxicated with their herrenvolkism to be making such brazen demands of people whose right to life they have been violating for decades without any compunction.

One does not have to be a genius to realize that direct pink cold-blooded murder is now largely outmoded, and that proxies are in vogue as the new "refined" methods of achieving the same end without soiling the hands of the architect of the murder. Intensified economic deprivation, whose consequences are all the possible afflictions like disease, starvation, and crime that can devastate a disinherited nation, is yet another one of these vile methods. The fatal effects of this economic inhomanity are glaring, but the perpetrators hold up their hands to show that they are not literally dripping with blood, although they cannot claim not to have pulled the trigger that caused that blood to shed. But they know that the culling of undesirables in this manner is a big part of their plan to eliminate these impediments to their sole and absolute control of twin world, as we will see in the next chapter. What we see in the hands of these Krustans and those of other faiths who behave like them are multiples of the proverbial thirty pieces of silver harvested from the shedding of that innocent blood.

# Chapter 13
# Economic Inhomanity

The pink Krustans of twin world have devised many devious ways of promoting their insatiable quest for money, even to the extent of diverting it from its intended benevolent purpose where it is meant to be used to save the lives of poor browns and members of their own pink tribe. Their high priests have learnt to capitalize on the intellects of their flocks that imbibe any kind of information without analyzing it critically, accepting irrational and unfounded utterances that are inconsistent with the facts of their existence, and rejecting those that are consistent with rational, well-founded, and publicly provable facts in the same period of time and circumstance. The point is sadly brought home by protesters who have been marshalled by religious and other bigots and by those who exploit their naïveté to promote their own slanted agendas to demonstrate against what they call infringement of their autonomy by brown civic authority, an ignominy that their vain pride cannot stomach. As we have noted, these ignorant common folk boastfully re-affirm their negative stance by citing irrelevant reasons for their participation in marches into which they have been huddled like unthinking cattle by malicious-minded racist characters like them who are advancing their own vested interests and ulterior motives at their expense. Encounters with some of them might go like this:

Johin: Why are you marching?

Soriah: I don't know; but I want to reclaim my country.

Johin: Your country? Reclaim it from whom?

Soriah: I don't know, but I have been told to come out and march to reclaim my country.

Johin: But this march is for protesting the extension of privileges and rights to browns, not to reclaim their country from them; they were never able to take it back after we confiscated it from them many centuries ago. So we don't have to reclaim it. It has been and still is firmly ours. Don't you understand? This is our country.

Soriah: So why am I marching?

Johin: I don't know; but I have a hunch that you are marching to save my investments and those of my corporate colleagues who, like me, are also milking browns, you, and the system.

Soriah: Which system?

John: You will never understand. Such concepts are difficult for simple minds to comprehend, if you even know what I mean by that. So just keep on marching; that's all you are good for.

Soriah: In that case, then, I will march and also attend a lemonade party to give vent to my ire at having browns occupy the higher echelons of our pink society. How about that?

John: Please yourself; perhaps the vitriol that you spew at your lemonade party will impress the other unintelligent, gullible sections of our pink society to see things through the distorting lenses that we are making them wear, although I doubt that it will make much of an impression on the intelligent ones who think for themselves. But who cares, the dolts are in the majority; they believe anything we tell them, and they will willingly execute our filthy agenda. Besides, lemonade parties are not the same. There are street parties for your kind, and there are elite champagne cruise parties meant especially for the rich and famous of our rabble, like me, to blow off the steam of frustration and lick the wounds of our losses to browns.

Soriah: I have been programmed to march until I drop; so I will continue marching. Good bye, enjoy your cruise, and don't forget that I am marching for you. Down with browns; more power to pinks. Backward march; right, left; left, right; right, left (confusion).

These credulous, unthinking, and ignorant buffoons are some of the superior beings who rule twin world. They can't see the idiocy of continuing to pay happily for the elite health care of guys like John who are using them to block extension of the same privilege to them under the pretext that it promotes state interference in what should be their personal choices, but, in truth, resent its inception by a brown when they successfully scuttled similar attempts by other pinks to dismantle their steady source of hefty pourboire from the corporations that fleece the people with the prices of drugs, forcing their supporters to seek basic health care from neighbouring states.

The minds of successive generations of the people of twin world have been taken over by these cabalists with simulacra of what life is about by making them believe in their canards and promises of well-being through a globalization that is aimed at self-enrichment at the expense of the trading and other rights and freedoms of all those who implicitly believe in them. Meanwhile, the burden of poverty carried by the poor ones has grown, while the amassing of wealth by the rich has increased, and greed and corruption have blossomed to the point of throwing their global economy into a tailspin, thanks to the selfish and incompetent cliques in their governments who, together with their cronies, are trying to establish economic empires for themselves at the expense of the common good i.e., the good of citizens that they govern and dominate with lies. It is regrettable that the trust of the citizens in their corrupt leaders blinds them to their disreputable actions, allowing them to misuse their elected positions, selling out them and their country to protect themselves from their own misdeeds.

These unprincipled types do not hesitate to invent lies about purportedly imminent collapses of those economies that they want to sabotage by scaring investors away from them, letting them collapse, and then moving in for the kill by acquiring them. When they squander their tax dullams on rewarding their friends for doing the dirty jobs of oppressing and exploiting citizens of other countries, when they willfully permit the disrespectful pillaging of the national treasures of their victim states, when they fail to account for billions of reconstruction dullams that have been placed in their care, and when their only record of success is the turmoil that they have left behind, their citizens should be in total revolt, instead of tractably accepting these misdeeds as part of their protection from the imaginary outside harm that these illusionists have promised them for surrendering their civil rights and freedoms to them.

On the other hand, browns do not have that freedom; they are trapped with every step that they take to improve their lot for a better life. When they need money, rich pink states, through their corporations, lend them overwhelming sums of money (with sizeable interest, of course) or undertake development projects for them at exorbitant and prohibitive costs, which are really projects meant to provide gainful employment for the personnel of their construction companies, because the people who are supposed to be benefiting from these projects are compelled to use the costly services of these companies for which they will foot the bill. There is no opportunity for them to choose who will do the job for them for less money or to involve their local experts in rebuilding their own infrastructure; it is all planned and done for them by their benefactors who must maintain economic superiority at their expense in cheap (low-down) but expensive (costly) exploitation. This forced arrangement amounts to a sentence to perpetual enslavement of poor brown states that are forced to borrow money and to keep coming back for more costly loans to meet commitments that they cannot cover with their denuded national incomes. Only irresponsible pink states share this fate; otherwise their leaders are all part of this coterie.

Before they acquire these loans, however, they are compelled to submit to the imposition of structural adjustment programs to their economies, which are meant to stifle economic growth and foster dependency on the unprincipled lender who will spare no effort to undermine all their efforts at self-sufficiency, while demanding that their programs in education, health, and social welfare be drastically slashed, ostensibly to pay off their debt (which is never paid off or forgiven), but in truth to cripple their development and ensure the elimination of potential competition from them and their successive progeny, even after they have all been starved to death and are no longer present to be a threat and a nuisance. They are also required to privatize all their state held enterprises so that the vultures and their lapdog local officials can take them over and exploit the people for the essential services to which they have hitherto had ready access, but which are now inaccessible to them, unless they can pay the hefty price that comes with enjoying those services. For this dirty piece of work, governments serve as proxies for their bedfellows in crime, the corporations, because certain governments control vicious hit-squads that can enforce these evil conditions by assassinations and changing regimes that resist these iniquitous revisions to their rational ways of self-direction. These corrupt governments of the leading states of twin world are a boon to corporations, because they can claim immunity from prosecution under the cloak of state security, which the corporations cannot do.

The chain of subservience is continued by the puppets that these governments install in brown states who then initiate reigns of terror and mass murder, pauperizing their own states to secure their lucrative positions and to gratify these monsters who are keeping them in charge to facilitate their shameless looting, which will take decades to eradicate. Their pink benefactors secretly aid and abet them to wipe out thousands of their own citizens for favours that only good boys receive, and these boot-licking maggots are proud of their despicable role in the murder of their brown brothers and sisters and their children for these demeaning favours.

After all the cruel lies that they have told the people about why their elected leaders are being forced out and replaced by their stooges, the perpetrators of this rape on the citizens of victimized countries still have the unmitigated gall to suggest that these people who are now starving are better off than they were under their previous governments when they had enough to eat, and when they had advanced educational and health care facilities with enviable standards, instead of their present lack of the same institutions by which they maintained those standards. Their decent living quarters have been replaced by shanties in which they are compelled to exist like rabbits in holes; their well paying jobs scuttled by retrenchments that are meant to boost the profits of the usurpers but leave them without the means to support their families; and their social and community relations that inspired them to strive upward in the midst of privation, have yielded place to degrading disarray imposed on their simple lives by the hardships to which they are subjected by their dispossessing oppressors who are motivated and ruled only by ugly, insatiable greed and racism, aided and abetted by their own brown brothers who should be uplifting them.

Newly minted brown states that come into being with the best of good intentions are compelled by the same pink trickery and treachery that tripped up their ancestors to yield to concessions that amount to a total sell out of the people that they promised freedom from the bondage in which they were forced to exist for centuries under the political and economic boot of the oppressor. All the pledges that were made and never kept by their guileful pink deceivers, like providing housing to replace the shacks in which they are living, employment with decent wages to improve standards of living and longevity, basic amenities and utilities that convert mere existence to living, health care services with free access to desperately needed drugs to control some of the most devastating diseases like AIDS, fair distribution of land so that the myriads who are squatting on the arid <13% of it and excluded from the fertile >87% of it that is owned unfairly by the few rich pinks can begin to live like homan beings, and many other essentials that infuse purpose into life have evaporated. Their brown governments reneged on their promises, because they have tasted the luxuries that come with their positions. Browns states are more broke than they were before they took nominal ownership of the home in which oppressors are still the occupants. Now they have to pay all the bills, the mortgage, and other enormous debts that the same oppressors incurred while they were trying to keep them in the gutter with their boots on their necks and the cheque book in their sole control.

The full pressure of the boots is off now, but browns remain helpless in the gutter where the oppressors and their foxy economists are keeping them chained with the many restrictions that they have improvised for that purpose with their iniquitous theories of how best to swing the open market economy to their sole advantage, leaving the browns thoroughly flabbergasted and impoverished by the unexpected turn of events against them. Where they have previously tightened the noose of death around the necks of their victims by forcibly prohibiting them from trading with other nations, they have now turned around and arrogantly declared their country open for looting under the guise of free trade that is directed by them. Ravaged by a globalized economy and faced with a rueful lack of economic independence, brown states remain economic slaves of the oppressors who have weaved intricate schemes into their monetary institutions to keep them dependent for easy exploitation and continuing subjugation. As we have noted, their goods of all varieties are sabotaged on the international markets, and the costly loans that they are forced to take from these institutions come with ridiculous, harsh conditions that demand structural adjustments like spending 40% of their meagre gross domestic product on servicing the interest on their debt, without making a dent on the principal. The result is the shameful ignominy of relegating funding for their health, education, social, and other portfolios to second and third place for the sake of paying off their crippling debt. Unfortunately for them, their initially impoverished state made it impossible for them to fund the expensive projects for which they were forced to reach out for enslaving loans that make it impossible for them to break the cycle of dependency on their unscrupulous lenders.

Such is the havoc wreaked on poor people by uncaring superpowers and twin world equivalents of this world's super-benevolent financial institutions whose laudable deeds are known to all who care to study their operations, especially their structural adjustment (now euphemistically styled "poverty reduction") programs about whose moral role in the lives of poor people Davison Budhoo, a senior economist in that organization, dedicating his resignation letter to "the more than two billion voiceless, starving and diseased people who share our planet"[1] wrote, on May 18, 1988:

> Today I resigned from the staff of the International Monetary Fund... hawking your medicine and your bag of tricks to governments and to peoples in Latin America and the Caribbean and Africa. . . . I have taken the first big step to that place where I may hope to wash my hands of what in my mind's eye is the blood of millions of poor and starving people. . . . the blood is so much, . . . it runs in rivers. It dries up too; it cakes all over me; sometimes I feel that there is not enough soap in the whole world to cleanse me from the things that I did do in your name and in the names of your predecessors, and under your official seal.[2]

Describing "western society and western morality and postwar intergovernmental institutionalism that have degenerated into fake and sham under the pretext of establishing and maintaining inter-national economic order and global efficiency"[3], and stressing also that "the poor are not the expendable garbage heap that our institution thinks they are"[4], he goes on to describe the fund, whose insider he was for twelve years, as a soulless fund that churns out hunger, despair, and death; a hypocritical fund that violates basic human rights throughout the developing world and commits economic crimes and statistical fraud by cooking numbers to reflect poor countries in a bad light, thereby precluding them from receiving the financial assistance that they need, keeping them under its heel through the actions of a single staffer who brings to bear on his decisions "all his own personal prejudices and arbitrariness and hang-ups and self-interest and lust for power and mad desire to control the destiny of peoples and of nations"[5], thus forcing them into further destitution through a genocidal fund that drives poor people away from their lands to provide industrial and residential space, and to construct dams to benefit rich farmers.

Twin world pinks have appropriated this style of running their economic affairs and have now also taken to compelling everyone to walk on their side of the clear, bold line that delineates base greed from generosity, cruelty from compassion, and inhumanity from homaneness, a cursed side that expunges all of the latter qualities with disdain and embraces the former qualities with unmitigated zest. When nations are decimated by imposed budget cuts that result in unemployment by the millions, homelessness, sky-rocketing prices of food and other commodities, poverty, suicides committed in the desperation of the inability to support starving families, harlotry by children to provide income for their destitute families, and treatable but also preventable disease, they shamelessly wring their hands in glee, while decrying them for their immorality. But they still firmly keep their boots on their necks, further cutting off the air that they breathe, instead of lifting the boots and letting them breathe freely to improve their chances of survival from the asphyxiation to which they have been subjected. To sign a deal with them is to sign in blood a deal with the same fictitious devil that their Krustan books and teachings use to cow the credulous multitudes into submission. The only possible outcome of that Mephistophelean relationship is death for the unsophisticated victim who falls into their snare.

They further impose foreign exchange restrictions on their own countries to protect the flight of capital, but they forcibly lift them from their victim states under their adjustment programs to facilitate their own acts of pillaging, and they allow their corporate friends 100% tax-exempt ownership of all local industries and commercial concerns, some of which deliberately charge high interest rates on all loans, well beyond the reach of the common folk. Meanwhile, these slick oppressors and exploiters still assure the poor folk that they are prospering by averaging the astronomical annual incomes of the fat cats with their meagre annual wages to get a tidy sum that is applied to all of them as their average income for the year, giving the false impression that every one is well off, when the four million less one are actually starving to death and virtually all the money belongs to one fat cat. (Fat cat earns $100million/annum; 9,999 other citizens earn a total of $100million; average income of all citizens amounts to $20,000 per annum. But, in fact, the other citizens average less than $10,000 per annum versus his $100,000,000. These crafty manoeuvres, displayed as evidence of the general well-being of brown citizens, ensure successful stifling of public clamour against the deceptive trickle down effect of their heinous governmental economic policies, while concealing their intended goal of perpetual socio-economic slavery of the brown peoples of twin world.

When they overrun a country under the pretext of bringing their sick kind of democracy to it, they arrogantly give orders left, right, and centre, placing their corporations in charge of every facet of government, because they are not interested in establishing reputable governance; they just want the money and other riches that can be harvested from their victim states. That is all they came for, and why they will lift price controls to open the doors for their expensive commodities to flood the markets exclusively; all of which tells everyone where their well-meaning intentions are focused.

At any time, the demands of this enslaving coterie of leaders of the closely intertwined complex of state and corporations exacts from the poor states of twin world, among others penalties, those of voting at international organizations in accordance with the direction of the rich states; surrendering their votes at these organizations to the creditor state or else suffering curtailment of certain monetary favours and other means of aid; surrendering control of their oil, minerals, and other resources to the same rich states; allowing them to establish military bases on their soil from which they can launch their empiricist expansion programs designed to realize their pipe dream of colonizing and controlling all of twin world; producing only the raw material for manufactured goods that are processed by the rich pink manufacturer and then sold back to them at a much higher price than if they manufactured those commodities themselves; and growing only those crops that are mandated by the rich for their appropriation and sole trade on world markets, including selling them to these same growers who must purchase them at a price that far outstrips the cost at which they produced them and which they cannot afford. Thus they cultivate crops solely for the enrichment of these unfeeling fiends. They may not and dare not use these crops to feed their families that are starving in the midst of plenty and are thereby rendered physically and mentally incapable of mounting any opposition to the abuses to which they are constantly subjected.

If they had just grown those crops on their agricultural lands to feed their families as they had been doing before the usurpers took over, they would have been able to stave off the hunger, starvation, and the resultant infirmities from which their children are dying. All these and other manoeuvres that restrict the sphere of activity and influence of browns are designed to thwart their attempts at becoming and being economically, politically, and educationally independent. They keep them at the mercy of the inhomane system of pink supremacy in which they are condemned to an unending, miserable, and ignoble existence. If these poor states, through their farmers, happen to be able to cultivate and market their crops, they are outmanoeuvred from deriving a modest income from their produce and commodities and thereby kept dependent on the rich vultures by the latter's imposition of contrived devaluation on their cocoa and other goods. Their market prices plummet, they get next to nothing for all their labours, and their economies totter to their fall. This evil scheme is the progeny of father pink corporation and mother pink government, whose relationship appears to be male dominated (corporation→government), although sometimes it can be tricky, like when the states use corporations as their proxies to carry out unethical operations that they hope will not be traced back to them, while keeping their own hands clean. Similarly, corporations use corrupt local authorities, who are ready to sell the citizens' rights to their national assets, to steal the people's wealth.

By and large, however, it is the corporations that use the state to further their own ends, which are always laced with elements of avarice and inhomaneness. The citizens dare not raise complaints against them, lest they be branded as unpatriotic rebels against state jurisdiction; not against corporation greed. That is why government watchdogs can penalize citizens who infringe rules laid by the corporations on the use of amenities and facilities that they operate in private, like some private highways (built by the people, but sold to the corporation for a song) whose new owners use state police and licensing bodies to penalize toll transgressors, still at the expense of the tax paying public. This exploited crowd should be paying less tax for the maintenance of all the state assets that have been gifted to politicians and corporations, who should be maintaining them, but their taxes continue to increase while corporations enjoy tax cuts, and their taxes are squandered on fancy war machinery and new jails that should rightly be housing this duplicitous cabal of thieves.

But they are not the only grand larcenists; their other partners in crime are the new breed of spin masters that has infested twin world with devices for siphoning billions of hard-earned dullams from people's investments. They dupe prospective investors with glowing accounts of the high yields that will flow from these enterprises, and then shamelessly defraud them by misrepresenting the true state of the finances of their enterprises, leaving the flabbergasted investors holding bags full of empty promises and lives lost in the blinding dust of their lies. They and like liars in government revel in making fools of the citizenry with intricate schemes to assist them in stealing control of their lives to serve their own advantages of power and money. Lying is their password to power and influence in all sectors of twin world, and poor browns have been selected to bear the biggest brunt of the suffering caused by this epidemic of lying by the unfortunate but well-planned circumstance of their position at the base of the totem pole. Everyone takes unfair advantage of them.

To add insult to injury, when some people think that they are moving up that pole and emerging from poverty and lack to a level where they can afford to invest in the markets at the instigation of the rich owners of those investment engines, they are exploited by the executives of those institutions who wipe out their savings and reward themselves for their misdeeds with millions of dullams, which they safely stash away offshore, while their comrades in government let them get away with these grand thefts, because the sordid practice of misappropriation of public funds is universal in all sectors of public "service", especially in governments; they are run by thieves. One would expect that their assets would be frozen and seized to compensate their victims, and that they would be prohibited from rewarding themselves for their heists with more stolen money in the form of enormous severance packages and bonuses to honour their dismal failure in their duty to their investors. But they are allowed to take off with these large sums of stolen money in an arrogant attitude of entitlement, whereas the average person would be mercilessly thrown into jail or shot by the fat cats for the theft of a loaf of bread to feed his starving family or for some inconsequential misdemeanour that does not even inflict a minuscule fraction of the hardship and suffering caused by these privileged thieves.

The ease and readiness with which the powerless are thrown into jail for trifles is clear proof that these idiots fail to realize that the financial ($147,000/prisoner/annum) and social cost to their societies in caring for these multitudes of jailed persons far exceeds that of providing them with social programs etc., (<$20,000/person/annum) to avoid incarceration and social disintegration. But the idiots know what they are doing; they are destroying brown aspirations, since they constitute the majority of inmates who are being jailed for social crimes resulting from the conditions in which they are forced to live by inhomane pink policies. That is why they would rather continue a costly form of racist economics by allotting a pittance to brown social programs to dehomanize them than help to raise them to a level of decency where they will feel equal to them. That is why they will not fund brown enterprises that ironically generate millions of dullams for their city economies, while they pour tons of dullams into their own enterprises. That is also why they undermine special programs designed to help aboriginals (4% of the population, but 20% of inmates in Canada) overcome the effects of the scourge of alcohol, with which they have showered them to destroy them, by withdrawing their funding and committing them to the all-inclusive barrel of aboriginal affairs where they are certain to get lost for ever.

These are the same groups of poor people who toil in the sweat shops of the rich, where even children are harnessed to the mill to provide cheap labour for rich entrepreneurs; who don't qualify for compassionate care of their ordinary illnesses and other rarer illnesses for which they require special treatments, like drugs for Malaria and AIDS, which could be made readily available to them if their lives meant anything to the fat cats who reap huge profits from their labour at the expense of their health. For all their sacrificial contribution to the prosperity of the pink state, they should be receiving deeply discounted AIDS drugs and free nets to protect them from mosquito bites and infection with malarial parasites; they should be getting protection against the inhalation of asbestos fibres in the ship-wrecking and other industries where they labour every day of every year to further enrich the rich; and protection from the carbon emissions of factories that drive the economy of rich societies, bringing in more riches for the benefit of the rich on their backs.

Amidst this endless cycle of riches begetting riches, the greed of these rich fat cats makes them forget that many of the ill effects of pollution and global warming do not, like them, favour rich over poor. They wreak their havoc on the ozone layer of the atmosphere indiscriminately, and the atmospheric mantle of retained greenhouse gases: nitrous oxide, fluorocarbons, methane, carbon dioxide, etc., does not target poor people preferentially. Rich snots who think they can escape the effects of destruction of homan habitation and natural habitats of polar and other animal life, as well as potential (and actual) flooding of small islands and coastal dwellings from thawing of polar ice caps with loss of lives about which they don't care a hoot, because they choose where to live, had better think again. All havoc wreaked by pollution catches up with them, like the warmer ocean waters that create stronger, more moisture-laden winds and fiercer hurricanes that have now found a favourable climate in which to come into being with intensified force and ferocity, destroying all that lies in their path, including their lavish abodes and furnishings, all of which are made from felled trees that could have broken the force of these winds.

Simultaneously, change and contraction of the eco-environment have allowed overcrowding and facilitated the spread of contagious diseases, making it possible for some viruses to jump the gap from animal to homan host with devastating results to the specifically non-immune homan species. Today twin world is also living under the threat of devastating viral infections that carry the potential of acquiring pandemic proportions, like our own bird flu, swine flu, and West Nile virus infections. But these cats are not moved by these perils. They appease themselves by arguing that these are natural weather cycles about which nothing needs to be done. By so doing, they not only miss an opportunity to prevent disaster, but they also choose to wake up to the dire situation, if they ever will, in hallum (hell), long after it has consumed them and after their lives have lost the sordid, selfish meaning that they ever had, long after lethal damage to the valuable lives of other people, and long after most corrective measures can be of only limited or no avail.

It is no exaggeration to say that the wealth of twin world is in the hands of these few scoundrels, while many of the rest of the caring people are labouring under the yoke of poverty, want, and hunger, which oftentimes degenerates into destitution, as evidenced by brown children and adults scavenging for food in trash bins and garbage dumps, which are conveniently located close to where they live, but far from the classy neighbourhoods of the rich, while the rich are throwing away the same food for them to pick up. Why not pack it in a dignified manner and distribute it among them instead of humiliating them and reducing them to the level of foraging animals that scratch around for food, unlike their own pets, of course. Their animals do not scratch the dumps for food; they are fed special diets at well laid tables or other dignified indoor facilities that have been specially fashioned for their feeding comfort. Meanwhile, their owners are oblivious to these depressing sights of people foraging the dumps for food. They do not create the least impression on the fat cows who rule the land with political and economic lies, twin territories that are as impossible to separate as the economic fat cows and their political counterparts, either because they wallow in the same gutter or because they are often the same people.

Everywhere rich pinks exploit the rest of the population, but mainly browns. They abuse them in their own lands where they give them menial jobs in their mining and other industries for which they are expected to be ever so grateful as to accept any piece of trash that is thrown their way. Protesting against ill-treatment is not an option, because it can be lethal to the protester at the hands of hired, uniformed assassins, while pink governments that are associated with these corrupt corporations provide them with protection by refusing to be involved in investigating their violations of the homan rights of browns, claiming that their cases are being probed by the courts of law, and that alone prohibits them from interfering. At the same time, rogue states that fabricate indictments against browns continue to abuse their homan rights with impunity, because they know that they will not be questioned by their pink citizens. Even after the innocence of their brown victims has been established, they will not apologize to them for the inhomanity to which they subjected them, although they are sometimes forced to compensate them without condescending to making that apology. After all, who cares how disrespectfully browns are treated or what happens to them? Meanwhile, the abuse continues in the name of the security of their country, and poor people continue to lose their lives from drug toxicities, poison gas accidents, and torture in prisons. Anyone who lets the cat out of the bag about these incidents is calumniated sternly by the government's barking curs who should have attended to these misdemeanours before they could no longer be contained but chose to ignore them, mainly because they involved abuse of browns.

In every world, twin world included, every person's success in life hinges on the freely given or indirectly coerced support of others who also owe their success or failure to the same persons and to others. The relationship is reciprocal, and it benefits all alike. It is not unusual to find, however, that some of the ones who succeed do so by climbing up the backs of those who cannot make it, even though they boast of having pulled themselves up from the pit of misery with their own bootstraps. They hold themselves up as enviable and envied models of economic success, conveniently forgetting to add the nature of their bootstraps, which often include corruption in government and selling out their tribe for favours from dividers and oppressors of the people. Many of them are happy to serve as fronts for pink-owned-and-operated corporations that exploit brown economic empowerment by using them as window-dressing puppets for a price, while they continue to prolong brown socio-economic slavery and misery with their exploitative manoeuvres.

Governments of brown states should be particularly singled out for this kind of outrageous behaviour (corruption), as almost all of these thieves indulge in large-scale pilfering, depriving pensioners, public servants, and small-scale investors of the meagre benefits that are due to them after years of hard work. Almost all of them come into office under the pretext of having the interests of the people at heart but knowing full well that they are there for selfish reasons, reasons that impel them to become dictators who silence opposition with incarceration, murder, and genocide. Where their powers are limited by their stations, they are content with stealing the people's wealth by denying them their constitutional rights and appointing their unprincipled henchmen to assume supervisory reigns of power over them, whether of chieftainship or other forms of lordship, as long as their appointees can allow them access to gold, diamonds, platinum, or other sources of wealth that should be benefiting the people but are now being plundered by them. These so-called liberators of the people, who put themselves up as fighters for their freedom and upliftment in every aspect of their lives, turn out to be nothing more than paltry opportunists who have rushed in to take advantage of a situation where corruption is the order of the day, and where everyone who can is busy stuffing her pockets with the wealth of the people, like the original and latter-day vultures who scrambled and are still scrambling for the wealth of the Afibikan continent. These scurvy low lives, who are ruled only by greed, are the unabashed sons and daughters of the soil who should know better than to steal from the people who have placed their trust in their leadership.

They also engage in the despicable practice of selling their lands, minerals, resources, and the people themselves (as slaves) to the oppressors for personal enrichment. Their secret bank accounts are bulging with stolen millions of dullams that should be supporting the people and the economies of their countries, while the pink oppressor is also enriching himself on the backs of the people who are hardly managing to keep their heads above water in the expansive ocean of life where they have neither lifeboats nor life jackets for survival. Meanwhile the luxury ocean liner that is carrying the oppressor-exploiter, his despicable brown tools, and their bounty bounces and bobs its greedy, gorged, but never satiated inhomane cargo to their respective destinations where each one can begin to stuff himself on the spoils of their joint plunder until he disgorges from surfeit, if he does not deservingly choke on them. These ignoble characters are not difficult to spot in all communities; they abound like weeds in the cornfields of twin world governments.

Once these brown thieves have qualified for the elite status of the "haves", they become partners with the legendary exploiters, and together they impose environmental and cultural burdens on the citizens as follows: toxic effluent from their industrial plants, which belch into rivers from which the poor obtain their only supply of drinking water, because they cannot afford boreholes that will provide them with potable water; deforestation, which promotes erosion of the little land that they are renting for cultivating meagre crops to feed their under-nourished families, provided that the structural adjustment plans of the rich don't force their governments to prohibit such small-scale crop farming for self-sustenance in favour of unsubsidized farming (unlike the heavily subsidized farming that farmers in rich countries enjoy) for production of commercial crops to supply international markets from which they derive no benefit; extermination of wild animal life for the sport of the rich, depriving the poor hunter of food for his family; farming of aquatic animals for the money markets, diminishing food supplies for the poor brown fisherman whose seaside home is also demolished to make way for erection of pleasure resorts for the rich; and devastation of many other self-sustaining pursuits on which the poor depend for their livelihood. In short, genocide is blatantly perpetrated on the poor.

This despicable attitude toward the lives of others proves that the meaning of life beyond the ambit of the self that is wrapped in itself has yet to dawn on those who look into their mirrors and see only their reflections in them, from which they conclude that there is no one else worth losing sleep over. Hence the need for finding more effective ways of eradicating the rampant and exponentially growing inhomanity of the privileged few of twin world that periodically emerges as a mere hollow simulacrum of genuine homanity. Laws can't change these attitudes; they only encourage circumvention and more skulduggery. Only force can stamp out this wildly spreading weed compounded of avarice, arrogance, entitlement, and racism, so that the seed of a veritable homanity can finally blossom and flourish for the boundless enjoyment of all the inhabitants of twin world.

Will browns take up the challenge, or will they continue to roll over to expose more of their paltry possessions to this larceny and themselves to this degradation, and inhomanity?

# Chapter 14
# Political inhomanity

Answering the previous question entails remembering that life in twin world, as we have seen, is a curious mixture of greed and strife, with the former breeding the latter. If one tribe has something that another tribe wants, the greedy ones do not bargain for it; they take it by force, especially if the owner is weaker than them. (See reference [4], page 80). If they have a difference for any reason, the stronger tribe prefers to settle it with bombs. War is no longer the option of last resort after peaceful means of settling legitimate — not trumped up — differences have been exhausted, but it is the first option of these cowardly bullies. Strength purchased with wealth gives imperialist bullies the audacity to victimize weaker states while they pussy-foot around those that challenge them on their own terms. In defiance of international laws of non-interference in the government and self-direction of other states, these bullies violate their sovereignty, their political independence, and their territorial integrity by arrogantly assuming the prerogative of changing their systems of government (regime change). They destabilize, terrorize, and undermine them to impose their warped representations of a self-serving democracy that is driven by capitalist greed and theft, executed by the conflated duo of corporations on one hand and corrupt, inept government officials and their families on the other.

Some of these gutless dictators who masquerade as indefectible embodiments of the democratic temperament lack the forthrightness to respond to searching questions about their misconduct; they are vilifying their critics and opponents and they are adept at running and hiding under the skirts of authoritative ladies in search of leave to extemporaneously dissolve the constituted legislatures of their states, while the persons to whom they claim to be taking their sham democracy continue to attend to those duties even during what should be their deserved break from work. How ironic! Regrettably, however, this cowardly behaviour becomes a demeaning habit that only reflects the kind of cheap opportunism that they are made of. To their arrogant minds, democratic dialectic consists in bickering.

Democracy as government of the people, by the people, for the people has become rigid control of the people by these cliques for the benefit of their members against the will of the people. It emerges as one or more of plutocracy (government by the wealthy), autocracy (by one person), kleptocracy (by a gang of thieves), monarchy (by free-loading "royalty"), timocracy (by seekers after fame and glory), oligarchy (by a few select people), theocracy (by a class claiming to have divine authority), and totalitarianism (by a cruel faction that suppresses dissent by intimidation, demonization, etc.), all of which amount to shameless theft of the rights and power of the people for the purpose of manipulating them with lies to promote the egoistic ends of the so-called leaders who have placed themselves above the people and expend most of their energies in promoting their own interests. Within these so-called democratic systems, the people don't really exercise their right of self-determination, even though they go through the motions of exercising what they believe is their political sovereignty and franchise, they putter in a franchise puddle that subjects them to the indiscernibly complexed religious and political whims of those in power over them, literally making them slaves of the elected and the unelected back room boys who control their lives.

These democracies of twin world are replicas of the fictitious Oceania of George Orwell, where Big Brother's oxymorons that we saw on page 17 abound: Peace Ministries wage war, Truth Ministries spread propaganda and lies, Ministries of Plenty ensure shortages, Information Ministries disperse disinformation and misinformation, and Ministries of Love deliver torture and persecution. Big Brother watches over every citizen; distorts the folk histories of browns; imposes his language and mores on them; controls their thinking, reading material, and actions; encourages and rewards citizens and families for snitching on one another; brainwashes and tortures them, even murdering those who oppose the corrupt policies of the ruling class; employs various psychological ploys to control the citizens with the aid of its Thought Police who can tell by looking at them that they are thinking subversive thoughts, just as in twin world where dark skin colour spells criminal thoughts and intent.

While all of this is going on, youth and adults are pacified with frivolous distractions and "show institutions" that serve as sources of contentment used by politicians who don't want them to have the time to devote to serious thought about affairs of state and their associated problems. These distractions are imposed on them from childhood to condition the minds of the children to dwell on trifles, facilitating the calculated, extended brainwashing and manipulation that will continue for the rest of their lives into adulthood. All these distractions are meant to secure triumph at the next election for the promotion of the new world agenda, while their architects engage in misuse of public funds, war, terrorism, and the indiscriminate killing of other people to justify the lies that they have been spinning about the nation being the victim of foiled potential foreign and domestic assaults, deserved or undeserved. As for the truth of these matters, it remains sealed and hidden for decades, while the perpetrators haul their accusers into kangaroo courts or simply make them disappear mysteriously with the aid of their state-sponsored hit-squads that go under different official names in different countries of twin world, but essentially all performing the same dirty work of liquidating non-compliant trouble makers who also ask too many questions, or those they consider to be terrorists, ignoring the fact that they are fighting for their freedom from occupation and repression. Heads of other states, even though democratically elected, are also not exempt from being the victims of these sordid activities, if they don't toe the line of the bully states. When will international courts of justice haul in these villains, instead of dragging in small time operatives at the behest of these same freely roaming, reprehensible characters?

Those who attend brainwashing sessions for journalists and the gullible dare not ask searching questions that are meant to reveal the insincerity of the rulers, lest they be hustled away to keep them from alerting the rest to the big bluff that is being imposed on all the people. Furthermore, anyone who dares to question the assumed sovereignty and infallibility of their leader or the inhomanity displayed by him and his gang of cronies, or that of their friends who are oppressing browns in other parts of twin world, already stands accused of treason or lack of blind patriotism, and is under the threat of having his tribe's "benevolent" financial assistance from their arrogant government cut off, in spite of their entitlement to these funds by virtue of paying their taxes. If the state happens to be engaged in one of its bogus self-defence wars, the people must shut up and listen to their rulers; they must not criticize their stupid and selfish actions; they must allow themselves to be brow-beaten and lied to for the sake of national security; they must be absolute fools who have stopped to think for themselves—their self-serving, doltish leaders will insult their intelligence by thinking for them, using them for photo ops to boost their own shabby images, consistently lying to them, and finally taking them to hallum (hell) with them.

How often are people lied to by bullies and warmongers who wallow in disinformation for the sake of their self-aggrandizement? We are prevailing against the enemy; they are on the run; we will emerge victorious from this conflict, and until we achieve that victory—even if it will be when the cows come home—we will not give up the conflict that we started; "we are not quitters"; but we will proudly continue to send other people's children to provide fodder for the cannons of "the enemy", because it will hurt our pride to be seen to withdraw from a conflict with a puny state that we thought we could dazzle with our thunderous might and walk over it in the wink of an eye, instead of being mired there as we are. The illogical argument is also made that to justify the deaths of those who were sacrificed for the glory of the "leaders", more should be sent to suffer the same fate; and to justify their sacrifice, some more should be sent to their deaths; and to justify the deaths of the latter, more should be sent; and so on and so forth *ad infinitum* – how ridiculous and idiotic. But since it is not feasible to challenge infinity, we will have to keep on sending *them* (not our precious families, but *them*) and stop only when we do not have any more of *them* to send to their deaths.

To the warmonger's twisted mind, that is the pith of intelligent justification of crassness, not far removed from one that says a peace activist can be maliciously listed with "violent criminals, terrorists and sex offenders [and be declared persona non grata] for minor [malicious] convictions relating to civil disobedience for her protests"[1] against wars that kill millions of innocent twin-worlders. Such people fail to bring peace to others, because they cannot keep peace within themselves. It is also pathetically amusing to hear these warmongers saying that they need to send more troops to fight their wars. One always wonders just how many offspring they have that they are so ready to commit to danger and death. They speak as if they have fathered (by genetic engineering!) thousands of children that they can mobilize and send off to do their dirty work. But the reality is that they mean other people's children; and that is why they will send them back for repeated rotations of duty when they could easily institute a draft to feed their hungry egos. But they are not that stupid to set their own highly valued children up for recruitment under a draft, and that is why they avoid that word like the black plague. Ask them if they have any children in the army and watch them run like frightened chickens from a hawk that is hovering ominously over them. Some of them avoid service by faking pedal pathologies that will render then unfit for marching, others hide behind parental privilege, while others just plainly state that they don't want to die in some horticultural fields of foreign lands – all lily-livered frauds.

It never occurs to them that bullying tactics (spurred by greed) are not the answer to the quest for honour, nor do conflicts engineered through lies by seekers after glory earn respect; and at no time does it also occur to them to end their insane behaviour by talking peacefully with those that they have demonized for foolish self-serving reasons. They precipitate situations in regard to which they tell the rest of their world that they have to intervene to save the weaker adversary and twin world itself from unfair annihilation — obvious lies. This way they colonize their victim state and begin to siphon its wealth. But circumstances dictating failure to prevail over their victims do knock some sense into the thick skulls of these egotists and into those of their disciples of demonization and skulduggery, and suddenly they all pretend to see the light of day and decide that they will now be quitters as well as negotiators. Expediency rather than genuineness determines how they react to any of their self-imposed predicaments (which the people have to bear), and for some of them who are only spineless lapdogs that have lost their bumbling master to the flow of the tide of time, that vacuum begins to tell on their pathetic lack of leadership, leaving them in search of hiding places far enough away from the arenas where they should be accounting for their actions. Nevertheless, the people should not be deceived by this apparent retreat. It is only a recess to "recalibrate" and return with renewed determination to continue to inflict more of their characteristic evil injury.

These imperialists forget that the other, whom they always depict derogatorily as terrorists and scumbags to compensate for their own decadent morality, are finally reacting to their assaults and jibes over many years with assaults of their own, instead of meekly submitting to the insults that have been hurled at them and their homan dignity. They are reacting to the arrogance and hubris of people who leave their homelands to come and destabilize the homelands of others, destroy them, murder the people, desecrate their cultural assets, deprive them of their freedom, and dictate to them how they will run their affairs so that they can control their sources of wealth, because they always know best what other people's limited needs are and how to run their affairs to their own advantage. But as the saying goes, even a worm will turn; and these worms are now turning, and in their ferocity, which the oppressors have provoked, they inflict mortal wounds that the arch-oppressor is anxious to conceal from the people for the sake of maintaining his propaganda. That is why he resorts to the low-down, insulting ploy of hiding returning fallen "heroes" from them and lying about only a few or no casualties.

These same invader warriors engage in and sustain a diatribe of lies against their defenceless victims, accusing them of planning the ultimate atrocities against homanity and of threatening the security of the whole of twin world — claptrap that their gullible citizens buy as readily as they buy the arrogant dictates of some of their religious theocrats who take advantage of them with outlandish claims of being Gudd's infallible vice-regents, with all their foibles and failings of other homans that they deny; who arrantly expose them to religious bigotry by uttering the most prejudicial, irresponsible, and cavalier statements about other peoples' religions; and who disgorge irrational pronouncements that result in injury from preventable ills like AIDS. Unfortunately, some of the so-called intelligent leadership of their own tribe read from the same book as the holy men and have chosen to be so doltish as to deny the reality of these ills and hence also deny their own people treatments that could save their lives. It is most distressing to ponder the homan cost of the foolishness that has come out of the mouths of these religious and political oracles who have denied vulnerable people the use of protective devices against AIDS, or denied the entire concept of the natural history of the disease and then gone on to prescribe ludicrous measures to combat it. Together they bear the blame for the millions of wasted lives that have been ruined and prematurely terminated by these preventable and treatable diseases. Their inhomaneness has remained untouched and unmoved by the deaths around them of millions of helpless homans who depend solely on them for their survival. Their hearts of steel do not have the capacity to bleed for their scandalous deeds. Like the odious prosecutors who blithely send innocent persons to jail to earn promotion by swelling their count of convictions, they would also act in exactly the same opprobrious manner if they had to do it all over again.

It is said that animals have been seen to exhibit behaviour that amounts to homan sympathy or empathy with those of their kind that are experiencing pain or suffering; but these cats do not have those feelings for their hapless victims. So, of what use are their so-called leadership, intelligence, and expertise when they only serve as discreditable catalysts for the unnecessary deaths of so many people who rely on them for guidance and assistance? To think that these people of power can misuse their positions to condemn to death entire nations of helpless twin-worlders who depend on them just to satisfy their own egos and stupidity is extremely distressing. They should be guilt-ridden for the rest of their miserable lives, instead of presenting themselves so boldly as leaders who know what is good for the people, because they don't know. They only know what is good for their inflated Mickey Mouse egos.

To sustain these egos many so-called leaders of twin world lie so often that they believe their own lies of mushroom clouds and other horrors; and those who are exposed to these lies also believe them implicitly, because they are recited *ad nauseam*. If the prevaricators are caught off guard exposing their real motives and intentions about the subjects of their lies, they want to claim that what counts is what they publicly feed the people at those times that they are lying to them on matters of state policy through the microphones, not what they say off the record when they presume that the microphones are off and they are caught betraying their true natures and devious plans. These off-guard moments are the ones that tell the truth about them and their lies. Oxymoronic truth in lies? Yes; but this pitiable state of affairs results from the ease with which people allow others who may be even less intelligent than they are to make fools of them, simply because they have blindly reposed their trust in these liars who have cheated their way into positions of power that they retain with the aid of their political pawns, the brutal police and the army, whose personnel will foolishly kill their own people (relatives included) to prop thieves and liars. When will these maggots acquire backbones to say no to doing the dirty work of these liars and selfish tyrants, if not rather turn the guns on them? How do they explain their pitiable conduct to their children, besides insulting them by saying that they are obeying immoral orders to earn a disreputable living for them? Do they think that the children respect them for that, or do the children secretly despise them?

But, of course, their servile behaviour isn't difficult to comprehend; they owe their positions of contemptible power and financial gain to the people that they are keeping in power, and if these people go, then they also lose their detestable clout. However, when a violent and reckless administration that is characterized by ineptitude bears its fruits of economic and social collapse that prove to be toxic to the citizens, but spares its powerful perpetrators, they suffer along with the rest of the people that they helped to oppress. Little wonder that some people assign porcine appellations to some of them out of sheer disgust with their undignified behaviour. All of them are cat's-paws in the power and popularity games of their masters who do not give a hoot about their lives and their social relations with those they are forced to brutalize or kill, as long as the ruling master gets his way while he is safely sheltered in the comfort of his home with his family but stays in the limelight as a twin world strongman, or a benefactor who dishes out tax dullams as personal early Christmas gifts to buy votes from the easily duped electorate. Regrettably, some women with power have also been involved in this disreputable practice of boosting personal political fortunes with the lives of citizens and military personnel in their own countries and in little, powerless, islands far away.

The whole system is as rotten as a week old carcass in a tropical climate, and the citizens are as guilty of self-delusion as those who are always trying to delude them and succeeding, because they allow themselves to be mesmerized with deceptive, unending chants of the snide patriotism of the gun, the bomb, religion, and the flag, while the hallmark of true patriotism is being violated: respect for persons and for the constitution of their state. Where in worlds other than twin world will one ever find rulers who swear allegiance to the constitution of their state and then turn around and violate it at will to cater to their own self-serving ends? What authority do they then have to compel the citizens to obey the laws of their state, if they, the so-called leaders, cannot respect the laws and principles on which their state is founded? Where is their moral responsibility to their citizens, or their ethics—assuming that they have some semblance of an ethical code, in spite of their regular and blatant display of an utter lack thereof? That alone should tell the citizens that their so-called leaders are unfit for the positions of trust and responsibility in which they have positioned themselves, and that they deserve to be removed from them, because they have demonstrated that they lack the essential virtues to qualify them for leadership. It does not matter how many times they repeat their chants of the trumped up evil that lurks in the mind and intentions of "the enemy" (which includes patriots who decry the rot that they are perpetrating on them in the name of "government"), their lies, dressed in glittering apparel and awe-inspiring as they are, continue to emit a nauseating stench.

Nevertheless, the war chants go on and the people of twin world allow themselves to be wrapped in flags and fed the manna (opiate) of warped patriotism and nationalism to keep them docile and to encourage them to continue the chants of patriotism and ultimate sacrifice—for what? To stave off actual invasion or to chase after will-o'-the-wisps conjured up by their vindictive, imperialist "leaders" in search of revenge, fame, and possessions? To sacrifice life for truth is a noble deed, but to sacrifice it for a lie is the epitome of foolishness on the part of the citizen, to say nothing of the contempt that is due to those who are pulling off that heist whilst giving the rest of the people the impression that their sacrifices are noble. Twin worlders need to snap out of this lethal attitude of self-deception and deception by others and take possession of their lives and their future, instead of entrusting them to the callous manipulation of persons who can clearly see the abyss ahead into which they are leading them, but are still trying to get the most out of the hopeless situation that they have engineered before they crash the capsule that is carrying all of them into the void created by fatuous dreams of dominating their world and their universe.

In this kind of atmosphere the history of nations as told by these liars can never be relied upon as being authentic, because they spare no effort to try to rewrite it so that they can appear like national heroes overflowing with benevolence, homaneness, and goodwill, when the people know them to be vain, shallow, vindictive, greedy, inept, and murderous villains. We could easily take the words of William Carlos Williams out of their context as attributed to the aboriginals of the American continent (and other continents overrun by pinks) and put them in the mouths of these liars' concerning their attitude to history, viz., "History, history! We fools, what do we know or care? History begins for us with murder and enslavement, . . ."[2] They incorporate their fabrications and prejudices into their children's school curricula and text books to make sure that their lies survive as authentic facts and warp their pliable minds for ever. What are they raising? Some of the lesser breeds among them even have the audacity to call browns who founded portions of their country that contributed to nation building villains, using language borrowed from our own racist world to denigrate one of them thus, "to mount a statue to him on Parliament Hill would elevate anarchy and civil disobedience to that of democratic statesmanship."[3] This is the response of oppressors to the gallant efforts of their victims to protect their self-determination against people whose egregious self-regard is as offending as their lack of respect for the personhood of others, and who traded off their lands as if they were uninhabited, making no effort to negotiate with them for the sale of those lands, but rather using overpowering brute force to improperly appropriate and dispose of property that did not belong to them. So, who are the real anarchists and villains?

This practice of substituting fabrications for historical facts that lately masquerades under the infamous tag of "fake news" seems to be universal in pink accounts of events in twin world, as long as it slants the odds in their favour, collectively or individually. They cower in fear from reprisals and then claim besiegement by their victims, and they perpetuate the lie to discredit their victims and make themselves appear as the victims. What a shame that their "leaders" habitually etch for themselves records of meanness and inhomanity in the pages of history and then find it necessary to scramble at the eleventh hour to change them by subterfuge, when they had the time and opportunity during their years in government to etch records of magnanimity and benevolence that will stand by themselves as monuments to their glory, without the mad rush to lift them out of the gutter where they have been wallowing for years and where they really still belong.

Distorting facts is a commonplace in many of their official

accounts of the corporate organizations with whose leadership they have been entrusted. They glibly alter the authentic minutes of proceedings to hide their shenanigans, and any account that they report as being reflective of situations in which they are participating bears the stigma of possibly being a lie, even if it is not, because of the many occasions on which they have been intentionally careless with the truth. This is a sad state of affairs where people have to start off assuming that what they are told is a lie, and then having to demand proof that it is not before they can accept it. Gone are the days when they first assumed and accepted that what they were told was true, and that the onus of proof rested with whoever claimed that it was not true; i.e., a lie. No onus or obligation should bind the truth teller to prove that her account is not a lie, until she starts to habitually substitute lies for the truth like some of these people. In the end, the whole history of twin world becomes one big lie on the micro as well as the macro level, because many of their historians and heroes are liars. But that means nothing to lowly minds that cannot appreciate the lofty implications of historical veracity; their mercenary minds cannot rise above the mundane level of the sordid concrete (money) to take in the sublime (the meaning of history to a people and to all of twin world). Unfortunately, this disreputable trend has rubbed off on some brown leaders as well.

 Against this background of the need and demand for sublimity, pinks are still unable to rise up to the occasion. They have chosen to block avenues in which browns can prepare themselves for self-sustaining, productive, and crime-free lives; and instead of providing them with opportunities to make up for the shortcomings that they have imposed on them, they have chosen to add to their misery by perpetuating the conditions that led, in the first place, to the state of affairs in which they find themselves the victims of disproportionate incarceration. And that is exactly what they had planned for them: to keep them in the gutter of crime. This attitude is the same one that allows them to stand by and watch while battles and wars that they have engineered between brown states to promote their selfish pink agendas are claiming thousands of lives, until the life of only one of their pink brothers is extinguished, and then they bring out their big guns and openly take the side of their proxy in the conflict.

 Theirs is the bigoted, racist ethic of imposing on others absolute respect and subservience to their supreme will and using their high positions, authority, and force to destroy, with the utmost cruelty, all who do not belong to their tribe. In the blindness of their despicable racist prejudice, inhomanity, and characteristic lack of empathy with browns, they do not hesitate to use their positions, in defence of their racist and brutally repressive brothers anywhere else in twin world, to take on the whole of twin world that is standing up for unjustly treated browns. They re-iterate their unwavering support for them and will victimize their own fellow brown and other citizens, who are labelled as the non-compliant enemy, for criticizing their obnoxious policies and actions, even when it is quite clear that their pink brothers are in the wrong. Pinks are never wrong, of course.

Such is the arrogance and hubris flaunted by persons who have lost their homanity during the process of dehomanizing others and cheapening their lives, while they arrantly masquerade their charade as democratization—a feeling of superiority based on what? Religion wealth, might, race, culture, or right (righteousness of heart)? Racism has many faces, and one of its ugliest faces, also its most entrenched, is betrayed by callous government officials who play obvious racist games with people's lives by clutching at trumped up constitutional and legal technicalities to disguise their malice. Anyone who cares to examine the trend of events in so-called democratic states of twin world, where citizens are supposed to have equal rights, cannot miss this racist stratification in which some are more favoured than others in every walk of life, based solely on the meaningless lighter colour of their skins. Meanwhile citizens of these states claim to be practicing "tolerance" devoid of moral rights. But who is tolerating whom? Are pinks tolerating browns in their own lands? How absurd! They speak of practicing tolerance as if it is their prerogative alone to tolerate, these arrogant usurpers who should be the ones tolerated, because they had no right to take what did not belong to them, in the first place. Ah, but they are the herrenvolk; they grab what they want with impunity, because they have miraculous power.

Twin world also has other community concerns that resemble those that are sometimes found in our world. Many an inhabitant lacks the objectivity that can replace his subjective prejudices and biases with the reason and common sense by which any straight thinking person can recognize and differentiate good from bad, and can, therefore, direct his actions into appropriate channels of genuine homanism. Some of the people (manipulators) delight in promoting a siege mentality of fear and hatred among all the people, and they cultivate an attitude of mistrust among them to keep them apart and to promote themselves as the only ones who can save them from internal and external attacks by less favoured groups and their "evil" associates who belong to despised faiths and nationalities. They promote vacuous loyalty, compliance, and allegiance to their reckless leadership that is ruled by clique mentality and boorish ideology to the exclusion of reason and nobility of purpose, and they demonize and punish rational non-compliance, dissent, or, in their depraved language, unpatriotic attitudes with public ridicule and vituperation. Others denigrate browns with every hate-filled word that comes out of their filthy mouths and then want to misuse their athletic prowess and skills to gratify their greed for money by owning them in sports teams to indulge their odious mentality of slave ownership and pink supremacy and to use them to enrich themselves.

Such irrational actions are not the types of actions that any person with a rational grasp of situations would adopt; they are guided by selfishness, narrow-mindedness, hatred, baseless fear, and above all, unlimited greed. What matters to those concerned is what suits them best, regardless of the obvious fact that their intentions and goals are grounded in the inconsistent complex of cupidity and lack of respect for the other, both of which can never be universalized with any semblance of pride. In a broader compass, they do not stop to think what their world would be like if everyone acted uncharitably, arrogantly, selfishly, and maliciously like them. They are content to improvise a circumstantial morality as they go along, creating an expedient ethic for every situation to justify their perverted and universally unacceptable behaviour that has proved to be deleterious to the rights, welfare, and survival of other people, e.g., waging war against phantoms and invading non-warring states, with resulting imprisonment of innocent persons and children in the inhomane conditions of their known and secret political prisons.

The simple truism that what is good for the gander is *eo ipso* good enough for the goose in the same situation escapes them, because they are wedded to a contradictory relativism that says what counts is what counts for me, and what is rational is what sounds rational to my small mind and not to other minds out there that can grasp a wider view of the many solutions to all the problems with which we have to deal in twin world. They wrongly believe that their point of view is the only right one by their own criteria, which may not be the criteria of other people. Who is to say whose criteria are the only right ones, they ask? There is no objective measuring stick, and every person's assessment is as valid as the next person's.

But they have yet to learn that for people to communicate with any measure of success and to co-exit peacefully, they have to share their moral values and worldviews and also be mutually tolerant of the inevitable constitutional differences that are bound to exist among them. The kind of games that are played by people who know that they have no intention of living in peace side by side with their neighbours, and whose every action betrays their insincerity and determination to accomplish their archetypal plans of dispossessing them of their land, do not fool anyone, although their architects think that they are successfully pulling wool over everyone's eyes. The pity is only that they are allowed to get away with this chicanery by others who have the power but are too weak-willed to put a stop to it, rather than aiding and abetting it with the games that they are willing to play by posturing, gesticulating, and hollering aimlessly while financing the inhomane hoax to the hilt. These deplorable games are so transparent and nauseating that they place the player in the gutter with the racist usurpers that he is supporting; or is this simply a case of being emasculated and held hostage by them, rather than of birds of a feather flocking together?

On the other hand, clashes of morality and religious affiliation in the worldviews of twin-worlders don't facilitate or promote peaceful coexistence. While some harbour noble intentions of homanity, others delight in promoting strife, simply because they have the weaponry with which to pound others into submission, so that their puny egos and images can be magnified by their dreamt-of victories. I justly call such failed victories dreams, because these idealized victories are never achieved, and the idealist dreamers end up being literal dreamers who are forced to retreat with their tails between their legs, after falling from lofty heights where they did not belong. The barrenness of their dark, immoral code has been exposed to the light of day by the inconsistency between the facts of their theory and the practice that is supposed to be based on that theory at that time. Their feckless behaviour is the true hallmark of the goal of their high-sounding, inane, and painfully dissonant assertions. They claim to be benefactors whose mission is to spread democracy throughout twin world, even while they are assassinating or deposing democratically elected leaders of the people to install their own dictators and tyrants, their surrogates and tools who will not question or protest, but will carry out their selfish programs of greed to the letter for handsome monetary favours. They have vitiated morality by pretending that their purported ends can be achieved by any means including the immoral means that they use to achieve the immoral ends that they have always intended under the guise of seeking moral ends, like the typical wolves in sheep's clothing that they are, always ready to pounce on and devour an unwary flock of sheep, which is what the people are; they do behave like sheep.

Young and ambitious, nationally-minded, democratically elected brown leaders who have been chosen by the overwhelming majority of brown voters in their own countries of origin, and who dare to protect the resources of their states by nationalizing them, or by simply instituting economic, educational, health care, agrarian, and social programs to advance the cause of their people, are quickly and wrongfully accused of corruption and exiled or liquidated by the agents of scheming twin world powers who see these foreign sources of their own wealth drying up before their eyes. On orders from the oppressors, they are treated like common criminals and murdered brutally by their own people who fail to realize that the persons whose lives they are sacrificing to earn accolades from their unscrupulous masters were only protecting their joint property from the clutches of these wolves. To replace the murdered brown leaders, they install puppets who will do as they are told and will leave the wealth of the country exposed to plunder by them. It is shameful that everywhere these thieves will always purchase the services of local brown "leaders" (collaborators) who are ready to sell out their people to the extent of adopting the language of the oppressor by calling their own freedom fighters terrorists. They have been brainwashed and brow-beaten to accept and use derogatory appellations for their saviours, and to be happy to live under the boot of the oppressor, as long as he continues to toss occasional favours their way. Sadly, some of the ones who should be following in the footsteps of their parents in the struggle to liberate their tribe from bondage and dehomanization by pinks have sold their souls to the oppressor and are snitching on their own people for these little favours. Brown collaborators, when will you acquire the good sense to stop selling out and calling your brothers and saviours terrorists?

At the same time, when a young brown leader is elected by sensible and enlightened pinks to lead their nation, the bigots, who are best defined by the term "verkramp" (borrowed from that other African language, Afrikaans), meaning mentally cramped up, spare no effort to scuttle his effort in the hope that he will not succeed, and then they can say: what did you expect from a brown? We are the only ones who can lead; they can only follow; they were created to be our eternal underlings. What is sadly strange about their attitude is that they have been comfortably sitting on their hands, quite happy while things were going awry under the "leadership" of their pink brother, because many of them are still profiting from the status quo; but now that someone else wants to make the system fair to every citizen and save the country from hurtling further into economic ruin, they suddenly come up with bright ideas that they wish to substitute for his proposals purely for the sake of upstaging him for obvious unpalatable reasons: political advantage, financial greed, racial hatred, jealousy, etc. Where have you been, guys? The house started burning long ago under your watch, but you did not do anything to save it. What roused you from your sleep; the sight of a brown at the helm? Sorry, guys, the history has been written, and nothing will change it, even if you resort to your customary lying and distortion of the facts of history. It will perdure from here to eternity. Can your closed minds that are stunted by intellectual myopia even conceptualize the meaning of persistence into eternity? The best that you can offer to undo his successes is a rabid nazi-type racist demagogue with an inherited hatred for browns that you hauled straight from the gutter to be your leader—what a shame.

The simple pink minds that presided over the perpetration of all the rot, and who have never touched any project without messing it up and having to be rescued from themselves, have the nerve to dub brown successes failures to compensate for their own ineptitude, even while browns are cleaning pink mess successfully. They still delight in denigrating brown successes to distort history and oxymoronically bestow on themselves the mantle of achievement for howling failure. Sadly, however, some misguided brown brothers who still retain the inferiority complex that was drummed into their heads by their oppressors foolishly ape them in maligning their brown brother's successes, instead of supporting him zealously and inspiring younger browns to aspire to analogous positions of leadership in their communities. These doltish traducers would rather save their accolades for members of the herrenvolk who became mentally torpid over time and subsequently went to sleep at the wheel, because undeserved success was handed to them on a silver platter as a birthright, as always, or else their monumental failures were condoned, because pinks never fail. If they appear to be failing, it is because the failure of browns is bounced off them creating the conceptual illusion that they are failing. Ludicrous as it sounds, that is how herrenvolk mentality operates.

When a brown has ascended to a position of leadership in the nation, citizens are fed the lie that everything bad that happens in the nation state is his fault, even if it happened long before his time. Sowers of dissension crisscross the country charging hefty sums of money for venting their idiotic blabber onto besotted crowds who cheer fatuously after every stupid utterance of vacuous attack on him, because both she and they do not have sufficient cognitive ability to offer constructive proposals for cleaning up their own mess. The rueful image of a country bumpkin who makes all of them feel smug in their collective ignorance and irrelevance will never be enough to lift their country and the rest of twin world out of the economic and other quagmires in which they mired them with their misguidance and irresponsibility? The blabbering fool who spews meaningless trash and malapropisms in shrill attempts at oratory on par with cultivated brown oratory urges all all of them to engage in collective obstructionist tactics, professing phony and corrupt family values and trying to upstage brown historic feats with lacklustre rallies, while she sows dissension with inflammatory language and imagery calculated to fan the gunfire flames of hatred that end up consuming honest, dedicated representatives of the people, instead of posing progressive ideas. The boundless ill will of their tribe makes one wonder how much culpability they must bear for the liquidations and attempted liquidations of those that they hate by the "left-wing nut jobs" of society who serve as their scapegoats. If you can't beat them, label them with gun-crosshairs for perpetration of the ultimate violence on them; suggestible others will pick up the cue and kill or try to kill them and clear the field for you to pursue your ambition and your vile task of continuing to sow seeds of dissension, rebellion, treason, and racial animosity, unencumbered by these left-wing liberals and lovers of browns—kaffir-boeties or nigger-lovers, as they are derogatively called.

The inhomanity of racism defies rationality at every turn, and it will always strive to rear its venomous head in the face of all odds against it. That is its nature; it cannot admit defeat; it must triumph at all costs; even the most profound rationality cannot convince it of its irrationality. And so the sowers of vitriol and dissension ply their trade ceaselessly to promote their heinous agenda of misinformation, disinformation, and lies, prompted, in some notable situations, by the "affront" of a brown as the first citizen of their state. In their book only pinks can fill that enviable position, and they are prepared to cause unprecedented turmoil in their country under the pretext that it is being taken in the wrong direction, when their own brothers are the ones who took it to the place from which the brown is trying to rescue it, until they settle on the disaster of a clueless, fumbling narcissist who comes into the picture for himself. All of them are helpless victims of vicious and despicable racism that is consuming their society and accelerating its already far gone decay and impending demise. Whether this evil atmosphere will burgeon or not depends on the balance of forces between its proponents and its victims. So far, the scales have been tipped in favour of the evil, lying, and irrational elements; but it is time now for truth and rationality to prevail, for sensible people to take a firm stand against this racist insanity and stamp it out, if twin world is to be saved from the Armageddon imposed on it by these liars and scum of humanity and the masses of simpleminded dolts who follow them instinctively, either because they belong to the same disreputable faction or because they are incapable of thinking, let alone thinking rationally.

# Chapter 15
# Racism and Inhomanity burgeon

In this thriving atmosphere of lies and make-believe that promises pinks serenity and perdurable comfort on the backs of browns, many of the more privileged and powerful elite of twin world have so ardently embraced the phantoms that have been crafted for them by their ruling brothers that they have drifted far away from the naked truth and stark reality of their inhomanity that is staring them in their faces. They have been conditioned by their mind-controlling brothers to thrive on the trio of misrepresentation of self and others, dissimulation, and disinformation, on a scale that is unimaginable in our world. In this world we tell white lies about other people, but we seldom become as vicious and vitriolic as our counterparts in twin world. We demonize those on the other side of the political aisle for our self-enhancement, but not as fervently and destructively as the scum of twin world to whom they are the enemy that should be met with malice and belligerence, not for taking the lead in serving their nations, which would be absurd, but for heaping shame on the self-service in which these incompetent liars revel and for which alone they vie to be elected to office, even if they have to kill their rivals in the ruthless competition.

The scum orchestrates its little colonies of proxies made up of mediocre media hosts and authors of illogical trash who betray the covert plots that they are hatching to engineer the failure of those who devote their service to the people and not to themselves. Their empty tins continue to rattle incessantly and pretend to co-operate with brown leadership by presenting alternative but clearly self-serving and subversive suggestions to stifle his progressive agenda. Their yelping attack dogs fervidly overshoot their big mouths that are used to spewing only venom by letting the cat of subterfuge out of the bag, exposing the bogus concerns of their shameless handlers for the welfare of the citizens without even fazing them. They expose the negative partisanship rooted in the exuberance of self-service that infinitely outstrips the phony devotion to service for their country and its people that they claim. This obsessive milieu of animus against those who do not subscribe to their self-exalting agenda often reaches gutter levels with select, viciously programmed yelping "curs of low degree" (Oliver Goldsmith: "An Elegy on the Death of a Mad Dog") barking endlessly at and about hit-listed competitors on the other side of the political spectrum, even inciting violence against them with their gun-derived subliminal rhetoric. If we could interpret dog language we would discern the lies of their programmers in their barks as easily as we discern their intellectual barrenness. But many of the simple-minded puppets who hear the barks and take them seriously to heart have also been brainwashed to believe the lies that are being disseminated, and they also bark and maim without thinking about why they are barking and maiming other people for no reason.

Perhaps it is not a fair statement to accuse them of not thinking. One cannot be fairly accused of doing what one is incapable of doing, and these people are incapable of thinking for themselves. Nature was unkind to them by shortchanging them with that innate ability; hence the ease with which their highly pliable minds can be twisted by cunning others who use them to promote their selfish agendas in the same way that they use their privilege and power to propagate their skewed values. One can always avoid censure for sowing dissension, ill feeling, and racist misanthropy by planting and letting loose these programmed attack dogs on one's opponent (competitor) while pretending and appearing publicly to be genuinely defending his honour against their slanderous barks. People have been known to appear publicly to be quelling attacks while secretly encouraging them. Those who are misused as attack dogs are not only the ones with limited understanding of the problems that burden them, and for whose never-never solution they depend entirely on their users, but also the enlightened cowards who willingly submit to this abuse in spite of their full and intelligent grasp of situations. Additionally, they could also be looking for favours from the same deceivers, if they are not running away from being demonized, ostracized, or purged by official hit-men for speaking truth to power, because no oppressor likes to hear the truth about his inhomanity.

Everyone in twin world knows the substandard housing in which the original owners of the land live, the body bags that they are given to bury their dead instead of vaccines or medicines to prevent or treat the ailments of the living, the slop pails for toilets, the contaminated water that they are forced to drink for years until widespread disease and the toxic effects of mercury hit their communities, and then the usurpers resort to their usual tricks of denial and procrastinating the solution to the problem by claiming that these issues cannot be resolved for another hundred years.

Meanwhile, similar problems encountered by their own people, not through the neglect that they impose on the aboriginals, but through the sloth of their own operatives, are fixed promptly, proving that the tardiness with which aboriginal predicaments are dealt is motivated by racism. When an aboriginal child is critically ill, they bicker about who has jurisdiction over her health care until she dies and her taxpaying parent dies of a broken heart and its sequelae; but when their children are sick, they don't die while their elders argue endlessly about who has jurisdiction over them and who is responsible for providing medical services for them, regardless of their domicile; they act promptly and also go to expected lengths of providing the best services for them. These are liberal governments that boast observance of homan rights theories (not practices) and even have the audacity to hypocritically lecture other governments about their equally glaring, abysmal homan rights records, which are no worse than their own that they have artfully obscured with their evil laws. Some of these kettles that are calling the pots black have also brazenly said that the only good brown is a dead brown.

Their biased laws and amoral proclamations are purposely framed to make it impossible for browns to qualify for the help they need by drawing a line on the ground to confine them to the ghettos where they have huddled them and to where the help required does not extend. Their movements are severely restricted, and they are now being zealously kept out of countries of twin world that pinks stole from browns, countries that prefer only pink immigrants. Today they lock them up separately in concentration camps and cages in the spirit of the Third Reich of our world with its dreadful results? In the execution of these heinous acts, are we seeing the rise of the Fourth Reich with the same dreadful results? What kind of fate are these innocent suckling infants and young children who are being used as pawns and ransom likely to face down the road after being torn away from their mothers? Will they also be liquidated to rid this part of twin world of its infestation when they can no longer be used?

Meanwhile, across the tracks in their upscale residences every kind of assistance is readily available to pinks. In their intransigence to making even one compassionate exception to their inflexible iron rules, they make it appear as if the heavens will fall if they relented just once in a while to accommodate a dying or a disabled brown child who needs basic nourishment to sustain his life to which they apparently do not attach any value. But compassion for browns is contrary to their herrenvolk mentality and agenda. Perhaps these bigoted, racist, and evil minds are prompted into their inhomane and immoral actions by fear of the potential threat that this child represents to the perpetuation of their racist dominance over his tribe, because the revolt of twin world's youth against the status quo has scared them into the realization that their monopoly is in danger of crashing at any time. The children do not accept and tolerate pink domination and discrimination as readily as their parents; hence the twin world equivalent of NSSM 200 (see pages 198-199).

Nevertheless, evil does not discriminate between adult and child; it sees both as threats, actual and potential, that must be eliminated by any means, vile, shameful, or unguddly. It is no wonder then that when they seek to elevate their ignoble standing in the progressive world and to varnish their tarnished images they resort to standing on the hilltop to belch rodomontade to their world about how they intend to steer the rest of their fat cow brothers into the direction of relieving the poverty of women and children in third worlds of twin world, neglecting to start at home where charity always begins, but where they treat their aboriginal peoples who exist in poverty like dirt. If their intentions come to naught, who can say they were not there? The bluff will have paid off, because they can then blame their brothers for failing to latch on to this noble intention. Yes, intention; just that, intention. Don't we all have noble intentions, but no blue prints and nothing concrete to show for them, except the strings attached to them and the long trail of unfulfilled intentions? Haven't children been left behind before? Haven't people been promised a loaf, only to receive a slice of bread or nothing? Haven't the same countries been called "s- - t" countries to reflect the total lack of concern for, and hatred of, the people who inhabit those lands? Haven't people goaded others into action while they stayed behind, leaving them to carry the burden alone while they take credit for the good that the others are doing? It has and still will happen.

Their flagrant lies are exposed in their unceasing suppression of opinions that are contrary to their dogma of pink superiority. They curry the favour of those who practice the same kind of oppression against women and children as they do by resorting to the cheap ruse of persecuting anyone who speaks against the base practices of these their brothers in crime by muzzling him with their iniquitous laws, maligning him, or withholding financial aid that is rightfully due to him under the pretext that he is spreading tribal hatred. That way, they hope to garner the votes of those of their pitiable citizens who fall for their ruse, because they are cheap and shallow like them, and they think like them. And so when public funds have been budgeted for the services of aboriginal populations, they subject them to their partisan interests by withholding them, claiming that these people are terrorists, only because they do not shut up criticizing them for the unjust stands and actions that they take toward them and the rest of the brown tribes who suffer dehomanization at the hands of the pink establishment. Any merited criticism of the murderous acts of their partners in crime to whom they pander for votes exacts harsh punishment, including suppression of the civil rights of their critics.

In their world, browns may hold and express only those opinions that the pink masters approve of; otherwise they face excoriation and jail for uppity conduct when they make their own contrary opinions (labeled hate speech) known. Their tortuous logic says: hate speech is a punishable offence; people make policies; therefore criticism of policies = maligning of the architects of those policies = hate speech = punishable offence. So, no one may criticize the policies of their friends that are oppressing and dehomanizing other homan beings, especially browns who have to say *ja baas* (yes boss) to everything that their pink masters command; they dare not say *nee baas* (no boss) — what the masters call being uppity — to their pink gudds of twin world without paying a hefty price for their insubordination. This illogical logic is further extended to construe criticism of inhomane pink government policy as antagonism to the entire nation whose government is persecuting browns. They call that anti-*x*ism, anti-*y*ism, or ant-zism = racism. Vilification of browns is always acceptable, however, because it accords well with the selfish pink agenda of demeaning browns.

In this strange and incongruous world, these oppressed people are profiled and arrested on mere suspicion of belonging to so-called terrorist groups. Their traveling experiences are curtailed or made hell on earth by the same racial profiling, while pinks endure the minimum of harassment in their travels. Browns alone are always "randomly" selected for searches and deliberate delays to humiliate them. One or more of the herrenvolk starts the compelling trend of calling freedom seekers of the other tribe terrorists, and the rest of their shallow kind follow thoughtlessly and blindly, like the rats that followed the Pied Piper of Hamelin to their deaths. Their *ad nauseam* chorus rings monotonously through the years: these terrorists are envious of our democracy of greed and our corrupt superior lifestyle; we must eradicate them or keep them at bay, lest they come into our midst and kill us for what we have that they don't have. At no time do these dolts appear to exhibit possession of the good sense to be able to extricate themselves from the big hoax in which they are entwined to view it objectively and recognize it for the sham that it is. They are trapped in the powerful snare of repetitious lies that their governments feed them, helping to entrench the eponym (terrorist) that every one of these pitiable characters now bandies around to assuage their ignorance and prevailing guilt of meanness by claiming that terrorists deserve to be treated with the meanness that their own terrorist governments have adopted to all browns.

Their governments pat themselves on the back for successfully brainwashing the gullible masses who need an idol on which to pin their false hopes and rally them into a programming mode. Having accomplished that mission, they can now also abuse the devotion of their troops to the service of their country by deceptively creating reluctant war heroes out of persons who have been under the tender loving care of "the enemy" that they want to demonize for injuries that have nothing to do with the imagined heroic deeds under which they were allegedly sustained. But they go even further to upstage a deserving brown comrade by shining the spotlight on the pink colleague who probably did nothing to deserve the honour that is being heaped on her and which she is denouncing. The glories of their fabricated, ephemeral war heroes sprout out of nowhere overnight and fade with the light of the setting sun after they have been used to achieve the devious goals of the fabricators.

Meanwhile, the pursuers of truth, freedom, and justice, inappropriately called terrorists, or sedition-mongers, are arbitrarily thrown into prisons where they remain locked away in these ignominious pits of twin world pinks for years, if not indefinitely, secretly held under all kinds of certificates that have obviously been designed solely for them. Lies are concocted about them and they are not given an opportunity to hear the lies told about them so that they can refute them, they are never given public and fair trials in accordance with the accepted democratic statutes of the land that the pinks boast about, and they are never allowed to see their loved ones or talk to their lawyers, probably because their captors know that they do not have a case against them. In short, they are stripped bare of every vestige of substantive homan and legal (procedural) rights and left to languish in some of the most inhomane conditions of mental and physical torture in "the legal equivalent of outer space", many light years away from twin world, where no one hears their wailings or even cares about them. Their captors would like to butcher them to gratify their inhomanity and spite, but they dare not do so openly for fear of the revulsion that this lawlessness and assault on justice will cause in the rest of "civilized" twin world. So they torture them indefinitely in secret while they pacify their soft critics with the most irrational drivel to justify their actions.

In response, the blind, unthinking masses who live sheltered lives laud their masters for saving them from certain death at the hands of terrorists who are hell-bent on killing them, not in response to the oppression to which they have been subjected, but because they are jealous of their comfortable way of life, democracy, and ostensible freedoms of speech and action. They will not think farther than the tips of their noses (incapable), and they forget that what goes around comes around, and that this kind of fascist mentality and practice will one day entrap them when their pink rights have also been systematically eroded and depleted to keep their captors in power. Poor wretches they can see the individual trees, but not the forest in which they are trapped. In fact, they are already being held hostage by their rulers under a variety of restrictive laws allegedly directed against terrorists and meant to protect them, but somehow denuding their rights and leaving them with nothing to show for their so-called democracy. Nevertheless, they still remain happy and oblivious to the systematic enslavement in which they are also ensnared, as long as they are led to believe that this rude erosion of the rights of browns (and their rights) is for their own protection.

In the process, selected brown children of twin world are also jailed and tortured to gratify the vindictiveness of their captors and to impress the blindly credulous masses. Evidence is fabricated to justify their detention and persecution to ensure their successful conviction for the sake of enhancing the status of those who are misusing the lives of others to boost their measly egos. In twin world children who are misused by adults as soldiers are not committed to rehabilitation as we do in our world when we capture them; they are imprisoned, tortured, and forced to confess to terrorist crimes, even if they have been critically wounded by their adversaries whose aim was to kill them fair and square in the pitch of battle (acts of pink heroism). The latter are not committing crimes against these children who may be so ravaged by their fire power that they are oblivious to the goings on around them; they are rightfully killing "the enemy" in war, and they invoke their own interpretation of twin world rules of engagement to justify murdering these brown children that they regard as adult soldiers. But they go further and deny all of them other protections mandated by the same rules of engagement to clear the way for torturing them indefinitely in their detention pits. The intentional confounding of categorial boundaries between children and adults on the one hand, and murder and sanctioned killing of an "enemy" soldier in battle on the other, serves to facilitate despicable practices of inhomanity on brown children; they are branded as the only "adults" who "murder" their potential killers in a war. They are also accused of committing war crimes by gutless war criminals who, while daring not to venture into their world for fear of being apprehended for their own war crimes, have the audacity to re-write their local laws extempore to exempt themselves from prosecution for deeds analogous to those that put others in their kangaroo courts.

That is pink racist logic and justice at its best; the kind that improvises its own rules of war to fit the expediency of the moment, the kind that holds back exonerating details of the truth of situations for the sake of having a sacrificial lamb to appease the masters who are hell-bent on convincing their sheepish and bigoted citizens how much they should be trusted to protect them from terrorists, and the kind that serves as a springboard for the upward movement of statutory accusers through the ranks of their establishment. It also reflects on the obvious racist prejudice of those who consider the use of child soldiers taboo to their "highly civilized" standards and can effectively intervene in this sordid miscarriage of justice, but bluntly and doggedly refuse to do so, despite clear overtures and goading from the implicated jurisdiction that it is willing to comply. Do we need to ask how this whole story would have unfolded if pink children had been involved instead of browns children? Hardly.

Similarly, in civilian life the unprovoked killing and maiming of browns by pinks under any kind of rule, especially minority pink rule, is called maintaining law and order, but the provoked killing of a pink by a brown under majority brown rule spells lack of safety for pinks and good reason to seek asylum in pink dominated countries. This illogical logic only goes to show that pink lives are sacred, but brown lives are dispensable — everyone knows that. What we would like to hear, however, is that the villains who foment wars that result in the deaths of millions of innocent people simply to boost their paltry egos and to gratify their insatiable greed for power and possessions should face firing squads to give them a final taste of what they have dished out to the millions of helpless others in their customary callousness and hubris. This rich reward should not be limited to the architects of the evil, but it should also be generously extended to benefit their lapdogs all over twin world.

When "terrorists" are released, if ever, from the pits of misery in which they have been kept for years on end without trial, they are expected to kiss the feet of their oppressors and thank them for wasting their lives. If they naturally take revenge for the undeserving injustice to which they have been subjected, they earn the appellation of bad boys who did not deserve to be released from their hell-holes. Where is the logic? First you round up someone for no good reason, throw him in prison, torture him for years, deny him a fair trial, and eventually release him at your pleasure, without the decency (which you lack, anyway) of an apology or any attempt to indemnify him for the heinous crimes that you perpetrated against him prior to and during his incarceration as well as those that you had in store for him, simply because you have the might, but not the right to do so. Next you audaciously claim that you should have kept him shackled, because he is still as dangerous as, and most probably more so than when you first detained him without reason and then turned him into the monster that you claim he is. Only herrenvolk mentality operates with that kind of warped and sick logic.

The practice is as old as the dehomanization of colonialism when the indigenous peoples of twin world were forced out of their lands and denied the right to protest their treatment in courts of law that were established by the invaders to redress all infringements of citizens' rights as embodied in the constitution of their country. The only difference is that their constitution declares universal equality before the law of only the superior persons who belong to their privileged race. The rest of the people have no status within this law. They receive equal treatment only within the already discriminatory law that is framed especially for them in their inferior status. The injustice becomes apparent only if the same law is applied to both groups, otherwise the parallel laws are applied with equal justice in their respective hierarchical domains. Hence the culprits feel free to violate the rights of discriminated browns as flagrantly as they do in their devious dealings with them, and as scurrilously as some of their extant heads of state who, in their pettiness and hubris, do not hesitate to defy their obligation of accountability to the people who elected them into office, justifying their expulsion from office. That is where and when the soldiers and police should wield their brute force to carry out the will of the people against that of tyrants, instead of slavishly killing them to aid these unprincipled thieves and opportunists to execute their ruinous and self-serving policies.

In days of yore, the enforcers of such discriminatory practices never had the moral decency to recognize the personhood of others whom they regarded with disdain as savages and whom they treated worse than their pets and livestock. Their basis for discriminating against them was that they were not Krustans. Justice and fairness were the preserve of Krustans only; the rest of the people could be treated unjustly and unfairly with the impunity that goes with being a Krustan. If they dared to complain about the theft of their lands, they were instructed to show their title deeds, which were promptly destroyed so that they had nothing left to show to prove their legal claim to their property. That is still what the immoral moral code of twin world decrees as the just, fair, and acceptable Krustan way of doing things. So we ask again, who needs their perverted religion?

But closer study of their bubel by sane minds indicates that these evil people practice not what their authentic bubels decree, but what they have laid down in their "Book of Greed" on which a succession of their generations have been raised since the beginning of time, and which teaches them how to furtively steal from others or else forcibly misappropriate their possessions (land, minerals, oil, etc.), while they use another version of this bubel to enslave the minds of their victims with noble pronouncements of their high intentions during their acts of theft and vandalism. Their outlandish holy books, which instruct them to spitefully burn the holy books of others, espouse a religion and an ethic that fosters ruination of the lives of others in every way possible. That has indeed been the pattern wherever they have gone and discovered uninhabited but well populated lands and continents in twin world with non-existent inhabitants who lived there and whom they enumerated with the wild life of the continent, and then went on to treat them like animals or even worse than animals in most cases. To borrow a quote from Susan Nathan of our world, they discover "land without people for people without land", and they would rather feed and tend their animals than do the same for any hungry or sick indigenous person, in most cases, and they would not kill off their animals as they killed these people in their millions. In their world animal rights transcend brown rights any day. Today they expose these people to toxins of all kinds, in the air, food, and water, and they carry out lethal medical experiments on them, but never on their own tribe's people.

The intelligentsia of twin world have adopted the same myopic view of its browns as that adopted by one of the civilized persons of our world who audaciously wrote of its so-called "savages" that "their consciousness has not yet reached an awareness of any substantial and objective existence . . . [they have] not progressed beyond their immediate existence."[1] By his anemic opinion, they lack spiritual interests and development, because they, like all the other browns, are "untouched by higher thoughts or aspirations"[2], since they eke out a merely sensuous existence in a continent that "has no historical interest of its own"[3]. Having "no determinate character of its own"[4], it "merely shares the fortunes of great events enacted elsewhere"[5], because "life there consists of a succession of contingent happenings and surprises"[6]. That is how a European insulted Africans, and that is how the Eubopans of twin world insult Afibikans today. The pattern is unmistakable.

But their big lie and ignorance have been exposed, as happens all the time in twin world where pinks are always trying to discredit and demean browns in the hope that by so doing they will elevate their own status against the background of lowly browns. In our world, more than 200 years before Hegel was born, Leo Africanus wrote, in 1526, about Timbuktu, Mali, then a city in Ghana (Africa), in these terms: "There are in Timbuktu numerous judges, teachers and priests, all properly appointed by the king. He greatly honours learning. Many hand-written books imported from Barbary are also sold."[7] So, have they really not progressed beyond their immediate existence? Are they really untouched by higher thoughts and aspirations? Does their continent really have no historical interest of its own? Does it have no written history? Joan Baxter's answer to these questions in "The treasures of Timbuktu"[8] also belies this lie.

Like Hegel, they further claim that these "savage" people harbour a primitive lack of self-consciousness and the incentive for directed development that prompts them to destroy one another, while also admitting to malicious suppression and callous decimation of them for their cultural inferiority that is no match for the more intensive cultural development of the more advanced pink nations of twin world—a mandatory and arbitrary death sentence for an allegedly inferior cultural development. They do not mention the element of greed that caused this situation, but they instead decry the achievements of browns who have been allowed the unusual opportunity to undertake and distinguish themselves in learning and the professions. Their racist mentor then goes on to say that "during their wars and forays, they behaved with the most unthinking inhumanity and revolting barbarity"[8], brazenly accusing them of behaviour that is matched only by the observation of someone else about his tribe in the war that they unleashed on his world. Like them these civilized pinks not only attacked armies, but also civilians, in contravention of the rules of engagement to which they were signatories, and they pillaged, destroyed, and desecrated other people's treasures in a glaring display of their barbarous spirits and base instincts, which they called superior civilization. They further engaged in the now familiar and reprehensible practice of executing innocent children and old people, while violating, humiliating, and torturing young girls and all women, and also executing those prisoners of war who escaped their murderous chemical weapons of war. To this day, all the so-called civilized, but disrespectful, nations of twin world with their high moral values still do these things with impunity; it seems to be inherent to the being of civilized persons to behave in this uncivilized fashion. So who needs their civilization?

The habitats of browns do not fare any better against the wanton murderous instincts of their conquerors who use scorched earth tactics of burning down their dwellings and destroying their crops, so that famine can wipe them out, if they should be lucky enough to escape extermination at the hands of callous, bloodthirsty pink soldiers. Their policy has always been to harm men, women, and children indiscriminately. Make no mistake; the soldiers do not engage in their beastly behaviour because the owners of the land are at war with them. They either take advantage of the welcome that has been extended to them, or they come with their devilish minds made up (by order of their superiors and for their own morbid amusement) to destroy the people and their property. The impunity with which they wield their vile, unrestrained power, and of which they stand accused, is backed by promises of protection from any kind of prosecution by their fathers in government. The parents teach the children how to be evil, and they in turn teach their children how to be evil, and so the immoral attitudes are perpetuated through generations without interruption. Naive little pink boys and girls who are born without racial prejudice have been misled by their racist parents and taught to call brown men and women who are entrusted with tending and raising them "boy" or "girl" to assert their superiority over them, to emphasize their insignificance and anonymity, and to rudely remind them that they do not merit the respect that is due to adults of their own race. They carry these attitudes with them into university where they should be sufficiently enlightened to know that they are wrong, but they go even further and disseminate them when they become teachers and leaders in those institutions of highest learning. Louise Brown pinpointed this attitude thus, "Students reported acts of overt racism: a Queen's University student said she was spit (sic) on and told to go back to Pakistan; a swastika was painted on a Guelph university washroom wall; the 'N-word' was scrawled on the door of York University's Black Student Alliance office."[9] Others have said, "blacks are necessary evils . . . the greatest curse ever inflicted on our magnificent countries"[10]. Lack of respect for the personhood of others governs these woeful, inhomane characters, reflecting their intrinsic cheapness and confirming their incorrigible brutishness.

On the contrary, brown children are taught to respect their elders whom they address as "uncle" or "papa" and "auntie" or "mama"; never ever as "boy" or "girl"! That is why as adults they will readily apologize for hurtful or inappropriate comments and actions with humility and remorse, a virtue unknown to pinks. Pink boys and girls are further taught not to credit browns with personhood, and not to try to copy anything that they do, including their good deeds. One little brat earned the ire of his equally brattish mother by remaking to her: "Ek wil koeldrank drink soos die

Kaffirs"= I want to drink cold drink like the kaffirs (browns), using the Arabic word, "kaffir", meaning non-believer in Islam, as a derogatory designation to denote Blacks, as he had been so pitiably indoctrinated by his ignorant parents. So what kinds of persons are pinks raising and how will this kind of education and upbringing benefit homanity at large. Clearly, those who engage in this kind of conduct are trying to excel in beastliness, climbing down the tree of evolution to antiquity. (Oops! They do not believe in evolution, only in creationism with them as demi-gudds). There is no doubt that if those children were removed from this toxic atmosphere and given to the same browns to raise them before they were exposed to the viperous influence of their parents and society, they would develop a close, loving, and colourless attachment to them, which they still do, up to a point, while they still spend the greater part of their waking hours with their brown nannies.

In other walks of social life, underprivileged people who were hitherto protected from excesses of inebriating beverages that cloud the clarity of their thoughts to what is going on around them have been enticed to avail themselves of the deadly liberty of imbibing as much alcohol as they wish, without interfering restrictions from their providers who also happen to be their oppressors. They are made to feel that they are enjoying a form of freedom that is really a form of disguised mental enslavement by their benefactors who know the intellectual dulling effects of strong drink. That's why from their very first encounter they degraded them and drowned them in liquor, as they are still doing today, to destroy them intellectually, politically, socially, economically, and educationally, and to keep them in a perpetual twilight state where they cannot even have the will to think about their besetting problems and organize effective protests against their imposition by those who listen to them with bias and contempt and react only with violence, but not with reason, to their feeble protests. Taking into account the fact that alcohol *per se* lacks commendable effects but abounds in deleterious ones, we can justly conclude that these people are being systematically eliminated by unlimited exposure to the following: arthritis; cancers of liver, mouth, rectum, pancreas, breast; kidney disease; liver disease; hypertension and coronary heart disease; malnutrition and abnormal blood sugar utilization; dementia, aberrant behaviour, depression and the suicidal propensities that accompany it; and many other ills. So, who needs alcohol to survive and why would anyone encourage someone else to drown himself in it? It is not unthinkable that someone might want to use it as a covert form of murder by drowning browns in it. Unfortunately, they, in turn, oblige by foolishly falling into the trap.

Like Hagala, these people also accuse browns of "contempt for humanity . . . [and] lack of respect for life, [because] life in general has no value for them"[11]. The smear is meant to deflect attention from pink contempt and lack of concern and respect for the lives of those that they kill in their wars and for the soldiers who commit suicide after breaking down mentally and emotionally from being forced to end the lives of children, women, and old people, not counting the lives of soldiers of their victimized states who were trying to protect the honour of their fellow citizens from violation and dehomanization by foreigners who had no business in their land. Browns don't "allow themselves to be shot down"[12] in their gallantry, as it is insensitively alleged; they are shot down like hunted quarry by greedy and arrogant intruders who use overwhelming numbers of them in their own armies to provide fodder for the cannons of "the enemy", while they exclude them from their victory celebrations and deny them deserved recognition for the gallant contributions that they made to the causes that contributed to the advancement of their selfish pink agenda, saving the butts of its architects from defeat and humiliation. The truth is that these wars do nothing for browns and their wrecked family lives, but everything for the pink herrenvolk agenda.

If some of the citizens dare to keep clear heads and ask tough questions of their leaders, the time-worn tactic of fostering sectarian hatred by driving economic, social, cultural, and political wedges among them for ease of domination rears its ugly head. The architects of herrenvolkism dangle carrots before the docile majority who promptly abandon their rights and dissociate themselves from "the rebels" who are asking embarrassing questions for the sake of receiving favours. They simultaneously bring the stick down quite heavily on the protesters, shoot them or unjustly throw them in jail for demanding due respect of their rights. It is not uncommon for pinks to cement these wedges among the people by creating the impression that the more honourable status is theirs, and that anyone who can qualify to be an honorary member of their tribe will be better off than the indigenous peoples on whose rights they could trample together (their way of minimizing opposition). Many fall for this ruse and scramble to cross the line with the sole purpose of availing themselves of the opportunities, privileges, and usurped rights that pinks enjoy. Those who meet the qualifications for membership of the chosen tribe find themselves in the ranks of people who believe that even the lowest in intellect and manners among them are better than those of other tribes who are of a darker skin colour but still surpass them in homaneness, deportment, and cognitive ability. In short, they lost their reason (if they had any, to begin with) to the irrationality and futility of attempting to stratify colours according to value criteria—the impossible pursuit of idiots.

But the schism does not end there, nor do they give up on their idiotic pursuit, as Willie Lynch (was he a lynching expert?) realized (See, reference [8], page 141). Some of these stupid browns can be pitted against others on the basis of their skin complexions. They are made to believe the fiction that the lighter the complexion, and hence the closer to the norm as established by pinks, the more superior the homanity of the owner. Among them also, some oppressed ones who happen to be living in so-called first world countries, under the yolk of pink domination, have been made to feel superior to others who live in Afibika and are self-governing (for what it is worth, with all the impoverishing, enslaving economic strings in which pinks have tangled them) so that they actually look down on the Afibikans whose ancestors begot their ancestors, aping the deplorable, idiotic, hubristic behaviour of the master. They do not want to be subjected to the disgrace of being mistaken for Afibikans, and yet they are not treated differently by the pinks that they are assisting in wedge-driving and with whom they want to identify but are still shunned for their skin colour. In other areas, pinks huddle aboriginal peoples into hovels (reserves), impose special aboriginal laws on them, and encourage them to weed out those who do not belong to their tribe and would otherwise dilute their pure blood. This is the "one drop" drivel being sold to aboriginals in their education for ignorance. The pure blood moronic concept will persist for as long as pinks are around as evidenced by xenophobic and racist tribal leaders of twin world who utter bigoted statements like: "We do not want to be a multicoloured country"[13] and "I think that all of this immigration has really changed the fabric of [Eubopa]. . . . allowing millions and millions of people to come into [Eubopa] is very, very sad. I think amoralyou are losing your culture."[14]

At all points of contact, the colonialists, who were welcomed among the indigenous peoples of twin world with magnanimous gestures that characterize the natural sense of hospitality of their gracious hosts, displayed this inherent ingratitude, inhomaneness, and lack of manners by taking advantage of their hosts and using guile to steal their lands, which was, after all, what they really came to do. They did not hesitate to use their hosts and then discard them like trash afterwards, as is still their vile nature to this day. In *Stolen Continents* Ronald Wright tells the story of one of the colonizers whose life was once saved by an indigenous man, but when the latter came to him to plead for fair treatment of his people, he dismissed him summarily and would not stoop to grant him further audience. Subsequently his armies dispossessed and humiliated an indigenous woman, prompting the man to articulate his regret that he did not kill the colonizer instead of saving his life, since the lack of class in his action was diametrically opposed to the reciprocation that he owed for the favour that was previously bestowed on him. Such attitudes of ingratitude are not a rarity in today's pink-brown relations, and no one should be surprised to encounter them in dealings with pinks; they just have no class. Their lack of class is further displayed in negotiation, which they execute with drawn daggers under their cloaks, intent on springing a surprise attack on the unwary negotiating party. How can anyone trust them?

If the original owners of the countries that they have colonized accept the choice of remaining among them in their newly stolen lands, they force them to be assimilated into their culture, so that there should be no trace left of the theft and other moral indignities to which they subjected the people—the same kind of arrogance as is displayed by those who try to avoid "woe" to their gudd-chosen tribes by assimilating into their superior religions others who marry into them. So it was six centuries ago, and so it still is in this modern age in twin world. Brown children were removed from their families ostensibly to attend schools in pink institutions where they were tortured and also forbidden to speak their savage language, practice their customs, or associate with those of their families who were left behind, so that their minds could be primed to think only in terms of the lies that their oppressors were feeding them, as against the truths that they knew from their traditional upbringing, truths about their lands, their culture, their rights, their freedoms, and their homanity. But they also paid a hefty price in sexual and physical abuses of all kinds, which broke their spirits and made them mere helpless possessions whose only choice was to acquiesce, however reluctantly, in their inhomane treatment for their own survival. Pink oppressors everywhere in twin world still mete out this kind of abominable treatment to their victims.

However, among the ranks of pinks are "collaborators" who recognize the injustices of their tribe, but who choose to remain silent when the rights and liberties of those they fear and dislike are infringed and eroded, because they cannot understand them. One wonders why they allow themselves to descend to the gutter levels of their pink brothers when they have a better understanding of the ethical impropriety of their actions. Perhaps doing so makes them feel assured that pink supremacy will remain secure from the threat of the challenge posed by brown quest for equality and respect for their rights and personhood, instead of pitying acknowledgement from liberals. They are also complicit in the rigged and unfair trials of certain others in which they are not allowed representation by counsel or allowed self defence, and they still call that justice. Such justice only demeans the stature of their respectable courts of law, reducing them to the mere kangaroo courts that these accomplished, wise practitioners of justice attribute only to so-called under-developed countries of twin world. But there is always a final price to pay for collaboration with evil in the loss of homanity and degeneration into tools that can be used and discarded at will, as well as becoming the victims of the same evil. Evil does not choose its prey; once let loose, it devours all persons randomly, even the racially privileged and sheltered citizens.

And so it is was and still is that to be able to use them to full advantage as blindfolded pawns in their power games and misdeeds, the manipulators wrap these citizens in the flag, subject them to partisan flag waving rallies where they cheer their pseudo leaders and hail them as national heroes for nothing, or for trumped up deeds of valour that amount to no more than intimidating and murdering peoples of other countries and nations in so-called wars of liberation and democratization, which also carry costs in the lives of their people and their economic well-being. These murders include children of all ages, as a soldier observed in conversation with his peers that he was obliged to shoot and kill a child who happened to pick up a gun, a toy gun; or a policeman who shoots and kills another child also for playing with a toy gun under the pretext of fearing for his own life. This is the same stormtrooper mentality that was forged and executed by the totalitarian and fascist regimes of our world and is still the norm in so-called rogue states and the yearning of other state leaders who want to wield absolute authority where people sit up, listen and obey when they speak. On this showing, the title of rogue state appears to be common to both in a case of the pot calling the kettle black. These are states that have used germ warfare (e.g., Smallpox infected blankets, Dengue 2 virus of twin world) on the defenceless indigenous peoples of the lands that they came to steal by intrigue and betrayal of their owners for trusting their conciliatory demeanour, or by decimating them to the extent of wiping out any resistance by them to their acts of theft.

These diabolical Krustans also tried their utmost to "extirpate this execrable race" (to borrow from Lord Jeffrey Amherst, 16 July 1763) and placed a bounty (£300) on each of their scalps to abet their murder, honouring the champions of these murders by naming state institutions and towns after them. To this day, their churches are still used as potent narcotics (the opium of Karl Marx) by occupiers to tranquilize the troubled minds of browns into submission. These religious rogues and machinators hope to allay the resentment and determination of the exploited masses to revolt against their insensitive treatment and to induce them with lies to lay down the cudgels that they have picked up to end their victimization. And so they are intensifying the preaching of their Krustan gospel of non-violence against the prevailing backdrop of their violent takeover of other people's lands, while they continue to vehemently soften their malevolent tones and deny their loudly speaking murderous actions and selfish motives.

Some knowledgeable persons have quite bluntly alleged that to date they still manufacture and use biologicals like AIDS and Ebola virus equivalents to gain control over and prune brown civilian populations of twin world. Their now open secret, heinous programs (equivalents of Global 2000 and NSSM 200 or National Security Study Memorandum, which has been aptly styled a "plan for food control genocide") call for exterminating browns all over their developing world, especially in those countries of "special political and strategic interest" that have the potential for gaining significant but unpalatable political power and influence, because of their large populations and youth who are more likely to resist the new world order of continuing pink domination, selfish investments, and exploitation. Little wonder that there are severe food shortages and famines from which browns are dying like flies in these countries, while those who can reverse the tragedy are looking on with folded arms and unconcern. Little wonder too that they are doing so little about the AIDS epidemic in brown states and even instilling the same inhomane attitude in so-called brown leaders who deny their citizens the appropriate treatment for their affliction, while they perish by the millions as part of the herrenvolk master plan of increasing the death rate outside the criminal arena of war, which is second only to hoarding money in their hierarchy of perverted goals.

These are the devout Krustans whose history includes burning their own brothers at the stake, or else keeping them under house arrest and forcing them to recant their rational scientific discoveries just so that the simplistic and self-serving theories of the church about twin world's central role in its relationship with other worlds could prevail. More ludicrously, however, they punished browns for treasonable ideas and offences against the pink gudd made in their image, as if he lacks the omnipotence to exact his own revenge. In this atmosphere, looking up to these Krustans for delivery from oppression is like expecting the devil to release one from hallum (hell), which happens to be another of their infamous fabrications to scare gullible people into believing in their big gyp, especially since some of their holiest authorities lavishly donated the stolen lands on which aboriginals lived to their pink sovereign friends in Eubopa without consulting (wishful thinking) the owners of the land. That is the irreproachable church of Gudd at work, ever perpetrating evil.

Those of this ilk who want to appear homane often express verbal sympathy with browns, while doing nothing to alleviate their misery, because they benefit materially from their oppression, or else they look the other way and let these atrocities continue when they can do something to stop them. We have seen champions of justice and fairness abandoning their stand and willingly compromising on principle for expediency, sacrificing the subjects of their wardship when their own family interests and aspirations were being threatened by their assumed benevolent role. The notable few who have taken up the cudgel to champion the cause of browns with any semblance of sincerity are to be commended for their commitment, bravery, and perseverance. Some of their kind have paid with their lives for their devotion to the task of improving the lives of the underdogs; and for those sacrifices the browns of twin world should pause to pay them due homage. At the same time, many who profess to be engaged in the same struggle are in it only to make money and to enhance their social standing, like the known empty-headed, glamorous, unprincipled bashers of brown civic authority who rush to devastated brown countries for vain photo ops.

Does the future augur amelioration of the multipronged plight of the brown tribe? That remains to be seen. So far, the prevailing snares of the religious, social, economic, and political hurdles that we have encountered, artfully contrived to enslave even those brown states that boast freedom of religion, social equality, and political self-determination, are some of the worst evils to befall them, and they promise to keep them permanently underprivileged, exploited, and enslaved. What else is left for them in twin world?

Nothing, unless they wake up and fight off oppression.

But does that deprive their lives of meaning? No; after all, they do not owe their advent in twin world and their very being to pink whim, although that whim affects and determines to a large degree their continuing survival in that world. Pinks may destroy the body, but they will never destroy the spirit that drives that body, and like the legendary phoenix, the person that they thought they had killed will, by the grace of that spirit, rise up to reclaim by force what has been taken from her by deceit and force of arms.

# Chapter 16
# The varied meanings of life.

The reader might wonder why the title of this chapter is not "The meaning of life", since life is considered to be the universal period of existence between birth and death that is experienced by all persons alike, and which must have an inherent meaning that they share (we will not enter into the fray of the personhood of the fetus and of life after death. I have discussed them in my *Philosophy for Medical Students and Practitioners* and *Our world and its Values*). But life happens to be an outwardly meaningless process in the sense that it just is; people are born, they live, and they die, all for no apparent reason. So, whether we believe that life owes its being to an uncaused cause or to spontaneous beginning, and whether or not we think that life has a purpose and meaning that is yet to be discovered and defined does not affect the fact of its being and the fact that its meaning starts from within itself, rather than from something else out there. Its being (ontology) is enough to vex our minds and keep us speculating about its multiple facets: origin, meaning, purpose, etc., even if we cannot find ready answers to these questions now or at any time in the foreseeable future. The problem is here to stay.

In our efforts to find the meaning of life, we should distinguish between meaning as reference or denotation of a set of connotative physiological processes: alertness, mobility, breathing, circulation of blood, reproduction, etc., and meaning as delineation of perceived causes and effects and their impact on the psyche of the living being. In the latter case, we decide the meaning of life based on the moral parameters that we have delineated as the pre-requisites for that meaning and how closely people's lives adhere to them, without implying that all lives are the same by virtue of satisfying the same essential, basic, measurable biological characteristics, because psychic qualities can't be measured by physical parameters. Lives like those of some modern national "leaders" that lack qualities like love, honesty, justice, fairness, respect, compassion, etc., may be complete, in their own mean and selfish way, but they have less than optimal moral value when compared with those that possess these qualities.

Understanding the past does not tell us life's meaning, nor does teleology. Past events may have some influence on many present and future events, and they may contain the seeds of flowers that are yet to bloom, but they do not determine the value and meaning of life, in as much as the etymon does not always determine the current use of a word (etymological fallacy) and the current value of an idea does not always depend on its origin (genetic fallacy); i.e., the history of the idea is not always relevant to its present value. Life can equally not be interpreted in terms of a future objective or telos, because it does not follow a rigid course leading to a pre-determined end, although it does yield to the reality and influence of past and present events. If it does have a telos, it is only the one that will satisfy projected future needs as reflected in the present needs of survival of twin world and its inhabitants; otherwise the telos of life resides in the oblivion of death. Therefore, it is absurd to imagine or postulate a life after life when the body that contains the elements of life decays after the demise of the person who is represented by it. The body is not the person but the necessary vehicle for the consciousness in which personhood reposes. Permanent loss of consciousness by that body results in the person ceasing to exist; and if the body that harbours that consciousness is annihilated, the person also ceases to be, because consciousness cannot exist without a body to harbour it.

The person does not, therefore, derive meaning for his life from a mythical future where only his consciousness will survive in a hodgepodge of consciousnesses. It is inconceivable that a nondescript, amorphous, and ethereal entity like it that lacks identification and individuation criteria can be the lodestar of life. Serving to further confound this already confused field is the invocation of faith in the post-mortem existence of the soul, a nebulous, conceptual entity posited without justification, and best characterized as a "ghost in the machine" by Gilbert Ryle in *The Concept of Mind*. People find comfort in claiming the existence of a fictitious transcendental chimera to assure the survival in it of their present and hoped for personalities. They will not accept the fact that they are merely the sum of their time-limited physical and psychic characteristics, and that they will be extinguished permanently when function ebbs out of these constituents of their persons. Life is so nice for only some of them (not the poor) that they invent a life after life for this fiction that they invest with immortality by unfounded faith.

These claims of irrational faith, as it obtains in twin world, can only be answered in the words of one author from our world: "Faith is when you believe something that you know ain't true."[1] Indeed, every thinking person will agree that when she believes something, she does so on the basis of credible evidence, because evidence forms the basis of authentic proof, and for belief to lead to truth, it must be authentic. Without truth, there can be no knowledge, and without knowledge the future of homanity is bound to be shrouded in uncertainty and loss of direction, because the morality of homan actions ultimately depends on the true beliefs that homanity accumulates over time to direct its thinking and action, and if it bases its beliefs on false evidence it will diminish its potential for collective intellectual and moral worth. In the final analysis, future events that can only be speculated about may serve as attractive teleological stimuli for the performance of present-day actions in preparation for hoped for eventualities, but they do not define the meaning of life, nor does what has happened in the past (genetic fallacy).

So, when someone says "my life has no meaning" we construe that to imply "meaning" in the qualitative or value sense rather than in the sense of being materially present and physiologically active, which is the ontological sense; and that prompts us to ask her for the qualities that are lacking in it: relationships, achievements, purpose, mental calm, morality, etc., while realizing that she is physiologically alive. From these questions it is quite clear that the meaning of life to different persons will vary with the manner of living of each one of these free agents who are living undetermined (often prosaic, vapid, mundane, inconsequential, but goal-directed) lives with the liberty to make decisions and rational choices on how they will act and assume responsibility for those acts, and not the meaning that some others claim that their gudd pre-determined it to have for them as their menials. These are cowards who shun responsibility for their actions but prefer to shift it to their gudd who should bear the blame for how they mistreat others, because he allegedly chose them to be rulers, and they are only carrying out, however inhomanely, duties that are consistent with maintaining their positions as divinely chosen rulers. They quote their bubels to justify their amorality.

However, if they are their Gudd's chosen people and his intention was to select them for *baasskap* (boss-ness) and oppression of other people, then it is pointless for browns to pray to the same gudd to liberate them from oppression by pinks; they might as well pray for a change in the entire order and natural laws of their world and the universe to have their wishes accommodated. If the infinitely omniscient one has foreordained the existing unjust arrangement, then finite little minds dare not question his decision, because as creator, he rules their world; their world does not rule him. So, even if oppressed homans think that his arrangement is inequitable, they are still compelled to accept it, because he alone knows what is best for them. But to try to attribute this irrational dispensation to the true

Gudd is to mock his omniscience (supreme wisdom and rationality), which is, in turn, to play dirty games with what he represents in the lives of all his people, unless he happens to be the pink created gudd that is partial to them. Such games are consistent with the wiles of scheming homan beings who contrive these vile situations for their own benefit and then sacrilegiously attribute their origin to the Gudd that they cannot control and command as they like.

In the language of our world, even if we fervently believe that we act in obedience to God's commands, we still have to decide that the commands came from God, and that they are not figments of our imaginations like those referred to above. Beyond that, each one still has to add her own interpretations to the meaning of the life that she is living, which is different from the lives lived by other persons whose interpretations of the meanings of their varied lives must necessarily differ among themselves and from hers. The mere existence of God does not alone give meaning and purpose to life, even though some transgressors of his will feel that without a transcendent lodestar, a being who is greater than life and humanity, life cannot have any meaning. The meanings of our lives depend on what each one of us brings to them and takes away from them from our daily interaction with our neighbours. Life's meaning lies beyond its physical self and its appearance, in that it has proved to be more than the sum of its corporeal components. Science can unravel the material constituents and reduce them to their elements (atoms, etc.), but it cannot assemble them to produce life *de novo*. The best chess playing computer may share its ultimate constituents (atoms etc.) with the people who designed and made it to mimic their intellectual performances, but it still lacks life. Unknown, elusive-to-science factors that make the difference between being alive and being dead, as well as factors that endow one life with meaning and value still remain, while another life that lacks these factors is found to lack that meaning and value, although both lives may be scientifically equivalent but not morally exchangeable; hence the title of this chapter.

No amount of faith can bridge the gap between the materials of which our bodies are made and the thoughts, values, emotions, and "spiritual" experiences that characterize our mental lives. Atoms, whose physical behaviour is determined by physical laws, are found in all material bodies, animate and inanimate, but not in minds, and there is no way that minds and values can be reduced to atoms, although they can be explained as products of atomic action. Somewhere in the interface between the physical and mental states, a transformation takes place that still eludes our understanding but shatters the rigid course of physically pre-determined, but chaos-prone, events in the lives of humans that science has delineated for their mechanistic bodies. Inexplicable changes occur in our lives in the same way that courses of events are altered by quantum effects that derail the anticipated physical behaviour of matter. Attributing all these mysteries to God is not answering the question or solving the problem, but just shelving it in the same way that some people deny and shelve problems stemming from their inhumanity, instead of acknowledging and addressing them honestly and seriously.

We like to think that we make our lives what they should be by virtue of our freedom of choice to act otherwise than we actually do; but even that freedom is often restricted by the barriers imposed by people whose delight is to determine the directions of our lives for their selfish benefit, in spite of our ability to do that for ourselves in most situations. The people of twin world do not fare any better. The inhomanity that prevails in their world, as in ours, makes us wonder what meaning its less privileged people attach to their lives of privation in the context of the good living that they see around them, but which is well outside of their reach. The best that they can do is only wish for it or dream about it, but they can never experience it, nor can their children and their children's children. They are caught in the downward spiral of self-perpetuating dispossession and poverty, not of their own choice, but which has been imposed on them by their Gudd-appointed Krustan guardians, and which is thus beyond their power to regulate, or even to try to terminate. For them, life and "living death" carry the same meaning, and it is not surprising to hear some of them wishing that they would rather die than face the helplessness of being unable to change their lives and also bring hope into the forlorn lives of their children. The dire circumstances of their existence make it impossible for them to seek out sources of basic happiness that they can add to their existence in oppression to make it bearable. They do not choose servitude or value it more than freedom; and rather than desiring their own oppression or choosing to wear the chains of slavery from cowardice, they "loose everything in their chains, even the desire of escaping from them"[2], because they are driven into the gutter by the elite oppressor who, ironically, is also forced to remain enslaved down there, keeping his foot on their necks to ensure that they don't get up.

For them it is not a question of choosing between investments and their projected returns, or comparing restaurant menus, but striving anxiously to procure the next slice of bread to feed their hungry families, even if they have to retrieve—at the risk of being jailed— untouched edibles that the same restaurants have discarded, instead of making them freely available to them. They do not have to keep up with the Joneses, because that is vanity that they cannot afford in their lives; instead, they have learnt to face the grave facts of life in their unforgiving cruelty, which are not the trivial facts that fill the competition-dominated lives of the affluent world. Their lives are under the direction of those who set the boundaries at the low level of mere existence where they have been deprived of their right to self-determination and have become the tools of their exploiters, much like the inert objects that all of them use to assist them in carrying out certain functions in their daily activities of living. But don't blame the guardians for the plight of their wards; everything has been decreed by their gudd, and they are the instruments through which he executes his plan for the poor wretches, in spite of having endowed each one of all his creatures with free will for self-determination. So, each one is paradoxically (oxymoronically) free to exercise her free will in her pre-determined situation (see chapter 5 of my book *Mind Your Ps and Qs*), like a shackled prisoner in a locked room who is told that he is free to go home.

Nevertheless, all persons are still presumed to have the freedom to make themselves into what they desire to be, and not to be pre-determined to be one way or another, and certainly not to be the objects of manipulation by others, or to be used by them as means to their own ends, rather than also as ends in themselves. Arrogance alone will impel someone to regard another person's personhood as less than his own and to want to use him as his object while blaming his attitude on circumstances beyond his control, an attitude styled "bad faith": the free market determines our fortunes, and if certain persons fall through the cracks because they are ill-prepared or unprepared for it, then so be it. This self-advantaged snob wants to pretend that every one has an equal chance to exploit the markets, when he knows that his tribe has made it impossible for the other person to even entertain any thought of taking a crack at the market; certainly not with his empty hands, which are all he has for tackling the world of money and competing with those who are labouring under the weight of their overladen money bags.

So, what is the meaning of life to these two categories of persons? For the affluent it consists in living in the present, hoarding more goods and money, and paying little attention to the dangerous conditions that he is creating for himself and others in callously polluting the environment and accelerating the pace of global warming with its devastating effects, some of which we have already enumerated. His sole interest reposes in the money that his polluting industries will bring him and his progeny that he is foolishly also sacrificing to his greed, because the disasters caused by that greed will affect them as much as they affect the rest of the people whose lives don't count with him, and they will not be around long enough to enjoy the money that he has left for them, since he can't take it with him to hallum (hell) when he blesses his world with his expiry. His policy of living for today only, because tomorrow may not come, is in direct conflict with his wish of hoarding for tomorrow, as surely as he believes that it will come; so he performs the impossible task of riding both horses at the same time, even though they are going in opposite directions. That cannot be the tension-filled kind of happy life that all people would want to aim for, because, while it might have meaning in its owner's perverted thinking, it fails to have any meaning for those of his clear thinking fellow twin-worlders who sadly cannot escape being affected by his surd selfishness.

Someone might argue that it is better to live now, rather than spend this life in preparation for a future life in hivana that might never come, or one that will come but continue *ad nauseam* and end up being quite boring. That frame of mind might accord well with the worldview of the hoarder who keeps everything to himself, while forcing other people to survive on less than the barest essentials of life; but it is cold comfort to the dispossessed who are made to bank on the argument that earthly life is short and it ends in oblivion for all; hence those who are forced to endure it while others are enjoying it can console themselves with the thought that it will soon be over for all alike, in eighty years or so (see page 45), after which eternal bliss will bless those who were temporarily deprived, as much as it will also unfairly accrue to those who monopolized the bliss of twin world. Finding it difficult and unfair to be expected to cling to this vacuous promise, they are nevertheless still compelled to derive their consolation from the indubitable, cold fact that death will level all of them. And so the ominous words of the poet (their cold comfort) ring in their ears all the time about the ultimate fate of both rich and poor:

> A heap of dust alone remains of thee,
> 'Tis all thou art, and all the proud shall be! [3]

On the other hand, the foolish man of privilege does not want to believe this fact, and he refuses to realize the futility of hoarding treasures that he must leave behind when he dies, because there is no way that he will be able to enjoy them in his decayed, disintegrated state; but denial of the facts keeps him hard-hearted. Swindlers of billions of dullams have died soon after their big swindles, leaving all those fortunes behind, but their brothers in swindle never learn;

they still pursue their exercise in ultimate futility ardently, and they continue to inflict misery fervently on the rest of the people.

At the same time, rulers and generals of twin world who have directed the slaughter of millions of innocent civilians in spurious, immoral wars of empire expansion, domination, and ethnic cleansing have fared no better; nor have those who have sacrificed the lives of many of their local citizens and of the citizens of their victim states to boost their political fortunes that were tottering under the weight of their baneful state policies. They have not attained immortality, in spite of extended efforts to keep their bodies alive devoid of their consciousnesses, as we discussed on page 202, but have instead all ended in the same dust as the one that they made their victims bite prematurely. The lurid legacies of their horrendous deeds have survived them, if only to mock their lives in the same way that they mocked the lives of those they murdered, because they thought those lives were cheap and did not matter, although they mattered a lot to their families who loved them as much as they (rulers and generals) loved their own families and were loved by them.

For the underprivileged, life means what his affluent brother is constantly trying to instil in him. The good things of life will accrue to him by trickle down from those who are enjoying them when they have had their fill, which is never, because their insatiable greed is fed by the flow of the deluge of prosperity towards them. What he does not manage to acquire and enjoy in this world, he will have in abundance in the next world, wherever that is. His privileged brother has awarded him the unknown bounties of an unknown world, and all he has to do is live in hope and not fret over the goods of this world that pass him by every day of his life on their way into the inventories of the rich. He should forgo the twin world slice of bread for the marvellous slab of cake that he will feast on in hivana one day, if he can bear the privations of twin world with the courage that is required of him to qualify for admission into joyful eternity where there is no want or labour, and where milk and honey flow freely for the satiety of all as they traverse streets paved with gold — funny. This is a special privilege to be shared with their oppressors by those who were not permitted by forces in their marketplace to acquire even the most basic necessities of life while their oppressors claimed ignorance of their dire circumstances: we did not know that you were living in such poor circumstances, because we did not want or care to know. We knew that our state was a fascist pink state where browns did not have the franchise or earn a living wage, because we voted alone and passed laws that repressed them and we paid them their meagre wages. We always regarded them as non-vital appendages that could be severed without any compunction, even though we depended on them for our identity and for sustaining our economy with their cheap labour. As far as we cared, they could moan and die in agony without adversely affecting our lives, but we also told ourselves the lie (one of the many that we are customarily propagate; call it second nature) that the religious pink state would continue to exist happily or better without them.

Such, according to his oppressor, should be the meaning for which the brown is searching in his life, even if he has to do so from the icy cold and wet discomfort of the bed of concrete slabs on which he sleeps on the streets, where the only music to his ears is the din of city traffic as it whisks past him and sometimes splashes dirty slush on him. Meanwhile his dispossessor is enjoying the comfort of his warm and sheltered repose on his king size water bed from which he can enjoy jazz, rock and roll, a Beethoven symphony, or a trivial show on his high definition plasma television set, if not watch (in a detached manner) a documentary on poverty and hunger in the "third" world, seeing images of starving people rummaging garbage dumps for food, living in tents and shanties without running water, sanitation, electricity, and other basic amenities that are considered essential for health and well-being and taken for granted in his "first" world. Like the nobility, about whom Charles Dickens wrote that "it was clearer than crystal to the lords of the State preserves of loaves and fishes, that things in general were settled for ever"[4], they also believe that this situation will endure for all time. What a grievous error; they don't want to see or feel their world of comfort changing fast around them and shifting under their firmly planted feet of clay; they feign blindness to the writing on the wall.

The best of their times in relishing an unchallenged *baasskap* (bossness) over browns is fast becoming their worst time as the spring of their hope of endless superiority is rapidly yielding place to a winter of despair in their ability to maintain the status quo, in spite of the application of brute force to stay on top. They may have everything before them now and believe that they are on their way to hivana, but after the tables have turned, they might end up having nothing, like the people that they have dispossessed, and also find themselves going directly to hallum (hell). Their monopoly on being the bosses has blinded them to any possibility of negotiating power sharing, let alone losing that power to browns. They deride them like the *white* oppressor of our world who, scoffing at a Black that he was prosecuting under the Terrorism Act 1967 of his racist state for his role in the liberation struggle of his people, said, "Oh, you would like some whites to call you *baas*, wouldn't you?"[5] The pink implication of this adopted attitude is that there is only one *baas*, and it is the pink *baas*. In his utter fear of brown potential and his asinine regard for the meaningless title of *baas* that he has bestowed on himself, he cannot conceive of a brown sharing that measly title of vacuous honour with him. Like the cowards that they are aping, the funks of twin world also seek refuge in the same kind of Terrorism Act when they want to suppress brown discontent with their evil ways.

In their denial, some of them have been known to soothe their absent consciences by remarking that the poor will always be with us, so why burden our minds with their lot and their problems when we could be making the best of our present comforts, because we might not be around tomorrow to enjoy them, and who knows where we will be; the world that we keep on promising them may turn out to be the real figment of abundance that we thought we were tricking them to believe in, to hope and live for. What they should go on to say is: let them find a way to resolve the problems that we imposed on them or else wallow in them; we have found our niche in life that we will not share with them or sacrifice for their sake. So, in these circumstances who has good reason to resent whom, and who should be following the gallant example of the French peasants who revolted, and some in our own times who are revolting against their unjust share of similarly blatant and equally arrogantly perpetrated injustice by similar breeds of conscienceless dictators and exploiters? There is no question about the fact that poor folk have never been given the opportunity to make it in the world, even though they are treated as if they are hankering for what they have not earned and do not deserve. The truth is that they have earned their place in the sun, and they want to be given a chance to continue to prove their worth, achieve more and contribute more, because they have pride in their untapped and unutilized abilities. They are not inert driftwood, as they have demonstrated so many times when they have been given the chance to prove their worth. They do not want to sit around waiting for handouts and crumbs that fall from the sumptuous tables of the rich, a situation into which they are being forced by the oppressor; they want to earn their keep. Is that what the dispossessor fears? Does the actualization of this pent-up potential for success that threatens his smugness at the steering wheel of this ship of life that is carrying all of them and that he is recklessly running aground on the deadly rocks of racism and senseless egotism fill him with awe?

The rich oppressors accuse browns of being envious of their hard-earned possessions and successes, which they earned easily on the backs of the poor who lay the railway tracks, labour on the roads, and do the menial jobs that keep commerce and industry flourishing. They are expected to compare themselves only with those who are equally oppressed, depriving them of any sense of ambition and nobler meaning in life that has been unfairly shifted beyond their reach by those who do not wish them well. But all that browns want is to try and succeed or fail. If they fail, they want to try again until they succeed, like everyone else. That process of trying and that achievement of success are what have given meaning to their lives, in a limited way, through centuries of oppression and exploitation, but they want to expand their scope to encompass the broader meaning of life for themselves, their progeny, and the rest of humanity. There is no greater joy than making of oneself what one wants to become (an asset to self and to one's fellow beings), rather than being made a tool for the use and sole benefit of someone else under the pretext that that is the will of the Gudd who directed the process of biological evolution (fatal error; it is the miracle of creation; evolution is blasphemy in the ears of these types) in twin world. Pinks claim that they are made in his image, and have been given a place above all others, nearer to him, from where they cannot be displaced, and from where they can re-create him in their own scurvy image and use their creation to oppress the rest who are not even made in the image of their false gudd, the one with pink features and repugnant attributes.

Belief in a benevolent pink gudd who acts without benevolence is as oxymoronic as belief in him as the source of life, its meaning, direction, and destination in the face of blind self-directed evolution. Believing is not the same as knowing; it is still clouded by doubt that deprives it of authenticity and often forces it to appeal to faith for support in the absence of convincing evidence. If the people of twin world believe in evolution, they do not need the gudd made in their image to explain anything; but if they seriously believe in Gudd as the sole architect of their world, they still cannot exclude evolution as an addendum to the creationism that some would like to see as the only meaning of life, viz., service to a gudd with tribally motivated differential purposes for his people. In that case, they do not have to rack their brains to find out why they exist as inhabitants of twin world, because the meaning of their existence can be found in their creation. It can therefore not transcend their handiwork (their gudd) or remain as inscrutable to their finite minds as the nature of the immense universe in which their planetary system represents only a tiny speck of no or very little significance, and in which their lives and their meaning represent an even tinier speck that is not even worth any consideration. There is no mystery of life for them, since they created the gudd who created life on their specifications.

This dust of twin world arbitrarily claim the authority to decide who shall live and who shall die from the wrath of their atom, cluster, and laser bombs. With hands stained with the blood of innocent victims, they reach out to their toy gudd that they claim gave them the right and power over the lives and deaths of their fellow creatures. This self-serving band of critters who have lost the only sliver of meaning that their lives might have had to hubris compounded with a generous proportion of greed, placing them well beyond redemption, at least not until they have learnt to respect the lives of others and allowed them to dream freely about their futures and that elusive purpose in life that they should pursue without hindrance from them, will not desist from behaviour that threatens to annihilate their species and the rest of the innocent species of homans and animals (and plants) of twin world with their devastating explosives that they have already detonated on some other tribes with shamefully horrendous effects.

So, the oppressed are left with only one source from which to derive the meaning and purpose of their lives: dying, while the vile oppressor finds it in living at the expense of everyone else's life. The oppressed are denied the opportunity to attain the good life by constraints on their communal development, because they are faced with their own individual struggles for personal survival. Their goal is one: survival. They do not have the luxury of entertaining multiple goals to fill their lives with multi-purposeful activity; they have no exhilarating results to anticipate; and they have no legacy to pass on to their progeny besides that of poverty, economic serfdom, but, above all else, self-pride. Their lives of drudgery constitute one long-drawn-out episode of misery and boredom. In the face of the affluence that prevails around them their limited options and liberties deny them the autonomous choices enjoyed by other citizens who have instead made the unenviable choices of greed, selfishness, and inhomanity to express their freedom of choice, and who are never satisfied with the amount and degree of oppression, dehomanization, and exploitation that they inflict on browns; they are always looking for more ways to accentuate and perpetuate their cruelty to boost their supremacy, but they have not crushed the pride of their victims in themselves and their homan worth.

These oppressed persons would like to think that freedom is an ideal condition in which choices are not preordained by antecedent events; that it evolves spontaneously from conscious deliberation. But the serfdom of some of them to ignorant fear, facilitated by the ease with which they succumb to brainwashing, makes a mockery of their fancied freedom; they have become free serfs. This oxymoronic state of being can be overturned only by revolution against enforced choices imposed by oppressors who claim to know what is good for them, what their needs should be, and what will satisfy those needs and keep them happy in their unhappiness and free in their fetters. The restrictive authority of pinks is the people's freedom, because it saves them from the emotional social harm that is likely to result from their unregulated idealistic yearnings for rights and liberties that they can never attain under the authoritarian supremacy of their oppressors, and they can be free only if they submit to bondage, instead of chasing after the futility of obeying their own consciences that hanker after unrealizable aspirations — superlative irony.

The oppressor defines freedom for them, including their freedom to stray into trouble, which they abet by fomenting civil war amongst them so that they can eliminate one another for money and also stifle the chance of a potential opposition that they might pose to oppressive pink authority if they are given the opportunity to unite against it. Regrettably, this kind of self-destructive freedom is made possible by some people's lack of discipline and self-pride, which they would like to blame on poverty, but for which there is no excuse, as it will keep them forever subjugated; at least, for as long as they are poor. The oppressor makes them believe that they owe the state their patriotism (to fight its stupid wars) for the freedoms that they enjoy when they are actually constrained on all sides to impede what little progress they make on their own. When it suits their purposes, they wrap them in their national flags and bombard their ears with anthems whose words express ideals that are not intended to apply to them, in the same way that their global laws discriminate against them within their liberal traditions and forms of government.

In the final analysis, life's meaning will have to emanate from each person as agent, making her individual choices and decisions freely, rather than having them foisted on her; not forgetting those collective choices that stand to benefit the rest of humanity, including those who do not belong to the select pink tribe. These choices will of necessity address material needs, but they must also and importantly address moral pursuits for their intrinsic values before addressing any of their derived values. Everyone should, for instance, exercise virtue for its own sake rather than for the benefits that it will bring her in the short or long run, because such priced virtue will not stand up to rigorous challenges that demand even a limited degree of altruism. At no time, also, should anyone pursue the elusive promise of faith in the unknown, because it does not add meaning to any life. No one in her right mind can, without good reason, elect to postulate a mythical or fictitious future existence and pin her faith on it. For faith to have meaning, it should rest on indubitably solid proof, such as the faith grounded in the mechanical soundness of my bicycle that assures me that it will carry me from point $a$ to point $b$ without breaking down, barring unforeseen mishaps, rather than resting on apocryphal, blind trust in its wished and hoped for performance.

The meaning of life can further be understood only through activity or agency. Where there is no activity, or where passivity has replaced agency, meaning ceases to exist, because only mechanistic determinism prevails in such an environment; and we know that the essence of mechanical tools is not to evolve into better tools. Their essence is predetermined by their manufacturer before they come into existence and they will not develop into anything else, although they may sometimes be newly designated and put to uses other than those for which they were originally designed, if they happen to be thus adaptable. So why did Hagala have the audacity to allege as fact his fiction that Afibika is a continent where nothing happens, where there is no activity? The homan agent exists before she uses her freedom to shape her essence as she tries to reach out to the nobler aspects of her life to make herself a better person. In that way she infuses meaning into her life by choosing to do $\delta$, which brings benefits to her and to other people, instead of $\beta$, which is lethal to everyone. Within the context of $\delta$ there will be variations on the main theme, and different people will prefer their own versions of the same theme, but that does not make for the kind of senseless killings and persecutions prompted by petty differences in religious or other affiliations that are being promoted by the domineering, hypocritical, and selfish Krustans of twin world who want every one to see the world through their unholy holy eyes.

If these hypocritical killers object to this characterization of them, why would they condemn dictatorship and torture when they are meting out the same injustice to other persons, as related by a mere boy held in the jail of a twin world state that proudly vaunts its human rights in the faces of others? They do it because they happened to see this extract from one of our own news media:

> Whenever they used to restrain me and put me in the chair, they would handcuff me, . . . Strapped me down all the way, from your feet all the way to your chest, you couldn't really move. . . . They have total control over you. They also put a bag over your head. It has little holes; you can see through it. But you feel suffocated with the bag on.[6]

Why would they chastise gay persons when they are living secret gay lifestyles? Why would they vilify unfaithful husbands or wives when they are also secretly unfaithful? Why would they murder "killers" of the unborn when they are killers of the living? Why would they lock children in concentration camps when they condemn dictators who do the same thing? Why would they kill children in their wars when they decry the same foul deeds at the hands of others? The list goes on and on. They do all these things, because they believe their own lies: that they are better than everyone else, that they alone know what truth is, and that only their warped version of self-indulging truth is valid. When people descend thus far into the abyss of hubris, ignorance, and authoritarianism they lose all sense of propriety (if they had any, to begin with), wanting to crush any and all who do not also wear blinkers and subscribe to their narrow-minded worldviews. Perhaps they should stop to think of the implications of their treatment of truth as relative to their own persons, their circumstances, and their intentions, and then they will realize that all truths have equal validity, and that their standards and their version of truth should, therefore, not be forced on other people. But that would be going against their own disreputable agenda of deluding other people into believing and trusting only in their duplicitous words and deeds, and in their promises of a better life hereafter. Their desire is to see browns get there by brute force, leaving the bliss and comforts of twin world to them, although some of their holy men are not in any hurry to get there.

    The problem with such faith and its promise of life to come rests with the ethics of the persons and societies that are promoting it: bigots and hypocrites who subscribe to dogmatic religions in their racist Krustan churches, institutions whose self-righteous, bubel-carrying members, especially those in high office, practice or have at one time practiced ungúddly persecution, exploitation, greed, lying, deception, murder, disrespect of other persons by depriving their lives of tenure and meaning, and all the sins against which they preach incessantly and hypocritically to their world. Their motto rightly deserves to be characterized as: do as I say, not as I do. They leave their humble flocks of sheep perplexed about the bona fides of their promise of the glorious incentive to life that comes with faith, and which offers salvation from the oblivion that results from death. It is held out as the answer to all who seek happiness in this life and in a life to come. In its loftiness and transcendent outreach beyond what twin world can offer on an equal footing, it promises to eliminate the proverbial elusiveness of happiness and contentment and the inaccessibility of true happiness to those who set out in search of it *per se* when they should be devoting their lives virtuously and truthfully to the noble cause of living in peace, love, harmony, and dutifulness with their neighbours, whence happiness will accrue effortlessly to them. As Cyril. E. M. Joad has so aptly stated,

> The kingdom of happiness is not to be taken by storm any more than it is to be purchased by wealth. . . . Set out to seek happiness and it will elude you; . . . lift yourself up out of the selfish little pit of vanity and desire which is the self . . . and on looking back you will find that you have been happy.[7]

There are some who look upon the preceding discussion as an exercise in futility. They maintain that asking for the meaning of life is as futile as asking for the meaning of the sun or of sleep. They say legitimate questions of meaning do not arise in reference to these entities; in fact, such questions are *non sequiturs*, because they have no logical answers and should not be asked. How does one answer a question about the meaning of the sun or of sleep? On the contrary, one can argue that such questions do have significant meaning in the contexts of the effects exerted by these subjects: the sun literally sustains life, and sleep renews the ebbing strength and alacrity of the homan body and mind. In that respect, therefore, they have meaning for all people, even if they may never stop to ask the question of their meaning, because their lives are sailing on an even keel sustained by the clockwork regularity of the appearance and the occurrence of each of these two entities. Their failure at any time will prompt questions about their purpose and crucial role in life and the gravity or matter-of-factness of the effect of such failure, and then people will not stop asking these questions until they have been answered satisfactorily and reassuringly. Right now, they have no reason to ask them, because all is well. But all is not well with stratified homan lives, and so we ask for the meanings of those lives to see if they can be improved for benefit to their owners and to homanity.

Furthermore, there are also those who reduce questions about the meaning of life to meaningless linguistic confusion that fails to refer to life per se, but instead refers to how we use the word "life", in the same way as we talk about time without implying that there is an identifiable entity named time that possesses distinguishing characteristics. Such a view is prompted by the fact that life is an abstraction derived from the totality of the acts of living to which distinguishing characteristics can be applied. But the transposition of meaning from acts to abstraction is deemed to be a meaningless manoeuvre, as meaningless as the attribution of a general meaning to an aggregate of individual meanings of life's facets; i.e., individual meanings 1, 2, 3, and 4 of different aspects of the lives of different persons do not add up to one big meaning, $x$, of life.

In my book *Mind your Ps and Qs*, I discuss life's meaning as follows: The meaning of life is as difficult a question to answer as the question why we are here, and why in this particular world and not another. There is no single general meaning in life, and no end is common to all people. We are all striving toward different ends, being true to who and what we are, bringing out the best in us and not trying to be someone else; and so we all look at life differently. Some want to be teachers; others want to be artists, doctors, lawyers, or even (God forbid) politicians. So our ultimate interests will differ, even if our basic interests may be the same. We may like the same pastimes, but we have different ambitions. Some believe that the meaning in their lives emanates from within them, from those things that matter to them and from the noble ideals that they cherish very dearly and will not sacrifice for lesser ones. They care about family, friends, pursuits and pleasures with specific goals, and all the other things in life that allow them to express themselves and their concerns for the happiness of all people every day as they strive to make this world a better place for them. If they did not have family support in everything they do, if they did not have friends to engage their minds in fruitful discussions and pursuits, and if they could also not indulge in innocent pleasures that make life interesting and worthwhile for everyone, without hurting anyone, their lives would be devoid of any value. The same conditions apply in twin world.

In addition, many people think of life as divided into periods: infancy, childhood, youth, adulthood, and old age. Every one of these periods in life has its own meaning depending on the kinds of experiences that they enjoy or endure during those times. For example, the infant is probably oblivious to most things and has no clue about what her life means. She cries when she is hungry or uncomfortable, she sleeps most of the time, and she is totally dependent on her caretaker for all her needs. She could not survive if she were left to fend for herself. The selfish toddler guards his possessions jealously from other toddlers who want to share them, and he is prone to tantrums if he does not get what he wants. The youth thinks that she knows the answers to all questions. She makes mistakes but will not readily admit to making them. When she is corrected her stock answer is: "I know". That makes one wonder what she knows and how much she knows about what she knows about what she claims to know and about what is right. The adult realizes how limited her time is to fill all the gaps in her knowledge about life. She looks back at her track record over the years, and she realizes that she is nearing the end of life's uncertain journey, with little time left to make up for lost opportunities and unfulfilled ambitions. She flits from task to task, sometimes achieving nothing, in a gallant effort to cover ground that should have been covered long ago, and if she is a politician, she tries to cheat by rewriting history to erase the rot that she perpetrated and to portray herself in an honourable light. Finally, the old person lives on the glory of the past. There is nothing more left for her to accomplish. She has either done all or most of what she yearned for in life, or else she has messed up her life. She cannot start all over again; she must live on memories, whether they are sweet or bitter. For all these people, if there is no happiness in their lives, then those lives are as empty as living death.

These perspectives of life convey a rationale for existence and for the sanctity that we claim for our lives. Transposed to twin world, they restore the respect for the lives of all persons that has been denuded by the overwhelming love of money, which has eclipsed the last semblances of homanity and the homaneness that should rightly characterize homan relations. The same perspectives should bring hope into their lives, assuring them of tomorrows that will be better than today and yesterday, in the same way that the evolutionary unfolding of present-day Homo sapiens sapiens in our world dates back to the primitive beings who never envisaged trips to the moon and the stars which are the routines of today.

If only they could deconstruct money, reducing its value to zero, and replace it with fellowship, sharing, and respect for all persons, their world would be the ideal place in which to realize an untainted moral existence; and so would our world. The immoral existence that is adorned with multiple possessions amassed through greed, lies, victimization, and racist treachery to gratify the nugatory delights and bigotry of some persons, while denying others the opportunity to live well, will never impart meaning to any life. Even those who think that they are living in paradise with their obscene wealth that is dominated by selfishness know that they live a life of serfdom to their possessions and the need to watch over them like hawks, because other greedy homans are ready to steal them at any time; there is, after all, no honour among thieves, as evidenced by daily occurrences in government circles where fellow pilferers are always ready to flip and testifies against their amigos to save their skins. All of them are reversing evolution to the days of taking what they want from those who have it, like the Englishman mentioned on page 78.

# Chapter 17
# The road ahead

The evolutionary trail left behind by homanity in twin world that parallels the track laid by humans in our world from anthropoid through Australopithecus and culminating in the hominids: habilis, erectus, Neanderthal, Cro-magnon, and sapiens is indisputable, even though the entrenched and enduring beliefs of fundamentalist Krustans about six-day creation are being proffered as the only true facts about the origins of homans in twin world. Homanity's present lamentable state is equally well known; but what about its future? The future of homanity is open to many questions, some with possible answers looming large on the horizon, others with answers shrouded in the same kind of mystery as life and its meaning. One could well ask if twin world is now in the new age of Homo super-sapiens, because homans are certainly not marking time with all the breath-taking scientific advances of the present age that mimic our own: lunar landings that have shattered the myths hitherto surrounding the moon about which sentimental poetry was penned; space stations that can be maintained for prolonged periods, heralding the scary colonization of space that was once a pipe dream but has now become an imminent and frightening possibility as nations vie for its control, claiming sections of it as their own territory from which to launch their lethal weapons that are meant only to extend their inhomanity to their counterparts in twin and other possible worlds.

Instead of striving to secure peace in their world, they prefer to spill over into the heavens to wage their wars, destruction, and death for others. Certain of their tribes are content to undermine the peace of their world if only to assert their might, but at great cost to the stability of their own states whose wealth and talent is dissipated in hubristic adventures. And yet the people are so gullible and pliable as to swallow raw all the propaganda that they are fed by their so-called leaders who are too insincere to solve urgent problems of their world, like global warming, but choose to divert their attention to exotic ventures whose practical value for their daily living and their future is highly dubious; e.g., proudly conquer space, but suffer the devastating effects of climate change at home for all time. Why not fund climate research adequately, instead of cutting its funding and crippling it to justify personal financial advantage received from industry for sinking to the immorally low level of sacrificing other people's lives for profits and pay offs made to rogue scientists and unqualified cockroaches who flaunt forged documents as authentic scientific credentials? Both of these industry stooges shamelessly distort the genuine scientific findings of honest scientists for money. So the question previously posed on page 16 in a different context still remains pertinent: whither homanity?

Of the many struts on which the future of homanity rests, one of the main ones is genetics and its extensions: stem cell research, genetic engineering, and cloning, all of which have proved their utility for homan survival, especially when cloning entails provision of new organs to replace failing ones, e.g., hearts. But it says nothing about the homane side of homan nature, which extends beyond these confines to embrace what, for lack of a better designation and in naïve language, I will call the spiritual side of homan existence or an aspect of homan nature that can be apprehended only with a virtuous attitude of mind, and not with scientific tools. At no time, though, should the fundamentalists of twin world construe this admission as pandering to their irrational anti-scientific attitudes and justifying their vilification of genetic and scientific advances that seek to improve on the deficiencies of the evolutionary process as it coursed through the ages to culminate in the modern rational homan animal with her adaptations and maladaptations to her environment.

There is, though, still legitimate moral concern for the excesses to which genetic engineering can be stretched in the prenatal period by the editing of genes to produce the desirable type of designer progeny tailored to the liking of parents, e.g., intelligence, height, eye colour, thereby shaping a different person from the one who would otherwise have been. This process also raises moral questions about whether these genomic changes will redirect the course of homan evolution into new and precarious channels where it might not have gone under the guidance of its inherent natural stimulus, and whether this "quality controlled, genetically programmed" venture might not go awry and theoretically, at least, bear hordes of marauding Frankenstein monsters who will erase homan civilization as it is known in twin world, a civilization that is already sadly decadent and ready for effacement under selfish pink guardianship that has prevailed for many centuries.

The obverse of this dilemma is what has been styled genetic discrimination against persons who carry the genetic constitution and potential for diseases like Huntington's Disease that manifests later in life at considerable emotional and financial cost to the individual and her family. Such persons are typically discriminated against by the insurance industry, because their assured abbreviated lives cut into the profit margins that accrue from possible extended lives of unaffected individuals. One dreads the thought of what will happen as geneticists discover many more late-onset diseases. But these are ethical problems that we will only pose without delving into their knotty ramifications.

On the other hand, the lessons learnt from past efforts by others to produce super races of twin world using eugenics have been sufficiently discredited to dissuade even the most daring of scientists from attempting to fashion super-homans with superior physical and brain power to give their parent tribe a false sense of superiority over all the other tribes of twin world. The carnage that resulted from this insane frame of mind, resulting in the inhomane use of devices that caused a) instantaneous vaporization of many homans, while also leaving a residuum of many others with severe lingering agony from burns to their bodies and radiation effects that settled them with destructive cancers that conferred agony in living and in dying on them, b) inhomane suffocatinon of others with gases of various kinds, should be enough to warn against the potential for indulging in that kind of fatuous self-annihilation by homans. That is the level to which homan inhomanity can sink, as evidenced by the many who, finding themselves to be victims of similar torture, have asked to be terminated rather than be subjected to the bestiality practiced in the prison cells of the oppressor to obtain their coerced acquiescence in unfounded accusations against them.

At the same time, difficult questions concerning the moral status of the progeny of 46XX/XY cloned somatic cells and their homanity will have to be faced when cloning becomes a routine procedure, as well as those concerning the transfer of donor cells across the species divide. Some might make light of these anticipated problems by pointing to the fact that identical twins are no different from the products of cloned cells, except that they develop from the fusion of gametes (mature reproductive cells carrying half the number of chromosomes found in body cells) that are specially fashioned biologically and genetically for this purpose, instead of body cells that are used in cloning. The difference resides in the fact that the fusion of gametes is a necessary and sufficient natural means of producing homan beings, whereas cloning is a corruptible, artificial means that is beset with a load of ethical conundrums, as indicated above, including the possible theoretical survival of the person who is perpetuated in in her successive clones into eternity. In consequence, philosophers of note in twin world have adopted arguments advanced by this world's philosophers that

> as soon as adults treat the desirable genetic traits of their descendants as a product they can shape according to a design of their own liking, they are exercising a kind of control over their genetically manipulated offspring that intervenes in the somatic bases of another person's spontaneous relation-to-self and ethical freedom. This kind of intervention should only be exercised over things, not persons.[1]

It is hard to imagine how genetically modified foetuses can lay claim to the right to shape their destinies and ethical freedom, but not difficult to apprehend how "the fundamental symmetry of responsibility that exists among free and equal persons is restricted"[2] by this procedure. The argument that homan dignity, which entitles persons to equal and esteemed regard, is threatened by subverting reproduction from its natural character to an artifactual and morally unacceptable intervention that should only be exercised over things, not persons, rests on the famous Kantian principle that persons who assume this role of designers of others by employing genetic enhancements that treat foetuses (potential persons) as mere objects offend against the admonition that no actual persons should be treated as means (objects) for achieving the ends of others, but always also as ends in themselves. But can a valid argument about actual persons be fairly applied to potential persons? (I discuss this issue in chapter 19 of *Philosophy for Medical Students and Practitioners*).

In the case of actual persons, the contravention of this Kantian concept is rendered defensible by the proviso that if persons are treated as means to the ends of others, it should be with their fully informed consent to such treatment; hence the admissibility of a procedure closely related to, but preceding, cloning in technological evolution and execution: that of organ transplantation. The many advantages that transplantation has brought to the longevity and the quality of the lives of persons who might otherwise have succumbed to the functional failure of their diseased or otherwise disabled organs is not in question. But, as mentioned above, there is looming concern about the ethics of the potential use of animal tissues to make up for a shortage of homan tissues in many areas. The likelihood that this xenotransplantation could result in the replacement of substantial amounts of homan body tissues with animal tissues is small, but it still raises fears of how much homanity will remain after sizeable transplantations, where the cut-off point should be before the homan is taken over by the animal, and which tissues, besides the brain, are crucial for retaining the homan moral character and identity of the animal transplant recipient.

For example, how do we determine the homan identity of Tom, with 51% of his body parts replaced by transplantation from Jack, or to carry the experiment to its extreme, after a brain switch with Jack? In the latter instance his body will be Tom's, but his memories and behaviour will be Jack's, leaving both friends and enemies confused as to how to shower him with favours or how to heap scorn and retribution on him for "his" past thoughts and actions that he will deny knowing about, since only Jack can know about them. In the case of transplants of animal cells or parts, we might be faced with the possibility of a chimera with 46XX/XY homan cells and 48XX/XY chimpanzee cells; and if chimpanzee brain cells predominate, we might end up with a horrendous problem on our hands. We won't even try to imagine the ghastly outcome of the transplantation of whole animal brains into homan bodies. Will such procedures facilitate the population of twin world with inferior animal-homans and give modern day homan brutes a good excuse for indulging in the inhomane behaviour that they now display in using their might to persecute, dispossess, displace, and crush those who are weaker than, and "inferior" to, them in a brutish way? Perhaps; except that brutes (animals) exhibit "compassion" for their kind who are in pain and distress, which some superior homans lack for their "inferior" relatives who are not pink like them, including children.

On the other hand, there are less morally controversial aspects of the future developments of medical science that homanity can embrace without reservation, such as the use of prostheses that have endowed people with mobility and access to areas of their world that would otherwise have been out of their reach and beyond their capability to experience, and the latest advances in public health measures of disease control that have practically eliminated the threat to the future of homanity from Smallpox, German measles (rubella), red measles (rubeola), poliomyelitis, whooping cough, and diphtheria, diseases that used to inflict a heavy toll on children by killing them or maiming them for life both physically and mentally. Thanks to the honest use of vaccines, these and many other infectious diseases can now be controlled better than diseases like sleeping sickness, malaria, leprosy, and AIDS, which have not yet come under control, mainly because they ravage poor people from whom some curative drugs are withheld, because investing in the development, manufacture, and dispensing of them to such persons does not generate profits, and it is not the best way of applying the population control plans referred to on page 199—another example of homan inhomanity unleashed. It is not enough that these people are dying from wars and contrived starvation; they also have to die from this other preventable scourge, because most of the people who can help to prevent these calamities don't care to do so. They are only happy to amass fortunes acquired "legitimately" in the marketplace, some-times or most times on the backs of the same poor, dying people. Even when natural calamities have crippled them, rendered them homeless, and killed thousands of them, there is a lack of gusto on the part of pinks to restore their lives to a decent level many years after their tragedies, in spite of the billions of dullams in aid that compassionate others have given for that purpose. On the contrary, similar but less devastating disasters in pink habitations are remedied promptly by the same groups. Is that the gist of pink krustan homanity that preferentially teaches browns the healing power of pain, if not its lethal power?

The weight of evidence thus far indicates that homanity has failed to halt and reverse its downhill trend along the precipice of self-destruction. The alleged superior faculty that the homan animal should be using to lead all of homanity into a series of blissful tomorrows has instead positioned him to be the victim of the famous Cartesian evil genius who has implanted computer chips in his brain to take sole control of his naturally limited intellectual ability and steer him into irrational and irresponsible actions. He and his tribe stand accused, on their own admission, of acting retrogressively and inhomanely by displaying the lowest forms of immorality: abusing unjustly jailed browns in their war and other prisons, roasting them alive, flogging and strangling them, engaging in germ warfare against them; lacing their beer, chocolate, cigarettes, and envelope flaps with poison; covering their bodies with poison and tying them to trees overnight to see if they will die, injecting them with a muscle paralyzing drug if they survive, and then dumping them into the ocean from airplanes. Their litany of heinous deeds is unending in detail and duration, and in some cases, they involved persons whose professional oaths (like the Hippocratic Oath) obliged them to save lives rather than desecrate and destroy them. Whither homanity?

All these filthy, monstrous cowards claim to have been obeying the orders of their morally bankrupt superiors, and they also claim that what they did was not as repulsive as what other pinks are still doing to browns in other parts of twin world, but they continue to hide behind legal technicalities to avoid justice. Their wicked actions reflect a prevailing attitude of inhomanity mixed with arrogance and hubris, underpinned by hatred that does not augur well for the future of homanity. The prevalence of perpetrators of evil among the tribes of twin world who lack the foresight to expend their energies for the benefit of homanity, who also lack the decency to accept the immorality of their inhomane actions, and who display a rude reluctance to assume responsibility for their impropriety, reflects a characterological deficit that has the tendency to make twin world a forlorn place where moral standards are devolving instead of evolving. But it is also a place of hope where computer chips that escaped the clutches of the evil genius can be the boon that drives lazy hearts and artificial extremities, keeping people alive and enabling them to perform tasks that they could not otherwise perform as a result of physical loss of parts of the extremities on which they depend for making contact with many aspects and sections of the world around them. They only have to guard against falling into the clutches and complete control of the monstrous evil geniuses of twin world who are waiting to take possession of their minds to make them do things that are pleasing only to them, at their moral expense and under the perilous threat of stopping their pacemakers if they resist their control. It is a pity that the pacemakers of some of the incarnated fiends of that world have not been disabled by their obnoxiousness, and by the venom that circulates in their abominable bodies and constantly leaks out of their oral orifices to poison its recently purified atmosphere.

So far, the architects of many retrogressive twin world policies have been reckless males whose products bear the imprint of their self-centredness, greed, and short-sightedness in many instances. They have created economies and living conditions that attempt futilely to meet and satisfy their own needs of today, needs that were caused by yesterday's lack of foresight, inclusiveness, and the desire to embark on measures that are aimed at anticipating the perils of the ensuing day and that place contingencies in place to confront and vanquish those perils for the benefit of all the citizens. They repeat this cycle of regression day after day and year after year without compunction, because they are motivated by selfishness rather than altruism and futurism. They have promoted a self-serving capitalism that they claim will benefit everyone in the long run when the deep and wide chasm that it has created and is perpetuating for the underprivileged is quite clear for all to see. To boost their odious capitalism, they have dispatched economic hit men, accompanied by women enticers, who claim to have unmatched expertise in many areas and wield devastating authority over their credulous victims. Their job is to delude heads of mainly brown states into signing on to costly but often unnecessary projects for their countries at great expense to their citizens and their environment, as we have already noted. Nothing that they have done has brought any measure of happiness, security, and moral stability to the ordinary citizen that they have exploited and whose futures they have obfuscated with their shenanigans, as John Perkins has so lucidly depicted in his book *Confessions of an Economic Hit Man*.

To further promote their detestable capitalist objective, these unscrupulous, self-serving adults will enlist teens in their armies, and they will not hesitate to misuse children and youth to brainwash and bombard them with targeted advertisements intended to condition their minds and entice them into thinking only along the lines that they lay down for them to derive satisfaction not only from a gravely perverted war mentality but also from seemingly harmless recommendations to eat only certain foods or imbibe select beverages for the sake of their money-making markets. They will espouse the glamour of the sexy look and appeal that goes with certain types of revealing attire, smoking certain brands of tobacco products, imbibing certain select kinds of inebriating beverages, and developing phoney personalities that are consistent with the cheap commercial propaganda that fortune and power-seeking individuals and groups are disseminating. It is regrettable that adults should see in children corruptible potential sources of the big dullams of today and tomorrow to gratify their own greed, instead of homan agents who should be moulded to save their fast decaying world from the certain disintegration that awaits it in the years ahead. But they choose not to see the writing on the wall; all is fine with them as long as they can see dullam signs and continue to accumulate wealth while destroying their values.

Equally regrettable, and unfathomable, is the shallow mentality of parents who lose control of their children to these illusory, barren, and disastrous goals that are being set for them by irresponsible adults who have lost their sense of decency to greed. For instance, they choose to remain naively oblivious to the known adverse effects and lethal complications of the obesity that results from uncontrolled indulgence in some of these advertised products; e.g., diabetes and its devastating ravages of heart disease, hypertension, stroke, kidney disease and amputations of parts of limbs, or to the potential moral decadence that results from the combination of untamed sexuality, unrestrained exhibitionism, and personalities designed for money markets e.g., strippers, hookers, children performing provocative, sexy dances on stage, etc. In this atmosphere of crass vulgarity, the values of homan lives are set by their utility for the markets, not by their intrinsic worth, which has been downgraded by the ascendency of money to being the supreme value in homan life. Everyone has a price for which she can be purchased on the market, and that is the meaning of the associations that they form with other states and of the valueless family values about which they brag to their world.

Using these warped values, they have tried to pull wool over the eyes of the citizens with a tripartite of symbiotically related entities: exploiter states, controlling corporations, and underlings who help them to exploit the citizens of their own countries and of countries that they have overrun. There is never any semblance of planning parochially for the tribe or universally for the sustained glory of the entire homan species, but always an abundant display of selfish personal entitlement at untold cost to the tribe and the species. Unfettered fabrication and conspiratorial lies that do nothing to advance the course of peace have taken over from fact peddling, impelling even overrun states to sing the praises of the invader for having saved their country from civil war, when both of them know that it was money that bought them the tranquillity that they are boasting of achieving with the sacrifice of other people's lives, not what they call their sagacious planning. The only planning that they are capable of is that of stealing the people's wealth and brashly craving for their victims to hang garlands around their necks and strew flowers at their feet. But they triggered only sectarian violence by exploiting religious differences among their victims with their practice of driving wedges among subjugated peoples for ease of dividing and ruling them after local leaders have done the dirty work of them selling out. That helps to reduce their numbers and their potential for mounting opposition to the thuggery of oppressors, but fails dismally to provide for the future of the tribe.

Perhaps this is the point at which a feminist approach to life and society could teach some persons how to conduct themselves for the present and future benefit of all people, rather than for that of the warmongering, egotistical, and power flaunting male elements of their species that is also shared by the occasional woman whose feelings have degenerated to the same level as those of these self-opinionated men. The macho point of view of these guys and their inhomanity has cost twin world heavily in wasted, precious lives that cannot be replaced like the man-made components of their societies. Feminism, to its credit, has waged and is still waging a courageous struggle for the emancipation of women from the bondage imposed on them by men. In its struggle for the recognition of women's rights and equality with men, it has repudiated the stratification of persons on the basis of sex and gender differences whereby males regard themselves as superiors and females as subalterns, and it has assumed a forward looking strategy to right the wrongs imposed on twin world by men who are enwrapped in the illusion of chasing after the fleeting expediency of the moment with little or no forethought of everyone's needs.

Women see their future and that of their children and homanity as dependent on attitudes that are similar to those engendered by their caring and compassionate nature, coupled with their mothering and nurturing instincts, all of which promote a heartfelt and serene sensitivity to the concerns of other people, a sensitivity that is likely garnered from their concern and attachment to their progeny with whom some of them had the most intimate relationship during their pregnancies. If these attitudes can be translated into unbiased regard for other persons and also inculcated into the behaviour patterns of the youth of the world, homanity can hope for a better future that will be free of domination, torture, cruelty, exploitation, insensitivity, injustice, strife, and global discrimination. Every person's autonomy will be respected, and no one will have to fight for rights that should be accorded her by virtue of her homanity; the darkly coloured woman will no longer have to contend with the multiple, crass discriminations of sex, colour, possessions, etc., while her male counterpart is also struggling to emancipate himself from colour, and other forms of discrimination. She will no longer earn a mere 53% and he just 65% of their pink male counterparts while facing the same cost of living expenses and doing the same jobs.

Finding themselves pushed further and further down the ladder of opportunity and survival, with no future chance of escaping from their grim situation through the prevalence of permanently crafted impediments that had been created by the inflexible system to keep them in perpetual subjugation, the brown people of twin world decided that a system-wrecking revolution was the only way out of their designed and foisted downward spiral. They took their cue from the French citizens who were dispossessed by their reigning nobility at the end of the 18th century and decided that a revolution was the only way out of their seemingly endless subjugation and exploitation by the nobility and the conniving church, with no relief in sight. Their revolution paid off, despite the resistance of the privileged vultures who tenaciously clung to power and would not accommodate the wishes of the poor for a chance at a decent life for themselves and their children, as is the case today. Among the rich of both worlds, only they and their children matter. Other people and their children are counted with goods and dispensable livestock; their sorry situation does not make a dent in the feelings of the rich, because those feelings are too precious to be wasted on these wretches; only they and their children deserve them. That is why they can manipulate their national census to obscure the problems that poor people face, so that they can discount them in their budgeting and not face criticism for this dirty trick. After all, who can fairly criticize you for neglecting the needs of people that you did not know about, after you designedly ignored them? Evil has an inexhaustible store of ruses for prevailing over good.

Those of the ruling class who remained to tell their sad story laboured assiduously to hatch new plans to re-enslave the people by letting them enjoy their new-found franchise, but strangling them with the wrath of their financial institutions whose trade regulations made it impossible for them to make economic progress. They took control of the banks and established large cartels in which the poor could not participate, because they lacked the financial background that gave the rich a head start; they set up money-lending systems that doled out large sums to the poor ostensibly to aid their development, but actually to burden them with a principal debt and interest that would take them generations to pay off and thus end up enslaving them. Before yielding to the chains of economic slavery, they were forced to sign contracts that committed huge percentages of their gross domestic product to service their debt, regardless of what social programs (including health care for the people) were being shortchanged. Any talk of debt relief by the oppressor is just that, talk. The results of these machinations show up in the lives of the people as persisting, massive unemployment, absolute control by the rich on the world stage, and, finally, rapid degeneration of social life with telling effects on the integrity and hence the future of the brown tribe. Conclusion: evil mission accomplished.

Some of the nation states that saw through these evil schemes tried to steer clear of their perpetrators, but the financial straits into which they had been forced compelled them to seek their help in weathering the financial crises that had been purposely thrust on their world by the greedy corporations, mortgage lenders, banks, and conniving economists. Coincidentally, but actually after realizing their pariah status in the esteem of the nations of twin world, these institutions of the rich now appear to be responding to this back-lash of being shunned by all who would otherwise appeal to them for financial help in times of need by soft-peddling their hard line, if only until they can ensnare their prey, and then sadistically impose the same mean-spirited conditions as before. As we saw above, they also created crises in education, national security, and other areas to cause confusion in the minds of the people, distracting them, paralyzing their thinking, and then pacifying them by imposing their seemingly magnanimous, but actually self-serving pseudo-solutions on them, while they carried out their shenanigans of devaluing their national assets and thereby forcing the states to sell them off to them for a song. This endless list of vicious manoeuvres of dispossession prompted by greed, which they call a new world order, ensures that the future remains bleak for the poor people of twin world, unless they stage another revolution; otherwise they can only continue to live in the depressing shadows of despair and with death, wishing that a cosmic cataclysm could end it all for them, who have virtually nothing to lose, and for the rich, who have the most to lose.

Turning to our own situation, the future is wide open for every human being as she strives to define herself and blend in with existing reality, which she is also actively trying to modify. Reality is what it is; not how we choose to represent it; although some people think that we can create reality by how we describe it to suit our purposes. As John Searle observes in *The Social Construction of Reality* (page 162), three discrete pieces of matter (stones) a, b, and c can be counted as such, or as seven objects: a, b, c, a+b, b+c, a+c, and a+b+c; but these arrangements do no alter the ontological fact that three separate pieces of matter exist as such out there. What we do with them does not alter the fact of their discrete being, but it can allow utility and convenience into our lives concerning how we want to deal with these three items. In the same vein, an existing nondescript collection of stars becomes the Southern Cross only after we have recognized its suggestive configuration. Naming it does not rule on its becoming, being, or function; it does not affect its nature, but only provides a common reference point within a sea of stars that facilitates our study of astronomy and its applications for our sole benefit. Naming star patterns does not make reality; it only gives us a better handle and new perspective on it. Similarly, exploiting natural differences in skin colour for selfish ends does not create a new species of homans with inferior personhood. All persons still remain moral equals, sharing the same homan dignity, worth for respect, and aspirations of a productive future for themselves and their kin.

So, while some people always work hard to make existing reality different by creating a new reality for the sake of producing better conditions for their existence and survival of all, others utilize this capability to create conditions that make other people's lives hell on earth. Present existence may be less than desirable, but everyone wants her survival into the future to be studded with successes in a background of general well-being. On that account, it is only fair that no one's life should be trammelled and channeled by other persons maliciously and only for the selfish promotion of their own good and supremacy. No one should have the right to determine the fate of a whole tribe of people as most so-called leaders of nation states are doing, literally dictating to a dopy electorate that put them in office to represent their wishes and then went to sleep, leaving these reckless and self-indulging opportunists to have a field day at the expense of everyone's welfare and future security.

Against this backdrop, trying to live in hope in the midst of the virtually hollow existence created by the accumulation of multiple daily inhomane experiences to which the less privileged persons of twin world are subjected by those who monopolize all the privilege sometimes proves to be futile. (See Rousseau, page 118). Despair should, however, not be allowed to dash hopes of a better future, even in the maelstrom of this witless institutionalized racism that permeates every crevice of society in both overt and mostly covert ways. If that is allowed to happen, even those pinks who feel kindly disposed to browns will be trammelled in their sincere attempts to make them feel like respectable homan beings, while those who thoughtlessly hold racist beliefs and execute racist actions will feel exempt from blame, because they falsely believe that browns have willingly accepted their assigned inferior status as the natural norm. Only if these racists are made to feel the squeeze by being exposed to the perpetration of the same debasing actions on them that they impose on others, to cause them similar qualitative and quantitative grief, will their inhomanity dawn on them. But that situation is not on the cards, and they know that such an eventuality is well beyond the realm of probability for now, as long as they control the bombs that they use to squelch brown lives and aspirations.

Still, there is no excuse for holding racist beliefs and executing racist actions, nor is there any merit in excusing unfair preferential treatment of pinks over brown as not necessarily being racist when one realizes that positive results will accrue to the preferred candidate, while the other candidate is denied access to those results and even exposed to the negative results that eventuate from this denial of opportunity. No one is quarrelling with preference based on fair competition, provided that each person possesses the basics that are required not only for entering into the competition, but also for survival and for upward mobility. That means the backgrounds of the competitors should not be adulterated by prevalence of unequal and unfair prior differential circumstances based on racial prejudice, which, in the end create a vicious circle that cannot be broken. Only if the racist element that has been injected into it is eliminated from it to provide uniform conditions where each one has a fair opportunity to make the grade or else fail to do so on her own, at which point she will need help to achieve a prosperous future life, not repression. The job cycle depicted here does not allow her to move upward from the inferior status that has been forcibly imposed on her and rendered her helpless to change it:

> deficient background and lack of training→ deficient equipment → failure to qualify for the initial competition to enter the job market→ failure to break into the ongoing competition from outside the job market
> ↓
> failure to improve capability for any worthwhile job

| failure to improve capability for | ↑ | ↓ | failure to qualify |
| jobs in the growing competition | | | for well paying jobs |
| ↑ | | | ↓ |
| failure to survive any job competition | | | failure to qualify |
| ↑ | | | for stiff competition |
| degeneration, degradation | | | for entry into these jobs |
| enslavement, and exploitation | | | ↓ |
| ↑ | | | failure to survive ongoing |
| isolation | ← | | stiff job competition |

Result: utter disillusionment in life's future.

That is why cavils against the principle of affirmative action, which is only meant to afford a chance at striving for those goods from which their skin colour has prohibited and would otherwise prohibit browns, even if they have the capability, do not make sense, especially when they come from those who are not the oppressed ones, and who would ordinarily be chosen in preference to browns because of their favour pink skin colour. Of course, it would be just the thing to do, if the tables were turned and they were getting the raw deal. They would clamour for it louder than they are crying foul now that browns are being given the chance they never had. Their hypocritical lament is like their equally pharisaic tactics of smearing browns with racism for citing their covert racist actions against them; turning the tables, as usual. They rudely reject progressive proposals from browns (especially those who hold the highest offices with the highest authority over them) even if it is at the cost of stagnation, retrogression, or eventual decay of their country, as long as their picayune egos can be gratified by their malevolent and venomous attitude. They would rather witness destruction and death around them than accord a brown the respect that is due to him in his high office or credit him with the intelligence that he possesses and the problem-solving aptitude that he displays, which many of them obviously lack; hence their cheap negativity. And these hoods pretend to be the infallible, superior, civilized beings who think that the precious future of the people of twin world should be left to their disreputable, self-centred bungling.

Viewed in perspective, this entire unpalatable situation appears to have evolved along clearly defined lines laid by the first crop of racists who conspired to establish their exclusive racist institutions to propagate their racist ethos to the uninitiated of their tribe, and to provide societal channels through which all of them could oppress the brown citizenry effectively, rather than leave the task to the individual racist oppressor and risk diluting its intended demeaning consequences. From this point on, the racism in these institutions became self-perpetuating as successive generations of pinks (good and bad) acknowledged and "innocently" continued their racist traditions and practices without giving thought to their deleterious effects on the welfare of browns. They claim not to be practicing racism as willing, individual participants, blaming their behaviour on the practices of the institutions in which they are participating and to whose perpetuation they are contributing, but over which they claim to have no control; as if their refusal to cooperate with the policies of those institutions and their mass withdrawal from them would not force them to change those policies. I submit that this is still a display of insensitivity to and lack of consideration for the plight of others to whose present and future existential predicament they give no thought in their daily lives, until their attention is drawn to it, and then their liberalism and benevolence awakens from its slumber and makes only seemly noises lacking decisive actions.

We of this world are fortunate to live in a world that is inhabited by people who are devoted to the promotion of everyone's future well-being, unlike the underprivileged people of twin world who have lost even their social and health assistance programs to the tax cuts of the rich supporters of their unsympathetic governments that must share the blame for periodically landing twin world in dire economic straits where the poor drown while the rich continue to swim in the comfort of their combined wealth. Poor browns are subjected to indignities that are crafted to make them feel insignificant and inconsequential in the daily affairs of the communities in which they live and are thereby stripped of the desire to participate in those affairs, because opportunities for them to participate are non-existent or severely limited. They know full well that their efforts to participate or run for public office will be ignored, if not ridiculed. They constantly endure unmistakable racial profiling and harassment by racist law enforcement personnel who always vehemently deny their blatantly obvious racist behaviour and try to cover it over with lies, until others of them realize the futility of denying the obvious and admit to the practice. All these vile manoeuvres are calculated to frustrate them, smother their ambitions, and make their present and future existence in their world the equivalent of torture in Krustan hallum (Christian hell).

These racists, who never do any wrong, will never admit to their biased fabricating of evidence by misquoting the public statements of browns that can be verified by anyone who cares to do so without blindly jumping on the racist bandwagon. To hear them retracting their lies and smear tactics for that time, only to engage in the same vile behaviour when they think that they have another opportunity to pull wool over other people's eyes and promote their heinous agenda is as amusing as it is exasperating. Their sole objective is to destroy the whole (brown nation) by destroying its elements (brown individuals) in their formative stages. That is why they are striving to scuttle the careers of young browns by suspending or expelling them from school for misdemeanours for which their pink counterparts are cautioned and pardoned. The idea is to demoralize them and eventually eliminate them from the educational system, pushing them into a life of crime that is certain to ruin their futures and hence also directly ruin the future of their tribe. So, at every stage of their intended academic careers, there are serious efforts from the other side not only to frustrate them but also to disable them from taking the next step. If they miss getting them in the early stages, they catch and decapitate them somewhere along the way that is over-laden with enough snares for that evil purpose.

A brown student of twin world was fortunate to be permitted to study medicine at one of the pink universities of his racist, brown-hating, "Gudd-fearing" country. In his third year of study he had a pink lecturer who habitually invited brown students to his home once a month for an evening of socializing, which was accompanied by subtle but obviously well contrived attempts at brainwashing and indoctrination into docility and acceptance of pink superiority as a permanent fact of life; not the crude, unsophisticated methods used by his forebears. This student and his friend ignored these general invitations, since they were not personal; but they also happened to hold leadership positions in the brown political groups of the university and in the night classes that were organized for the education of the illiterate workers of the university. At the end of the year, and to every one's amazement, they were the only two who failed the course, establishing a historical precedent. Before their supplementary examination, the lecturer summoned them to his office to warn them that if they wanted to pass his course at the end of the new academic year, they would have to give up the extra-curricular activities to which they were devoted, because one was unpatriotic (in their own land where aliens denied them citizenship and any kind of representation), and the other was useless to their students, because after learning how to read and write they would be reading communist newspapers instead of reading the bubel. This foolish, insulting, bigoted talk was obviously meant to inform the students that they had failed their course even before they sat the supplementary examination. Of course, they failed the course, but they did not give up their activities, in spite of the victimization.

Mean-spiritedness driven by herrenvolkism that does not brook self-assertion of the other or defiance from him, but desires only his non-negotiable domination, impelled a learned man to attempt to wreck the careers of two ambitious young men whose communities were in desperate need of their services as health care givers and educators, and who were answering the call by giving of their time to bring light to those of their people who were still in the relative darkness of illiteracy, while also trying to rectify the ills that the socio-political structure of the country had so selfishly imposed on the majority of the inhabitants that it dispossessed, persecuted, and disenfranchised. He just did not have the power that others of his breed have to capriciously expel brown students to wreck their careers and stifle the wave of brown awakening that threatens to overtake pink supremacy. They made it through that course and through medical school by refusing to yield to intimidation and brainwashing, but one of them died in suspicious circumstances in a state that was ruled by his own people, most probably because he opposed their despicable practices of pandering to the wishes and continuing domination of the same oppressors from whom they had won their independence and to whose daring control he would not yield or bow. As usual, these homan devils always get their man; they refuse to give up on their determination to wreck the future careers of browns and thereby ruin the future of their tribe. Their hatred knows no limits; if one of them does not get his victim, the others will get him, because they are united in their evil purpose of ruining the road ahead for browns.

Probably every brown who has attended a predominantly pink institution of higher learning has a story to tell about being discriminated against or victimized for the colour of her skin, like the story of the brown who was studying in a foreign land where his professor invited his entire class to his home for an evening of social interaction. On his arrival at the venue, he was met at the door by the professor's wife who promptly made him understand that he was not welcome by insisting that he had come to the wrong place. The student left without argument, but humiliated and thoroughly disgusted; who wouldn't be? His professor asked him days later why he did not attend or send an apology for failing to attend the occasion, and he was shocked to hear how callously the student had been treated by his wife. Needless to say, he did not take kindly to his wife's bigotry, and he made her apologize to the student for the undignified treatment that she had meted out to him; which makes one entertain the absurd idea that bigotry is hereditary among these people, although it happens to be a learned behaviour pattern for which the genetic basis is as lacking and preposterous as it is for race.

In this putrid atmosphere, no one from the underprivileged tribe can ever look forward to realizing her hopes and dreams of a better life; at no time can she also entertain the sentiment of living as if her world were meaningful; at no time can she believe in the "efficiency of courage, hope, and trust", because her experiences never seem to tend toward corroborating that kind of belief. Everywhere she goes, she is expected and required to perform ten times better than her competing pink counterpart to receive even marginal recognition for consideration in any enterprise, as is clear in education, housing, workplace, and community leadership. The power that is alleged to reside in optimism will for ever elude her and her tribe, because the gloom and doom in which they eke out their deprived existence does not admit of any measure of optimism. It is designed to inculcate persistently depressing thoughts of forlornness, submissiveness, and pessimism whose only possible culmination is a death-wish waiting to be fulfilled. That is the aim of the oppressor, and that is what he would like to see transpiring; but it is up to the tribe to disappoint him and rise up against this evil practice of upholding pink supremacy via the use of devices that have been specially forged to scuttle brown aspirations, subjugate and eventually annihilate them by dehumanizing, exploiting, and oppressing them in every avenue of their lives.

The way out of virtual economic, social, political, and educational slavery is always difficult, but never hopeless, and those who are victimized and oppressed by the unjust justice meted out by the system (in spite of denials and sweet talk about the fairness of pink courts and juries in dealing with browns) do not have to resort to the use of deadly mood altering drugs to dull their pain, giving these brutes the satisfaction of seeing them destroy themselves. They must cultivate and nurture a universal pride in their being and their humanity by holding themselves to standards of behaviour and performance that are consistent with their sanctity as homan beings, and they should not allow others to demoralize them for their selfish benefit. They must not apologize for who they are; they must not curry favours or solicit approval from their oppressors by selling out their folk and allowing themselves to be used as pawns in the oppression of their own people. They must not be grateful to their oppressors for worthless privileges, when they should be demanding and getting their rights to deserved basic necessities of life. They must force their disparagers to respect them for who they are, while they continue to discriminate against them. They must not give them ammunition to debase them by conducting themselves unseemly, because their disparagers are always looking for ways to discredit them and drag them into the gutter where many of them reside. They feel exonerated when browns debase and destroy themselves and their future, while professing innocence in their plight.

One only has to look at the efforts expended in this regard in the unfair punitive treatment meted out to sports figures and other so-called brown celebrities in contrast with the forgiving treatment given to their pink counterparts. Also the futile vulgar efforts of enforcing worship of their national flags and the cheap shots that they hurl at them while harping on the millions of dullams that they are earning and blatantly suggesting that their sponsors should ditch them to halt their flow of cash. They will also blatantly impede them or cheat them of their fairly earned successes to promote their own kith who have been relegated to the shadows of brown success. Of course, they will deny engaging in all this obvious intrigue, which is also consistent with how they treat the rest of the folk like cattle, in keeping with their agenda of ensuring that pink supremacy prevails for all time to thwart brown aspirations and wreck their future.

Browns should, therefore, constantly work hard to liberate themselves from these snares, and if it will take extra sacrifice to rise to respectable heights where they can wield influence, out of the pits of misery into which they have been forced by the oppressor, then that will be just fine, because it has been done before. If, on the other hand, it will take a revolution of some kind to realize the suppressed ambitions of all the underprivileged, then so be it, because that has also been done before; but things must change, the worm must turn. As the saying goes, it is a long lane that has no turning, and this lane is bound to reach its turning point sooner, rather than later. The sun has set in many empires of exclusive pink privilege before; it will set in this one as well. That fateful day of final sunset must dawn.

If oppression of brown tribes continues on the same disastrous path, it is bound to terminate in nuclear Armageddon and a fitting end to a world that has lost its bearings and has corrupted itself beyond the point of redemption. Depending on the redeeming power of religion (the "necessary evil" that fills the logical gaps in knowledge of the cosmos) in general and Krustanity in particular, both of which have been corrupted and subverted by the oppressor to his own advantage, will never liberate the oppressed, because those were the sops that were fed to them initially to subdue them and render them compliant. Regurgitating the mantra of turning the other cheek only makes pinks feel more and more secure in the evil that they are perpetrating as they slap it too. This fiction of turning the other cheek to someone who has no conscience that can dissuade him from slapping it too will never help to achieve freedom, justice, fairness, and homan dignity for browns; their vile oppressors know and understand only the languages of lies and violence in which they deal, both of which can never be justified or legitimized, but have kept them in control of the rest of their world. That is all they will heed, that is all they will respond to, and that is what they should be fed (lies excluded, because lies do not beget truth).

The brutes should be made to face the hurtful truth of their vicious insensitivity, inhomanity, and unforgiving heartlessness that have cheapened and devastated the lives and entire future of millions of browns all over twin world through many centuries of ruthless exploitation, oppression, and murder that they have been allowed to get away with. The fashionable cop out of extending the withered olive branch of "truth and reconciliation" at which they scoff, which they insincerely exploit to save their butts, and which they do not and will never deserve should never be extended to them, because they will always remain inexorably committed to their amoral, self-serving ideology and agenda of enduring pink supremacy, regardless of prevailing circumstances.

Browns must take back determination of their destiny from these pink usurpers, because the sole aim of pinks is to misdirect it by turning back the clock of their tribe's progression into projected avenues of advancement, and by stifling their plans for molding themselves into prominent players in the world for decades to come. They should take full control of their lives and ensure that the future of their tribe rests squarely in their own hands, unlike their past that was misdirected into retrogression from the vile, baneful sanctums of pink supremacy. Their war cry should be "never again shall we become the door mats of pink brutes". This is the moment of decision; to die for truth or live for lies, to be a hero in the struggle or to sell out like a quisling. Right now the liars may be sitting snugly but precariously on their thrones and sending browns to the scaffold; but it is that scaffold that will shape the future for all (see page 228).

# Notes

Chapter One

1. Twin world: The concept of twin world is derived directly from Hilary Putnam's thought experiment of "Twin Earth", a planet in the galaxy that is exactly like our earth and also has a liquid called water, which resembles our water in all respects and tastes like it, but has a different chemical formula, so that inhabitants of both earths could not tell the difference between the two waters without resorting to their physico-chemical analysis.

Chapter Two

1. Personhood: The quality possessed by individuals compounded of mental and physical characteristics and endowed with the ability to make morally acceptable choices and act responsibly on them. The minimum necessary conditions for possession of this quality are considered to be consciousness (alertness and awareness) and autonomy. Autonomy, which is postulated as a necessary and sufficient condition of consciousness, refers to a person's capacity for rational self-governance and the right to hold clearly understood personal views, values, and beliefs that determine his free and competent choice and initiation of actions, within the bounds of universal causality, in his own interests, without pressure or threat from anyone. These concepts are discussed at length in my book: Philosophy for the Medical Student and Practitioner, chapters 4(c) and 16(a) (i).

Chapter Three

1. Miriam Webster's Online Dictionary, http://www.merriam-webster.com/dictionary/oxymoron
2. Edward Makhene, *Our World and its Values*, (self-pub., 2017), 169.
3. Lewis Carroll, *Through the Looking Glass*, London: Harper Collins, 2017), 83.
4. Richard Poe, *Black Spark, White Fire*, (Roseville, CA: Prima Publishing, 1999), 495.
5. George G. M. James, *Stolen Legacy*, (Trenton, NJ: Africa World Press, Inc., 1998), 3.
6. James, *Stolen Legacy*, 6.
7. James, *Stolen Legacy*, 42.
8. Poe, *Black Spark, White Fire,* 365.
9. Georg W. Hegel, *Lectures on the Philosophy of World History*, trans. H. B. Nisbet, (Cambridge: Cambridge University Press, 1984), 171.
10. Martin Bernal, *Black Athena - The Afro-Asiatic Roots of Classical Civilization*, Vol. 1: The Fabrication of Ancient Greece, 1785-1985, (New Jersey: Rutgers University Press, 1999), 2.

11. Bernal, *Black Athena,* 198.
12. Bernal, *Black Athena,* 211.
13. "The Scramble for Africa: Berlin Conference of 1884-1885 to Divide Africa", http://wysinger.homestead.com/berlinconference.html
14. Naomi Klein, *The Shock Doctrine,* (London: Penguin Books, 2008), 69.
15. Deut. 28: 1 RSV
16. Deut. 15: 6

Chapter Four

1. "The Protocols of the Learned Elders of Zion", Protocol No.12. trans. Victor E. Marsden, http://www.jewwatch.com/jew-references-protocols-full-text-1-basic-doctrine.html#TABLE OF CONTENTS
2. Andrew Feinstein, *After the Party,* (Johannesburg: Jonathan Ball Publishers, 2009), 250.
3. Feinstein, *After the Party,* 284.

Chapter Five

1. John Milton, *Paradise Lost and Paradise Regained,* ed. Christopher Ricks,(New York: Signet Classic, Penguin Books, 1968), Book 1, 1, line 26.
2. Richard Swinburne, *Is there a God,* (Oxford: Oxford University Press, 1996), 106.
3. Thomas Nagel, "What is it like to be a bat?", in *Mortal questions,* (Cambridge: Cambridge University Press, 1996), 169.
4. Coloss. 3: 22-24 RSV
5. Swinburne, *Is there a God,* 107.
6. Giannis Stamatellos, "Xenophenes of Colophon", http://www.philosophy.gr/presocratics/xenophanes.htm
7. Cotter, Joseph S. Jr., "And What Shall You Say?", in *The Book of American Negro Poetry,* ed. James Weldon Johnson, (New Haven: Yale University Press, 1912), #23, http://artleby.com/269/86.html

Chapter Six

1. Ex. 20: 13 RSV
2. Num. 31: 17, 18 RSV
3. Matt. 6: 19 RSV
4. Mark Bowen, *Censoring Science,* (New York: Dutton, 2008), 43.
5. Bowen, *Censoring Science,* 307.
6. Bowen, *Censoring Science,* 238.
7. Robert Stone, "Patterns of Jim Crow in South Africa", transcribed by Einde O'Callaghan, *New International,* 14 No.7, September 1948, 204-207, http://www.marxists.org/history/etol/newspape/ni/vol14/no07/stone.htm
8. 2 Nephi 5: 21-23, http:/criptures.lds.org/2_ne/5
9. Stone, "Jim Crow".

10. Ex. 20: 23 KJV
11. Ex. 17: 16 RSV
12. 1 Sam. 15: 2, 3 RSV
13. Deut. 25: 19 RSV

Chapter Seven

1. Matt. 25: 43 NIV
2. Hegel, *Philosophy of World History*, 178-179.
3. Hegel, *Philosophy of World History*, 179.
4. Hegel, *Philosophy of World History*, 179.
5. Hegel, *Philosophy of World History*, 179.
6. Hegel, *Philosophy of World History*, 179.
7. William K. Clifford, "The Ethics of Belief", in *The Experience of Philosophy* 3d ed., ed. Daniel Kolak and Raymond Martin, (Belmont, CA: Wadsworth Publishing Company, 1996), 236.
8. Thomas Hobbes, *Leviathan*, (St. Paul's Churchyard, 1651; Project Gutenberg, 2013), chap. 19, sec. 4, http://www.gutenberg.org/files/3207/3207-h/3207-h.htm #link2H_4_0115
9. Matt. 6: 3 RSV
10. David Ben-Gurion Quotes, http://thinkexist.com/quotes/david_ben=gurion
11. Deut. 28: 11 RSV

Chapter Eight

1. Hegel, *Philosophy of World History*, 177.
2. Hegel, *Philosophy of World History*, 177.
3. Hegel, *Philosophy of World History*, 217.
4. George Bernard Shaw, "The Man Of Destiny", http://www0p.wepapers.com/Papers/20179/George_Bernard_Shaw_-_The_Man_Of_Destiny
5. High Arctic exiles still feel raw, *Toronto star*, November 30, 2009.
6. Poe, *Black Spark, White Fire*, 363.
7. Immanuel Kant, "Physical Geography", in *Race and the Enlightenment*, ed. Emmanuel C. Eze, (Oxford: Blackwell Publishing, 1997), 59.
8. Kant, "Physical Geography", 64.
9. Thomas Jefferson, "Notes on the State of Virginia", Query 14, http://etext.virginia.edu/toc/moderng/public/Jefvirg.html
10. Jefferson, "Notes".
11. Jefferson, "Notes".
12. Jefferson, "Notes".
13. Frederick Douglass, "What To The Slave Is The 4th Of July?" http://www.freemaninstitute.com/douglass.htm
14. "American Anthropological Association Statement on Race'"(May 17, 1998), http://www.aaanet.org/stmts/racepp.htm

15. Acts 17: 26 RSV
16. Hegel, *Philosophy of World History*, 185.

Chapter Nine

1. "Dred Scott case: The Supreme Court decision", http://www.pbs.org/wgbh/aia/part4/4h2933t.htm
2. "Dred Scott".
3. Rodrigue Tremblay, "The Neo-Conservative Agenda: Humanism vs Imperialism", http://www.topplebush.com/oped367.shtml
4. "Winston Churchill, To the Palestine Royal Commission (1937)", http://en.wikiquote.org/wiki/Winston_Churchill
5. Oakland Ross, "Former Israeli soldier bears witness to 'dirty' occupation", *Toronto star*, September 13, 2008.
6. John J. Mearsheimer and Stephen M. Walt, *The Israel Lobby and U.S. Foreign Policy*, (Toronto: Penguin Group, 2007), 89.
7. Ross, "'dirty' occupation"
8. John Locke, *Two Treatises of Government and A Letter Concerning Toleration*, ed. Ian Shapiro, (New Haven: Yale University Press, 2003), 114.
9. Ilan Pappe, *The Ethnic Cleansing of Palestine*, (Oxford: One World, 2006), 112.
10. Linda Greene, "Race in the Twenty-first Century: Equality through Law", in *Critical Race Theory*. ed. Kimberlé Crenshaw, Neil Gotanda, Gatty Peller, and Kendall Thomas, (New York NY: The New Press, 1995), 299.
11. Adam Hochschild, *King Leopold's Ghost*, (New York: Houghton Mifflin Company, 1998), 67.

Chapter Ten

1. Clarence S. Johnson, *Cornell West and Philosophy*, (New York: Routledge, 2003), 20.
2. Hannah Arendt, *On Violence*, (San Diego/New York: Harcourt Brace & Company, 1970), 19.
3. Jean-Jacques Rousseau, "*A Discourse Upon The Origin And The Foundation Of The Inequality Among Mankind*", (Project Gutenberg, 2004), EBook #11136, http://www.gutenberg.org/cache/epub/11136/pg11136-images.html

Chapter Eleven

1. Milton, *Paradise Lost*, 51, lines 58-60.
2. Andrew Buncombe, "Assassinate Chavez", *Independent*, August 24, 2005, https://www.independent.co.uk/news/world/americas/assassinate-chavez-pat-robertson-tells-a-stunned-america-307946.html
3. Buncombe, "Assassinate Chavez".
4. Hegel, *Philosophy of World History*, 185.

5. Hegel, *Philosophy of World History*, 185.
6. Hegel, *Philosophy of World History*, 188.
7. Rom. 13: 1-2, 4 NIV

## Chapter Twelve

1. Pappe, *Ethnic Cleansing*, 69.
2. Pappe, *Ethnic Cleansing*, 64.
3. Pappe, *Ethnic Cleansing*, 79.
4. Bryce Courtenay, "The Power of One", www.msward.org/powerofone.org
5. Tony McGregor, "What was Bantu Education?", http://www.scribd.com/doc/6008415/What-Was-Bantu-Education
6. "The Protocols of the Learned Elders of Zion", Protocol Nos.9 and 10, http://xroads.virginia.edu/~ma01/Kidd/thesis/pdf/protocols.pdf
7. Megan Ogilvie, *Toronto star*, July 15, 2010.
8. Carter G. Woodson, "Mis-Education of the Negro", http://oislc.org/html/ManThinking.html
9. "Willie Lynch's Speech On His Methods For Controlling Slaves", http://www.duboislc.org/html/WillieLynch.html
10. Locke, *Two Treatises*, 111-112.
11. Locke, *Two Treatises*, 112.

## Chapter Thirteen

1. Davison L. Budhoo, "Enough is Enough", http://www.naomiklein.org/files/resources/pdfs/budhoo.pdf
2. Budhoo, "Enough".
3. Budhoo, "Enough".
4. Budhoo, "Enough".
5. Budhoo, "Enough".

## Chapter Fourteen

1. Funston, Mike, *Toronto star*, February 27, 2010.
2. William C. Williams, "The Fountain of Eternal Youth", BROOM Vol. 5, No. 2, SEPTEMBER 1923, p73, http://bluemountain.princeton.edu/bluemtn/cgi-bin/bluemtn?a=d&d=bmtnaap192309-01.2.6&e=------en-20--1--txt-IN-----
3. "Liberals demand apology after Tory MP calls Louis Riel a 'villain'", *Toronto star*, February 25, 2010.

## Chapter Fifteen

1. Hegel, *Philosophy of World History*, 177.
2. Hegel, *Philosophy of World History*, 174.
3. Hegel., *Philosophy of World History*, 174.

4. Hegel, *Philosophy of World History*, 176.
5. Hegel, *Philosophy of World History*, 174.
6. Hegel, *Philosophy of World History*, 176.
7. Leo Africanus, "The Description of Africa", http://www.historywiz.com/descriptionofafrica.htmcks
8. Joan Baxter, *Ummah*, "The Treasures of Timbuktu", https://www.ummah.com/forum/forum/islam/general-islamic-topics/74568-the-treasures-of-timbuktu
9. Hegel, *Philosophy of World History*, 176Hegel, *Philosophy of World History*, 176.
10. Brown, Louise, *Toronto star*, March 23, 2010.
11. Maloney, Mark, *Toronto star*, February 12, 2011.
12. Hegel, *Philosophy of World History*, 185.
13. Hegel, *Philosophy of World History*, 185.
14. Marc Santora, "Hungary Election Gives Orban Big Majority, and Control of Constitution", *The New York Times*, April 8, 2018.
15. Tom Newton Dunn, "Migrants 'Harm UK' ", https://www.thesun.co.uk/news/6766947/donald-trump-britain-losing-culture-immigration/

Chapter Sixteen

1. William James, "The Will to Believe", in *The Experience of Philosophy* 3d ed., ed. Daniel Kolak and Raymond Martin, (Belmont CA: Wadsworth Publishing Company, 1996), 243.
2. Jean-Jacques Rousseau, *On the Social Contract*, trans. Donald A. Cress, (Indianapolis: Hackett Publishing Company, 1987), 17.
3. Alexander Pope, "Elegy to the Memory of an Unfortunate Lady", http://www.bartleby.com/101/441.html
4. Charles Dickens, *A Tale of Two Cities*, (New York: Bantam Dell, 2003), 3.
5. Michael Lobban, *White Man's Justice*, (Oxford: Clarendon Press, 1996), 65.
6. The Associated Press, "Young immigrants detained in Virginia allege they were beaten while cuffed, left nude in cells", CBS News, June 21, 2018, https://www.cbsnews.com/news/shenandoah-valley-juvenile-center-virginia-young-immigrant-detainees-allege-beaten-stripped-of-clothes-strapped-to-chairs/
7. Cyril. E. M. Joad, *Philosophy for our Times*, (London: Thomas Nelson and Sons Ltd, 1940), 275.

Chapter Seventeen

1. Jürgen Habermas, *The future of Human Nature*, trans. William Rehg, Max Pensky, and Hella Beister, (Cambridge UK: Polity Press, 2003), 13.
2. Habermas, *Human Nature*, 14.

# Index

action, affirmative: cavils against the principle of, 232; strategies, 107; they gripe about, 137
*ad hominem*, 35
Adler, 66
agenda: 237; disreputable, 215; evil, 139; filthy, 152; heinous, 181, 234; of pink herrenvolkism, 124; of pink supremacy, 101, 141, 238; of zealots , 145; self-exalting, 182; self-serving financial, 70; selfish pink, 175, 186, 195; supremacist, 92, 100
AIDS: 132, 170, 233; devastating diseases like, 155; drugs for, 161; epidemic, 199; protective devices against, 171; sufferers, 57, 62
Afibika, 19-21, 102, 191-192
Africa, 77, 100, 131, 156, 191, 240
Africanus, Leo, 191, 244
alcohol: imbibing as much, 194; scourge of, 161
Alice, 18
Amherst, Jeffrey, Lord, 198
apartheid: apostles of, 143; dirty tricks styled global, 138; discreditable, 68; or apart hate, 149
ape, in heels, 33
apologists: 90, 108; vote-pandering, 68
aptitude: fabricated genes for, 86; more pigmentation have less, 85; problem-solving, 232; tests, 8
Arendt, Hannah, 242
Armageddon, 38, 144, 181, 237
assimilation, 142-143
atavism(s), 91, 141
Australia, 100
autonomy: 10, 133, 228; definition, 239; infringement of their, 151; respect for the, 95, 118

*baas*: 22-23; *ja*, 186; meaningless title of, 209; *nee*, 186; pink, 105
*baasskap*, 23, 203, 209
Bantu, 14
barbarism: acts of, 101; and savagery, 95; disgusting, 20; German, 77; pink, 80, 96; savagery and, 76
Barbary, 192
bat, 45
Bath, Patricia, 120
Baxter, Joan, 192
being-with-the-otherness, barren, 26
Beister, Hella, 244
Berlin: 24; Conference, 240
Bernal, Martin, 19, 21, 239, 240
bigotry: 20; legacy of, 64; of Krustans, 57; religious, 10, 40, 171
bigots: 58, 68, 85; a following of, 136; and haters of other persons, 25; and hypocrites, 215; in scholarly garb, 52; moronic, 91; religious, 36, 92, 151, 179; self-serving, 42; world of, 7
blood: 52, 87, 150, 156, 157, 211; and body, 62; black 85; blue, 112; brown, 84-85, 109; cold, 101; contaminating, 58; menstrual, 102; money, 165; one drop of, 58, 89; pure, 109, 196; transfusion, 58, 89
Blumenbach, Johan, 84
bogeymen, 130
Bowen, Mark, 56, 240
brown, definition, 8
Brown, Louise, 193, 244
buddies, hypocritical, 30
Budhoo, Davison, 156, 243
buffoons: bossy, 22; ignorant, 152; power hungry, 127, 157
bullies: 98, 123, 146, 166, 168; evil, 72; cowardly, 166;

imperial, 166; international 146
Buncombe, Andrew, 242

calamities: 23, 224; natural, 62, 224
Canada, 161
capitalism: 113; odious, 225; self-serving, 225
Caribbean, 156
Carroll, Lewis, 18, 239
Carver, George W., 120
Caucasian, 148
charlatan(s): 69-70; and xenophobes, 88; avaricious, 64; religious, 40
chickens: 105; coming home to roost, 3, 29; frightened, 169
Chinese, 148-149
choice, war of, 29
Christians: be like real, 71; bible-butchering, 39
church: 4, 79, 198, and state, 41; as potent narcotics, 199; bigoted, 41; conniving, 228; corrupt, 75; irreproachable, 200; pink, 39; racist, 73-74
churches: are their businesses, 52; bombed, 5; pink supremacy teachings of their, 57; racist Krustan, 200; tried to justify discrimination, 68
Churchill, Winston, 242
cleansing, ethnic, 96, 145, 208
Clifford, William, 241
climate change: devastating, 56; effects of, 219
cloning, 220-221
coin, 26, 55
colonialists: 196; descendants of the original, 117; erstwhile, 125; our world's, 24; predate the arrival of, 121
colonization: and occupation, 116; of space, 219
colour: 83, 86, 87, 151, 196; biases, 90; -blind, 10, 65, 108, 116, 126; -coding, 83-84, 107-108; consciousness, 99; light skin, 45; pink, 36, 86; -seeing pink laws, 65; —sensitive eyes of their justice system, 10; skin, 8-10, 80-83, 85-89 91-92, 148-149
colours: 116; gradation of, 86; juggling simple, 144; mere, 83; mixed with others', 196; myth of the, 144; pink, 1, 44; skin, 59, 91, 105; stratify, 196
commodities: 5, 11, 71, 124, 142, 157, 159; common, 24; currency for the purchase of, 101; expensive, 158; marketable, 23; persons as profitable, 14; unnecessary, 37
Cone, James, 44
consciousness: 76, 191, 202, 239; colour, 99; moral, 77; self-, 100, 192
conservative: brown, 36-37; judges, 132
conservatives, 36
continents of twin world, 17
corporations: 153-154, 166, 169, 236; complex of state and, 158-159; controlling, 227; corrupt, 163; greedy, 229; interests of, 131, 152; pink-owned-and-operated, 163; schemes of, 35; vulturish, 11
corruption: 178; allegations of, 37; and filching, 132; dominated by, 40; government, 106; greed and, 152; in government, 163; is the order of the day, 164; legalized theft and, 135; self-service and, 33; ubiquitous 125
Cotter, Joseph Jr., 240
Courtenay, Bryce, 243
creationism, 41, 65-66, 194, 211
Crenshaw, Kimberlé, 242
cronyism, 37
culture: 196; assimilated into their, 197; of duplicity, 147; of entitlement; of pink racism, 99

*de facto*, 107, 110
*de jure*, 107, 110
dehomanization: 85, acts of, 25; acquiescence in their own, 44;

bondage and, 179; brown exploitation and, 114; by foreigners, 195; despicable process of, 95; exploitation, and attempted annihilation, 85; many decades of, 74; of colonialism, 190; rejecting their, 126

democracy: 113, 158, 166, 178; garb of, 5; of greed, 186; illegitimate way of spreading, 98; rape of, 132; self-serving, 166; scourge of, 131; sham, 166; usurpation of, 131

denominations: 101; prestigious, 62

Destiny, Doctrine of Manifest, 142

dialetheism, 17

Dickens, Charles, 209, 244

discrimination: 85, 121; earmarked for, 4; churches have tried to justify, 68; crass, 228; de facto, 107; double, 237; genetic 220; global racist, 110, 228; immoral forms of, 74; institutionalized, 240; institutions of, 9; laws against, 92; naked, 114; pink, 185; racist, 137; reverse, 137; tribal, 58; victims of 145-146

dissertation, MA, 120

dogs: 98, 135; and browns not allowed, 77; attack, 37, 128, 182, 183; in a manger, 146; treated like, 81

dogma: 65, 66, 67, 75, 185; autocratic and corrupt, 36; crass, 118; foreign, 32; herrenvolk-tainted, 145; ignorance-driven, 55; Krustan, 64; religious, 13, 41, 53, 145

domination: 122, 195, 208, 228; of Krustans 75; pink, 108, 114, 140, 185, 196, 199; subordination to, 235; they worship, 35

Douglass, Frederick, 241

Dunn, Tom Newton, 244

duplicity: 75; culture of, 147; cunning and, 20; disgusting, 33

dystopia, 54

E9-551, 81

egos: 41, 171; absent, 52; hungry, 169; hypocritical, 117; measly, 188; Mickey Mouse, 171; paltry, 189; petty, 11; picayune, 232; puny, 40, 178; vain, 34

electorate: 127-128, 139; dopy, 230; duped, 172; gullible, 16; powerless, 42

elites, 28, 62

empathy: 62, 80, 118; characteristic lack of, 45, 175; with those of their kind, 171

enemy: 51, 173, 182; damn the, 60; fodder for the canons of the, 169, 195; non-compliant, 175; prevailing against the, 168; rightfully killing the, 188; tender loving care of the, 187

environment: 14, 15-16, 66, 147, 206, 220; deprived, 137; eco-, 162; racial, 148; schizophrenic, 4. terrestrial, 55

equality, unequal, 76

evolution: 41, 65-67, 69, 218; biological, 211; homan, 220; self-directed, 211; technological, 212; tree of, 194

excesses: 194, 220; measured, 30

experience: 64, 79; Canadian, 107; daily, 48; job, 107, 139; Konatian, 137; mystical, 69; of bats, 45; past, 128; religious, 69

Eze, Emmanuel C., 241

fairness: 4, 46, 201, 238; for all, 116; justice and, 62, 72, 118, 190, 200; no sense of, 116; of pink courts, 236

fallacy: 93; etymological, 202; genetic, 202, 203

fear: 69, 142; among the citizens, 122; baseless, 177; constant, 56, 140; domain of; 144; from reprisals, 174; guided only by 53; ignorant,

212; irrational, 109, 110; of being outnumbered, 100; of brown potential, 209; of the potential, threat, 184; 184; of the revulsion, 187; of their Gudd, 52; or blind faith, 72; siege mentality of, 176; unbalanced state of, 144
Feinstein, Andrew, 37, 240
feminism, 227
food: control genocide, 199; march without, 96; morsel of, 54; prices of, 157; rations, 34; rummaging garbage dumps for, 209; scavenging for, 162; throwing away, 124, 162;
fools: 22, 58, 172; absolute, 168; arrogant, 86, 115; bigoted, 33; blabbering, 181; miserable, 11; of wise men, 79; of the citizenry, 160; we, 174; wishful thinking of, 6
franchise: 134, 167, 208; new-found, 229
Frankenstein, 220
freedom fighters, 32, 55, 179
free will, 63, 206
Funston, Mike, 243

genes: analysis of, 87; ancestral, 91; deleterious, 86; editing of, 220; fabricated 86; neutral 86; 71, 88, 90, 94, 230
genius: 85, 149; evil, 224-225; inventive, 21; physiological, 83; superior, 21
genocide: 30-31; food control, 199; indirect, 143 slaughter amounting to, 97; 114, 164, 165
Ghana, 191
global warming: 56, 147, 219; effects of, 161; pace of, 206
Goldsmith, Oliver, 182
Gotanda, Neil, 242
Greece, 21, 239
greed: 2, 16; agenda of, 60; altars of, 72; Book of, 190; capitalist, 166; corporation, 159; democracy of, 186; economic, 132; financial, 179; for money, 38, 55, 176; for power, 35; insatiable, 3, 64, 71, 154, 189, 208; of lenders, 126; uncontrollable, 40; unlimited, 177; wars of, 5
Greeks, 21, 239
Greene, Linda, 99, 242
Guelph university, 193
gutter: 3, 6, 33, 83, 92, 155, 174; in which the leaders exist, 130; out of the, 136, 174; wallow in the same, 162; where many of them reside, 237

Habermas, Jürgen, 244
Hagala, 20-21, 68-69, 76-77, 140, 195
Hamelin, 186
happiness: 125, 218, 225; basic, 205; collective, 40; elusiveness of, 215; ethic of, 97; greatest, 116; illusory, 40; maximizing, 80; socialized, 122
health care: 11, 141, 155, 184; basic, 36; 152; benefits, 10, 122; elite, 152; facilities, 63, 154; free, 22
Hegel, Georg W., 200 years before, 191-192; lectures, 239, 241, 142, 243, 244
hegemony: 52, egregious, 46; racial, 99; wars of, 52
Herodotus, 19
heroes: 33, 36; are liars, 175; butchering, 32; ephemeral war, 187; fallen, 170; national, 173, 198; reluctant war, 187
herrenvolk: 27, 176, 186; agenda, 195; ideology, 143; master plan, 199; mentality, 82, 180, 184, 189
herrenvolkism: 93, 149, 235; architects of, 195; pink, 124
Hobson's choices, 129
Hochschild, Adam, 100-101, 103, 242
Holden, Paul, 37
Homanism, 13, 133
Homo super-sapiens, 218
homosexuals, 57

humanism, 13-14
Humono, 79, 81, 82
Humpty Dumpty, 18
hypocrisy: 30, 31, 85, 111, 146; abject, 109; blatant, 144; Krustan, 62; pink, 143; rampant, 75; religion of, 5; religious, 78
hypocrites: 50, 59, 62, 215; pious, 52; the way of, 56; the worst of, 57

*ignis fatuus*, pitiable, 84
ignoramus, 69
Immorality Amendment Act, 1950, 143
imperialists, 70 -71, 99, 170
indignities: 65, 233; moral, 197
injustice: 85, 110, 140, 190, 210, 214; hubristic, 2; undeserving, 189
institutions, money-lending, 16
inventions, 120

jail, 160-161
James, George, 19, 239
James, William, 244
Jefferson, Thomas, 241
Joad, Cyril E. M., 215, 244
job cycle, 231-232
Johin, 151-152
Johnson, Clarence S., 242
Johnson James W., 240
Jones, William, 43
Julian, Percy L., 120
justice: 93, 187, 198; and fairness, 62, 72, 119, 68-69, 73, 97, 131, 205; avoid, 224; champions of, 200; colour-blind, 109, 112, 131; colour-coded, 108; ethical principles of, 76; equal, 190; foreign systems of, 126; international courts of, 168; miscarriage of, 189; miscarry, 103; pink, 48, 188; system, 10; they profess, 4; unjust, 126, 236

Kaffirs, 193-194

Kamkambwa, William, 120
Kant, Immanuel, 241
Kantono, 80-82
Klein, Naomi, 240
Kolak, Daniel, 241, 244
Krustan, definition, 39
Krustans, diabolical, 5-6, 53, 198

Lacka, 78, 81, 83
lands: 48, 51, 72, 115, 190; agricultural, 158; brown, 117; coveted, 49; foreign, 169; mineral-rich, 71; occupied, 85, 94, 236; other people's, 61, 199; promised, 51, 74, 85; steal, 20, 29, 98, 100, 196, 198; stolen, 74, 98, 113, 116, 143, 197, 200; theft of, 190; their own, 101, 162, 176; uninhabited, 120, 174, 191
language: 7, 17-18, 74; African, 23, 179; and mores, 167; depraved, 176; despicable, 74; dog, 183; figurative, 64; inflammatory, 180; naïve, 220; of lies, 238; of racism, 116-116 ; of our world, 102; propositional, 67; racist, 139; racist vitriolic, 3; savage, 197
lapdogs: 37, 189; favoured, 104; spineless, 170; vying for favours, 131
Latimer, Lewis H., 120
level, gutter, 106, 182, 197
Latin America, 156
Lawrence, David H., 43
laws: 90, 93, 131, 165, 208; aboriginal, 196; abortion, 41; against discrimination, 92; biased, 184; civic, 57; emergency, 83; evil, 184; global, 213; iniquitous, 185; international, 166; local, 188; moral, 81; natural, 81, 203; 108;  new, 125; nonsensical, 81; parallel, 190; physical, 204; pink, 9, 65, 72, 73, 76, 81, 115; pink tribally discriminatory, 39; rational, 132; restrictive, 188; self-indulging

abortion, 41; state, 99, 108, 117, 137, 173; unjust, 51; virtuous, 72, 73
leader, brown, 32-34, 179
leaders: 16, 51, 61, 73; brown, 37, chimerical, 79; depraved, 74; hypocrisy of, 75; pink, 33; so-called, 35, 71, subsequent, 32; sybaritic, 37
leeches, bloodsucking, 112
Linnaeus, Carolus, 84
loans: 157; costly, 153-154, 156; enslaving, 5, 156
Lobban, Michael, 244
Locke, John, 242, 243
logic: 35, 64, 81, 189; and decency, 37; bizarre, 144; -defying, 64; distorted, 76; fuzzy, 90; illogical, 8, 186, 189; odd, 85; pink, 98, 188; racist, 148-149, 188; sick, 190; tortuous, 186; twisted, 81; vicious, 80, 102, 125; warped, 82
loot, 37, 52, 72, 75
looting: 155; shameless, 154
Lynch, Willie, 140, 196 243

Maccas, Leon, 77, 86
Mali, 191
Maloney, Mark, 244
market(s): 124, 138, craftily constructed, 137-138; global financial, 129-130; flood the, 158; free, 206; international, 101, 156, 165; invest in the, 159; job, 232; money, 165, 226; open, 155; prices, 159; world, 158
marketplace: countries are traded in the, 101; fortunes acquired "legitimately" in the, 224; persons as profitable commodities for the, 14; the forces of their, 137-138, 208; trade its peoples in the, 24
Martin, Raymond, 241, 244
Marx, Karl, 40, 198
McGregor, Tony, 243
Mearsheimer, John J., 242

media: 30, 132; biased news, 122, 247; mediocre hosts, 182; myth, 30, 34, 65, 75; puppet news, 29, 56, 131
Mills, Charles, 43
Milton, John: 123, 240, 242; tried in *Paradise Lost* 44,
minorities: 113; invisible visible, 25, 105; majority, 125; visible, 25, 121
money: 47-48, 56, 106 135; bags, 206-207; deconstruct, 218; flow of, 31, 54; generating factory, 75; greed for, 38, 55, 176; stolen, 160
monuments: 36; execrable, 90; statewide, 144; to their glory, 174
morality: 12, 60, 83, 178; bankrupt, 61; circumstantial, 177; common, 51; decadent, 170; gutter, 58, 74; paradigmatic, 58; religious140; superior, 117; timeless, 58; western, 156
Morgan, Garrett A., 120
morons: 87; reputed thinkers and 84; vulgar, 24
murder: 8, 29, 164, 215: abet their, 198; and enslavement, 174; and sanctioned killing, 188; brutality and, 113; charge others with, 6; cold-blooded, 10, 108, 149; covert form of, 194; evil acts of, 97; evil and, 64; from their pulpits, 73; get away with, 127; inciting, 74; licence for, 95; mass, 154; of the millions, 39; oppression and, 144, 238; pillars of, 47; quondam victims of, 32; to maintain superiority, 117; wars and, 130
murderer(s): heartless, 28; branding their resisters as, 113

Nathan, Susan, 80, 191
Natives, 138
neighbours: 67, 177, 215; against their, 60, 61; defenceless, 146; in strife with, 15; interaction with, 204; live well with, 26;

respect for, 6; starving, 15; their Krustan, 62
neoconservatives, 36
Nietzsche, Friedrich, 50
Nomebika, 17
NSSM: 185, 199; initiatives like Global 2000 and, 121

occupation: 99, 138; freedom from, 168; the, 95
Oceania, 167
Ogilvie, Megan, 139, 243
oligarchy, 166
one drop: 58; drivel, 196; of contaminating blood, 58; nitwitted concept of, 89-90
oppressors, definition, 3
opium, 40, 198
oracles: 88; political 171
Orwell, George, 167
oxymoron, definition, 13

Pakistan, 193
Pappe, Ilan, 96-97, 242, 243
paragon(s): 2, 14, 25; of morality, 83
pawns: blindfolded, 198; brown, 58; children used as, 184; fawning, 99; in executing the dirty work, 16; in the oppression of their own people; 237; in their own exploitation, 33; political, 172; proxies and pawns, 8
Peller, Gatty, 242
Pensky, Max, 244
people, chosen: pinks are the, 75; their Gudd's, 31, 47, 203
Perkins, John, 226
personhood, 10
Pied Piper of Hamelin, 186
pigment: abundance of, 104; amount of, 89, 91; gene for the, 85; less, 24
Plato, 19
plutocracy, 166
Poe, Richard, 19, 239, 241
pollution, 161
Pope, Alexander, 244

poster-boy, spineless, 33
prisons: 125, 164, 187; christian, 102; feed their hungry, 83; political, 178; their many secret, 94, 125, 177; torture in, 163; war and other, 224
profiling: and harassment, 233; euphemism for, 108; made hell on earth by the same, 186
programs: 153, pauperizing structural adjustment, 126
propaganda: 74, 170; and lies, 167; cheap commercial, 148, 226; disreputable holy, 47; greed-driven, 55; spread their, 65; swallow raw all the 219; tools, 31
property: 2, 48, 72, 142, 190; attacks on, 29; destroy, 113, 123, 193; dispose of, 174; loss of, 78; pillage y's, 29; protecting, 179; rights to, 113; stolen, 116; taking his, 28
pro-lifer, 42
punishment, collective, 29, 32, 100
puppets, 31, 59, 72, 154, 178; brutal, 103; simple-minded, 183; window-dressing, 163
Putnam, Hilary, 239
Pythagoras, 19

raciology, 87
racism: 8-10, 18, 77-79, 83; agenda of, 60; definition, 87; egotism and, 31; has many faces, 176; hatred-based, 3; hubris and, 29; inane, 33; inhomanity of, 181; institutional, 104, 231; malevolent disposition to, 8; overt, 193; overwhelming, 97; pink, 86, 99; prejudice based on, 77; rabid, 40; skin colour, 91; victims of, 80, 92
Ramose, Mogobe, 14-15
Red Indians, 94
Rehg, William, 244
relationship, parasitic, 22-23
reservations, 48, 71, 75

restrictions: 111, 155; enslaving, 4; foreign exchange, 157; interfering, 194
revolution: 237; against enforced choices, 213; another, 230; bloody, 106; system-wrecking, 228
rights: 16, 29, 65, 68, 80, 100, 114, 188, 195; aboriginal, 74; animal, 92, 191; basic human, 156; civil, 28, 63, 153, 158, 185; constitutional, 103, 141, 164; drinking, 96; equal, 110, 176; homan, 9, 22, 23, 25, 77-78, 95, 163, 184; inalienable, 93; individual moral and legal, 14; legal, 187; lost their possession, 142; moral, 14, 45, 176; of non-extant posterity, 16; of other people, 72-73; of savages, 117-118; recognition of their, 102; to life and other values, 4, 76; trading, 137; to which they are entitled, 10
rogues: of homanity, 25; religious, 199
Ross, Oakland, 94, 242
Rousseau, Jean J., 118, 231, 242, 244
Ryle, Gilbert, 202

sacrifice, ultimate, 51, 173
Santora, Marc, 244
savages: 116; a nation of, 85; and wagers of war, 71; depict their victims as, 113; disgusting, 82; label them as, 120; regarded with disdain as, 190; rights of, 115; so-called, 191; well known, 20; who are the real, 102-103
Science: 55, 66, 84, 204-205; classes, 41; deniers of, 56-57; denying the, 147; knowledge of, 70; medical 223; teachings of, 65
scientists: 41, 148, 221; browns lack, 79; honest, 220; persecuted, 55-56; pseudo-, 147; rogue, 220

scriptures: allegorical 66; depraved, 52; dogma and, 75; say, 57; their own, 26; this world's, 26, 136
scumbags: brown, 61; terrorists and, 170
Searle, John, 87, 230
Shapiro, Ian, 242
Shaw, George Bernard, 241
silver, bloodstained, 126
Sisyphus, 23
slavery: 77, 111, 140; chains of, 205, 229; economic, 229; educational, 236; socio-economic, 158, 163; sold into, 101-102
slaves: 24, 72, 78, 109; breeding ground for, 143; economic, 155; light skin, 140; of backroom boys, 167; pink, 84
sociologists, 17
Socrates, 19
soldiers, bloodthirsty pink, 193
Somebika, 17
Soria, 151-152
South Africa: 143; oppressors of the brown people of, 14; Patterns of Jim Crow in, 240, 241; the barbarians of, 57
Stamatellos, Giannis, 240
states, brown: 154, 163-165, 175, 200, 225; accuse, 137; adjacent, 99; AIDS epidemic in, 199; expense of, 131-132; leaders of, 35-37; newly minted, 155-156; oppressing, 96; poor, 153; victimized, 146
Stone, Robert, 241
students, Negro, 115-116
subhomans: 3, 8, 101; discourse with, 83
superiority: 8; 67-68, 84-86, 142-143; complex, 3, 118; contrived, 120, 141; decadent, 87; economic, 153; endless, 209-210; European, 21-22; myth of, 106-107; of the few, 117; pink, 94-95, 118, 185, 234; racial, 105; shadowy claims

of pink, 19-20; spurious, 86; vaunted pink, 22-23
supremacy: 133; delusion of pink, 77; economic, 105; fabricated robe of, 29; ideology of, 38; pink, 107-108, 138-141; regional, 99, 145; self-assumed, 9; tout their, 15; tribal, 3
Swinburne, Richard, 240
system, the: 179, 236; absurdity of, 141; milking browns, you, and, 151; that imposes more rigorous demands on browns, 110; unjust justice meted out by, 236

tactics: 56, 59; bullying, 169; gutter, 61; lies and smear, 234; obstructionist, 181; of our world, 56; pharisaic, 232; pressure, 31; rogue, 103; scorched earth, 192
terrorism: 55, accuse brown states of 137; acts of, 32; and the indiscriminate killing of other people, 167; claim to be the real victims of, 100; freedom from their tyranny and, 55; from oppressors, 100; so called, 99
Terrorism Act 1967, 209-210
terrorists: 55, 70-71, 95, 168, 185-189; calling freedom fighters, 179; eschew communist agitators and 22; incorrigible, 32; laws allegedly directed against, 188; who have to be exterminated, 55
theocracy, 167
theocratism, and religious right, 42-43
theodicy, 44-45
thieves, colonialist, 62
Thomas, Kendall, 242
Timbuktu, 191-192
timocracy, 166
totalitarianism, 167
treaties: land, 71; phony, 72; sign, 20-21
Tremblay, Rodrique, 242
tribe, definition, 18

truth: 10, 30, 46, 91, 202-203; and reconciliation, 238; assaulting the, 131; aversion to, 31; crushed by the, 120; denial of the, 89; hiding from the, 49; impervious to reason and, 30; in lies, 172; killers of, 50; lack of, 145; muggers of, 56; real, 68; sacrifice the, 88; self-indulging, 214; to power, 183

*Ubuntu*: 26, 29, 77, 102; families governed by, 132; practice of, 20; thesis of, 14-16

Walt, Stephen, M. 242
warming, global: 56, 147, 161; pace of, 206
warmongering, 1, 129, 227
warmongers: 169; bullies and, 168; immoral, 12; Krustan, 72
wars: 11, 48, 51, 130, 143, 169, 175, 132, 189, 195, 214, 219, 223; and forays, 192; bogus self-defence, 168; evil, 10; immoral, 208; inhomane, 135; life-squandering, 132; money-generating, 56; of greed, 5; of hegemony, 52; of liberation, 198; self-serving, 130; stupid, 213
watchdogs, 56, 159
water: 20, 96-97, 239; contaminated, 183; cost of, 119; dirty, 48; drawers of, 22; drinking, 165; running, 209; wells, 96
West Nile, 162
Williams, William C., 174, 243
Woods, Granville T., 120
Woodson, Carter G., 243
Wright, Ronald, 100, 196
world: first, 15-16, 196; pink-dominated, 89; possible, 7, 17, 18, 27, 219; third, 16, 185

xenophobes, 88, 196
xenotransplantation, 222
Xuza, Siyabulela L., 120

yoke: of pink oppression; of poverty, 162; of serfdom, 26
York University, 193

zealots: 89; religious, 50; selfish agendas of 146
zoos, homan, 75

www.ingramcontent.com/pod-product-compliance
Lightning Source LLC
Chambersburg PA
CBHW031310150426
43191CB00005B/163